ORLOG
Yesterday and Today

The Shapings of the Norns

Winifred Hodge Rose

With contributions from

Sara Axtell

Daniela Svartheiðrinn Simina

Wordfruma Press
2025

Text copyright ©2025 by Winifred Hodge Rose. All rights reserved. Brief quotations with full citation are permitted, for the purposes of criticism, teaching, or scholarship.

Text that is authored by Sara Axtell or Daniela Simina is copyrighted by them ©2025 under the same conditions.

™

Wordfruma Press
Urbana Illinois USA

WordfrumaPress.net
WordfrumaPress@gmail.com

ISBN 979-8-9898337-1-9 (paperback)
     979-8-9898337-2-6 (hardcover)
     979-8-9898337-3-3 (EPUB)

Library of Congress Control Number: 2025921517

This book was originated and written directly by humans; none of the text was produced by AI.

Cover and book design by Winifred Hodge Rose.

My own title for the cover image: "Moonlight on the Well of Wyrd." The ripples look like the first movements of things coming into being, moving from the depths of the active, bubbling Wellspring to the shores of Midgard to take shape there.

Credit for the image is listed under "Photo Credits."

Dedications

From Winifred:

There is a well of wyrd and mystery within each of us.
We each have roots
plunging into the depths of Being.
We each have branches
reaching higher and wider than mountains.

This book is dedicated
to the deep places and the high spaces
that echo the Wells and the Tree:
the profound depths and soaring heights
within each of our hearts, minds, and souls,
within our friendships, kinships, loves,
within our Heathen troth and those we trust in,
reaching across the Worlds
from depths to heights,
growing together in the mystery of Being.

From Sara:
To *Healing Roots,* and everything we are creating together.

From Svartheiðrinn:
To Cat and Morgan, thanks for pushing me into the deep end. It was the fastest way for me to learn to swim in elven waters. To Kellene, thanks for reminding me to never dim my light. To Winifred, my gratitude for the teachings, books and mentoring - they made a difference in my life. To my elven allies, ancestors, and deities.

Statues of the three Norns at Ribe Viking Center, Denmark.

TABLE OF CONTENTS

Dedications 3
The World of Orlog 1
    Multiple Lenses 3
    Contributors 4
Part I. Orlog Yesterday: Laying the Layers 7
    1. The History of 'Orlog' 9
        Table 1. Time-periods of Old Germanic Literature 10
        Primary Meanings of Orlog 12
        Table 2: Etymologies of Orlog 12
        Evolution from 'uslagjan' 14
        Svartheiðrinn: Orlog as Fateful Inner Struggle 17
    2. Orlog, Layers, and Laws 19
        Comparing Roots of Orlog in Multiple Languages 19
        Inner Law and Outer Law 23
        Sigrun and Helgi II 25
        A Common Denominator 26
        Defining Orlog 28
    3. The Shapings of the Norns 31
        The Roots of Skǫp 32
        Table 3. The Roots of 'Shaping' 32
        Hallfreðr: Skǫp Norna as Heathen Troth 35
        Examples of How the Word 'Shape' is Used 36
        Do Runes Play a Role? 39

Speaking Orlog 43
4. The Ancient Role of Symbel 45
    Shaping Speech in Symbel 46
    The Fateful Oaths of Hedin, Helgi, and Svava 49
5. What Do the Norns Shape? 55
    Aldr: Lifespan and Life-Soul 56
    Table 4. Examples of Anglo-Saxon Ealdor Words 59
    World and Werold 60
6. Time, Tense, and the Norns 63
    The Names 64
    Past versus Non-Past 67
    Passing the Strands 68
7. The Curious Case of the Missing Wyrd-Word 71
    The Missing Word in Gothic 71
    Haliurunnae 74

Part II: The Work of the Norns 79

8. Orlog and Wyrd 81
    Personification and De-Personification of Wyrd 82
    Anglo-Saxon *Wyrd* 85
    Synthesis 87
    Wyrd: A Case Study 89
9. Causality and Determinism 93
    The Norns as Caretakers of Causality 94
    What if we were Orlog-less? 97

    Free Will *and* Determinism 99

    Significance: Making it Personal............................102

  10. The Norns as Beings of Fate.................................107

    Tending Causality, Shaping Fate..............................108

    Nornir / Valkyrja: Choosing Life / Choosing Death .109

    'Fate' versus Causality...112

    Wyrd and Will Together..112

  11. Foresight and Predestination..................................117

    Foresight...117

    The Influence of 'the Future' 121

    Predestination..123

    The Ambiguity of Time...126

    Destiny: A Pull or a Push?..128

  12. *Svartheðrinn:* The Nornir Walk Among Us 131

    The Roles of the Nornir...132

    Lesser Nornir..133

    The Valkyrja of Darraðarljoð 133

    Human Deeds..135

    Orlog Influences the Gods..136

    Seeresses, Spákonur, Völur..137

    A Co-Creative Process 138

Part III. Orlog Manifesting in Human Life..... 141

  13. Dealing with Orlog: Yesterday...............................143

    Table 5. Roots of Dreogan / Drýgja / Dree 144

    Odin and Loki 'Ørlög Drýgðuð'..................................... 145
    Völund and the Swan Maidens 146
    Dreeing our Wyrd... 149
    Or-deal.. 150

14. The Role of Luck 151
    Some Differences Between Orlog and Luck 152
    Varieties of Luck 154
    Hamingja and Other Luck-Bearing Spirits 157
    Similarities between Hamingja and Orlog.................. 160
    Between Fire and Ice 163
    The Insignificance of Random Luck 164
    The Mediating Role of Luck-Spirits........................... 165
    Luck versus Ordeal.. 166

15. Legacies 169
    Hamingja as Legacy... 170
    Ethical Implications of Predestination 172
    'Reputation' versus 'Karma' 175

16. Orlog at the Time of Death.. 181
    Orlog as Death, and the Question of 'Why?' 181
    Heathen Afterlife Beliefs 184
    Does Orlog Influence the Afterlife State?.................. 186
    Does Orlog Stop when Midgard Life Ends?............. 193
    Alda Vé 194
    Summary of Aldr's Roles 198
    What Happens to Aldr at Death? 199

Synopsis and Some Unanswered Questions 200

Part IV: Orlog Metaphysics 205

17. The Evolving Nature of Orlog 207
Process versus Substance 207
The Process of Orlog 208
The Substance of Orlog 209
Process Creates Substance 211
Orlog Evolves as Process Creates Substance 214

18. The Body as Orlog 219
Orlog as Nourishment 219
Genetics and Epigenetics 220
The Conditioning Effects of Orlog 220
Process and Substance 221

19. Time and the Time-Body 223
Bodies in Space and Time 223
Time as Change 226
Causality and the Time-Body 228
Time as Relationship 229
Time as a Container of Meaning 230
Time-Body / Aldr Soul and Werold 232

20. The Quantum Nature of the Norns' Work 235
Gatekeeper of the Quantum Realm 236
Norns and Three Phenomena of Quantum Physics . 238
Verðandi's Domain: Collapsing into an Eigenstate ... 240

    Skuld's Domain: Quantum Entanglement 242

    Urð's Domain: Wave-Particle Duality 245

  21. The Work of the Three Wells................................ 253

    Mimir's Well 254

    Relationship between Mimir's and Norns' Wells 256

    There's Quantum here too.. 258

    Hvergelmir and the World-Mill 260

    Entropic Inversion and Orlog 263

Part V. Heathen Perspectives on Orlog Today 267

  22. Orlog and Wyrd: Some Modern Perspectives 269

    A Modern Summary 270

    A Nature-Psyche Approach...................................... 270

    A View from Heathen Magic 271

    A Devotional Perspective 272

    A Tale-Teller's Insights... 273

  23. Collective and Group Orlog 275

    An Overview of Collective Orlog 275

    Sara: Personal Orlog Embedded in Group Orlog 279

  24. *Sara:* Orlog of Our Relationship with Land.......... 283

    Weaving Patterns.. 283

    Primstav... 284

    Relating to the Land... 286

    Gift for a Gift 287

    Land Consolidation in Norway 289

    Emigration and Becoming Settlers.............................290

    Development of the U.S. Food System 291

    Reworking the Pattern 292

    References and Resources for this Chapter 294

25. Beyond Individual Orlog: Deep Suffering and the Role of Frith 297

    Do we Blame the "Wretched Norns"? 298

    Comparing Orlog and Karma 300

    The Role of Heathen Frith 301

    The Orlog of Signy the Volsung 305

    Orlog is Context 306

26. Oathing in Symbel 309

    The Modern Heathen Symbel or Sumble 309

    Oathing in Symbel 310

    A Modern Heathen Concern 314

    Risking Luck versus Risking Orlog 316

    Oathed Bonds and Group Orlog 319

    Individual Oaths and Group Orlog.............................321

27. The Symbel Mysterium 323

    Gathering at the Well of Wyrd 324

    Meeting at Mimir's Well 326

    Actions of the Two Wells 327

    Our Choice in Symbel 329

    Which Well Fits Well? 330

Part VI. Orlog Awareness in Practice 333

- 28. Ordeal: Dealing with Orlog Today 335
  - Orlog is Personal 336
  - Working with the Knots.. 337
  - The Formal Ordeal... 339
  - Heroes of Our Own Time 342
- 29. *Sara:* Tools for Working with Orlog 345
  - The Big, Sticky Velcro Ball of Orlog......................... 345
  - Some Tools for Working with Orlog 346
  - Runes 346
  - Spells or Charms... 347
  - Ritual and Ceremony 348
  - Shild 350
  - A Bind Rune to Hold this Work 352
  - References for this chapter.. 353
- 30. *Sara:* Healing Orlog Journaling Questions............ 355
  - Verðandi: Feelings and Conditions Unfolding in the Present Moment... 357
  - Urð: Understanding the Patterns in the Well 357
  - Skuld: Healing, Transformation, Coming into Balance 358
  - References for this chapter.. 360
- 31. Wyrd and Shild: A Ninefold Rite of Life Renewal 363
  - The Symbolism of the Ninefold Rite 364
  - Shild and the Actions of the Norns.......................... 366
  - 'Turning' 368

Step One: Forming Your Intent 369
  Step Two: Paying Your Shild 373
  The Shild-Rite 379
  Step Three: Weaving Anew 380
  Sara: Testimonials on Using the Ninefold Rite 384
 32. Unfolding Destiny, Weaving a Werold 387
  Destiny Unfolding from Orlog 387
  Werold 389
  Werold as a Work of Art 390
  Mosaic: An Example 390
 33. Meditations 393
  Svartheiðrinn: Meditating on the Web of Wyrd 394
  Sara: Healing from the Roots of the World: An Embodied Visualization 401
  Being Shaped by Orlog 404
  Layers of Time 407
34. The Song of the Norns 411
  Expanding the Scope of *Sköp Norna* 411
  The Meaningfulness of Orlog 412
  What the Norns Ask of Us 414
  The Song of the Norns 415
Word Hoard / Glossary 419
Book-Hoard: References and Further Reading 441
Photo Credits 449
Authors 454

Winifred Hodge Rose.. 455
Sara Axtell 457
Daniela Svartheiðrinn Simina 459
A Word about Wordfruma Press...........................461

The World of Orlog

We live in a world that seems consumed with reactions piled upon reactions: conflicts around the world whose roots run deep into complex layers of history, culture wars and clashes of values that escalate with each reaction of one side to the other, natural systems and human needs conflicting with each other and disrupting both natural and human systems of feedback, balance, and stability. Everything is the effect of some action or process; everything is a cause resulting in some effect. Welcome to the world of orlog!

Academic scholarship on the subject of orlog and wyrd seeks to understand what these concepts meant in the past. This provides the necessary foundation for our work here, but this book goes further. Here we try to *evolve* an understanding of orlog from its basis in the Heathen past to its living manifestations today. 'Evolution' is very much a part of the nature of orlog, a perspective we'll explore in this book, and evolution applies as well to the personal experience of, and work with, orlog that each of us may pursue during the course of our life.

Orlog is a fundamental pattern that shapes life in Midgard, the work of the Norns, of Deities and humans, and

The World of Orlog

of natural processes. It is inexorable and inescapable. It is also supportive of all life and natural phenomena, of culture and civilization, learning and discovery, of growth and change as well as stability and stagnation. Patterns laid in orlog tend to take over our lives, on individual levels, group levels such as family or workplace, and larger collective levels of cultures and societies. Some of these patterns are beneficial, others are harmful, some are adaptive and others maladaptive in the context of any given circumstances.

Their natures and the balances among these patterns are always subject to subtle or sudden changes and disruptions—apparent eruptions of 'fate' into the pattern. As individuals, we often feel like pawns in the greater fluxes and flows of shifting patterns around us which tend to impact our lives substantially even when, as far as we can tell, we have little to do with those greater patterns other than being a leaf in the forest, so to speak.

Ancient Heathens saw all this, and—looking deeper—found metaphysical roots of orlog that are expressed in mythical, spiritual, and religious ways as well as practical and ethical terms. Other cultures, religions, and philosophies have done so as well, and structure their belief systems around their understandings, such as the concept of 'karma' among Hindus and Buddhists, and 'God's will' or 'Providence' among Christians.

Heathens have our own take on this phenomenon of orlog, as well as our own words for it from the old Germanic languages. Ours is at least as deep, subtle, and consequential as any other interpretation, and as deeply embedded in our own world-view. That is what this book explores, as we modern Heathens take our places among the many philosophers and philosophies that strive to make sense of this multi-layered world of Midgard and our places within it—and beyond it.

Multiple Lenses

A profound understanding of orlog requires the employment of multiple lenses, approaches from many directions. In Part I of this book, "Orlog Yesterday: Laying the Layers," we take a look at linguistics, history, ancient literature and lore from multiple old Germanic cultures to lay the groundwork for our understanding and provide more specific definition of the concept. To facilitate this cross-cultural Germanic view, throughout the book we're using the generic spelling 'orlog' rather than spelling from one specific language such as Old Norse *ørlög* or Anglo-Saxon *orlæg*, except when the word appears in quotations.

In Part II, "The Work of the Norns," we consider some of the most common philosophical questions associated with orlog, such as determinism, free will, causality, fate, predestination, foresight, the nature of time, and the roles of the Norns and Wyrd in those contexts.

Part III, "Orlog Manifesting in Human Life," explores ways that we experience and deal with orlog and related phenomena, including the roles of orlog- and luck-bearing spirit-beings, from the beginning of our life to the end of it, and beyond that, to the legacies that have been passed down to us and which we can pass down to others.

Though the metaphysical aspects of orlog permeate the whole book, in Part IV, "Orlog Metaphysics, or Some Weird Ideas about Orlog," we go into more depth and explore some more metaphysically-daring ideas, such as the evolutionary nature of orlog, analogies from quantum physics to understand aspects of the Norns and orlog, the idea of the

Time-Body, and mysteries of the three great Wells that relate to orlog.

Part V, "Heathen Perspectives on Orlog Today," offers what it says: various modern Heathen perspectives including the orlog of our relationship with land, the ethical connections between 'orlog' and 'ordeal,' and considerations relating to the practice of modern Heathen symbel or sumble and to oathing in symbel.

In Part VI, "Orlog Awareness in Practice," we bring the book to a close by offering some tools and methods for developing and applying orlog awareness in daily life. These include a ritual for addressing personal wyrd and shild, suggestions for ceremonies, journaling, rune-work, artistic expression, and meditations relating to the subjects we've explored in this book.

There's a great deal of material in this book; you may find some chapters of definite interest to you, and other chapters less so. I've provided a detailed table of contents so it's easier for you to find topics you're interested in, and can skip over subjects of less relevance to your interests. The Word-Hoard or glossary includes definitions of important concepts and indicates which chapters discuss those concepts, for ease of reference.

Contributors

This is an in-depth exploration of orlog and approaches it from many directions: both scholarly and traditional directions, and more exploratory and speculative ones. We present both theoretical and practical aspects of orlog, while considering ancient views and modern ones. I'm honored to include in this book the inspiring contributions of two wise and experienced Heathens, Sara Axtell and Daniela

Svartheiðrinn Simina, whom I refer to here as Sara and Svartheiðrinn. Their contributions are identified by name, both at the beginning of the chapters or sections they've written, and in the table of contents. We come to these explorations of orlog from similar but not identical directions, which is the value of including more than one author here!

Many of the references and resources listed in the Book Hoard, and included at the end of some chapters, offer more discussions, practices, and viewpoints on topics we discuss here, and we encourage you to explore them. We all hope that, whether you agree or disagree with specific points throughout this in-depth exploration of orlog, you will find this book thought-provoking and worthwhile as you follow your own unique path on the way toward Heathen wisdom.

~ Winifred, Sara, and Svartheiðrinn ~

The World of Orlog

'Os / Ansuz / Tree arising from the Well.'

Os / Ansuz is the wellspring of all speech,
The foundation of wisdom and useful to the wise,
And to everyone it is gladness, prosperity and hope.
(Anglo-Saxon Rune Poem for Os, my rendition.)

Part I. Orlog Yesterday: Laying the Layers

Manuscript of the Beowulf poem, kept in the British Museum. Layers of orlog are preserved in these layers of pages!

The History of Orlog

1. The History of 'Orlog'

We'll begin our explorations into this mysterious phenomenon, orlog, by taking a look at the history of the word 'orlog' as its meanings developed in the main Germanic languages. For ease of discussion, we are using the generic spelling 'orlog' as the general term for the phenomenon that is the subject of this book, except when discussing the specific term in a given language. By using 'orlog' as the neutral umbrella term, we can discuss various aspects of the word without choosing the spelling of one or the other Germanic language as the 'only correct' version of its spelling and its meaning. Not to mention that 'orlog' is easier for modern English speakers to say and to spell than the original words are! So, let's turn now to the history of this word, beginning with Gothic as the oldest written form of the Germanic languages.

Though the Gothic word *us-lagjan* = 'to lay, to lay upon,' lay hands upon' exists, which would be the form that the word 'orlog' would take in Gothic, it does not have the meaning of 'fate,' as far as one can tell from the available texts. The oldest written texts where 'orlog' words do have the meaning of something like 'fate' are in Anglo-Saxon *(orlæg, orleg,* pronounced 'orlay'), Old High German *(urlag)*, and Old Saxon *(orlag)*. Anglo-Saxon, Old High German, and Old Saxon texts where this word appears are several centuries older than manuscripts written in Old Norse, such as the Poetic Edda which was written in the 13th century based on oral poetry composed during the period around 800 to 1100 CE.

Table 1. Time-periods of Old Germanic Literature
(all CE / AD)

Gothic Bible: around 350
Anglo-Saxon / Old English literature: 650-1100; some is based on older oral poetry
Old Saxon literature: 700s-1100s
Old High German literature: 750-1050
Old Norse Eddas: Written during the late 13th century, based on oral poetry composed during 800-1150.
Note: By the time ON Eddas were written, OHG, OS and A-S / OE had already shifted to their Middle forms, no longer 'Old.'

Note that there is a period of about 900 years between the earliest substantial Germanic-language text that we have—parts of the Bible translated into Gothic—and the written forms of the Old Norse Eddas and early sagas. (I am not counting runic inscriptions here, many of which are much older, but rather written texts of more substantial content and length where forms of the word 'orlog' are used and can be understood in context.) In tracing the history of our word-concept 'orlog,' this 900-year time span is significant. Words may have shifted meanings, and new meanings for words developed during almost a millennium of time, as we shall explore here.

Non-Norse Germanic writings were composed earlier in time and are useful for tracing the development of the 'orlog' word and concept. On the other hand, much of the Old Norse writing offers more of a Heathen context and thinking than the earlier Germanic language writings, which are often focused on Christian topics and show more signs of Christian influence. The Old Norse oral literature period, from which most of the early written literature was drawn, covered centuries during which many were still Heathen, and others were struggling with conversion. In other words, some of the texts we examine here are older in time and language development (the non-Norse literature), while others may be 'older' in terms of more Heathen-oriented, less Christian perspectives (Old Norse literature). Thus, all of these resources have something to offer our explorations here.

We need to keep in mind that this information does not necessarily tell us anything about the age of the orlog-concept itself in the different cultures, since the words would have been in use for centuries before finally being written down when those cultures were introduced to textual writing. But it is worth asking whether we can see evidence of some kind of evolution of the concept, or its branching off into different directions, based on the ages of the texts in the different languages.

Primary Meanings of Orlog

Here are the etymologies, the word-roots, of orlog words in the main Germanic languages, followed by a discussion of their implications for our analysis.

Table 2: Etymologies of Orlog

Proto-Germanic (PGmc) *ut-* became *uz-* = a preposition meaning 'out, out of,' from Proto-Indo-Europoean *ud-* = 'up, out'. Then became Gothic *us-*; and ON *ór, úr*, meaning 'out of, from.' In the other Germanic languages this prefix took the forms *or, ur, yr, ar, er, ör* (deVries p. 419). I do not find any meaning of 'ur = origin, beginning, primitive' in Proto-Germanic. The Proto-Germanic form for orlog would likely be *uz-lagjan,* but I don't find this word in the Proto-Germanic dictionary.
Gothic (Go): *Us-lagjan* = 'to lay, to lay upon, lay hands upon,' from *ligan* = to lie (down). This is the form that the word 'orlog' takes in Gothic.
Anglo-Saxon (A-S): *Orlæg, orleg* means both 'fate' and 'battle, war, strife.'
Old Saxon (OS): *Orlag* means 'fate' and 'war,' *urlagi* means 'war, fighting.'

The History of Orlog

Old High German (OHG): *Urlag, urlagi, urlac* means 'fate' and 'war.' **Middle High German:** *urlouc* with the same meanings.

The prefix *ur- / or-* in all three of the above languages (A-S, OS, OHG) refers to 'original / primal / ancient.' The root *læg / leg / lag* in all three languages means 'to lay, to lay upon.' So *orlæg* becomes 'ur-layers, ancient layers,' or 'that which arises or comes from (ur-) layers'.

Old Frisian (OFr): *Orloch* means 'fate' and 'war'. Its descendant, modern Dutch, has the word *oorlag* meaning a naval battle.

Old Norse (ON): *ørlǫg* = 'fate,' a plural word, from *or-* meaning 'out of, from' and *lǫg* meaning both 'layers' and 'laws.'

Proto-Indo-European (PIE): I do not find a word resembling 'orlog' in PIE, but looking up the Latin roots of 'origin,' *oriri,* we find the meaning 'to arise, appear, be born.' This traces back to PIE *ori-yo,* and to the prefix *er-* 'to be, to exist.' In the Germanic languages this takes the form *ar-* and *or-* and appears in the modern English verb 'are': 'you are, we are, we exist.' It is also the root of 'earth' and its Germanic cognates. (Watkins p. 24.) In none of the etymological sources I've searched do I find the suggestion that the 'or' of 'orlog' relates to this PIE root *er-*. All of them trace the *or-* of orlog to the PIE root *ud-* 'up, out of.'

The History of Orlog

To me, the PIE meanings of 'to arise, appear, be born, to be, to exist,' and the concept of 'origin, originate' seem to be closely related to the concept of orlog and to the meanings of 'up, out of.' Whatever the true linguistic connections may be, in my personal understanding and my own spiritual practice, I find a meaningful linkage between the concepts of 'orlog,' 'origin,' 'arising,' 'birth,' 'coming into being,' 'existence,' and 'earth' itself. Earth is 'that which is laid down in layers' and is the foundation of earthly existence. I offer these thoughts for your consideration as well.

Evolution from 'uslagjan'

Looking at these roots in the various Germanic languages, it seems that either Gothic was the only main Germanic language that did not have the meaning of 'fate' for orlog, while the others did, or else at some time and in many places during the three hundred-plus year span between Gothic writing and the earliest writings in Anglo-Saxon, Old Saxon, and Old High German (textual writing came later for Old Norse), the meanings of orlog that are familiar to us today developed within the latter cultures.

Here is my thought about how the meaning of orlog could have evolved from Gothic *uslagjan* 'to lay upon, lay hands upon' into the orlog meanings of 'fate' and 'war' in later Germanic languages. 'Laying hands upon' someone often indicates a fateful event in their life. Here are a few examples of how *uslagjan* was used in the Gothic Wulfila Bible to imply fateful outcomes.

Luke 9:62: Jesus said "No one who lays a hand *(uslagjans handu)* to the plow and looks back is fit for service in the kingdom of God." Here, 'laying a hand to the plow' is used as a metaphor for a fateful, lifelong decision and commitment.

John 7:29-30: Jesus claimed a mission from his God, whereupon the temple authorities "tried to seize him, but no one laid a hand on him *(uslagida ana ine handu)*, because his hour had not yet come." Here, it is recognized that the fateful moment for laying hands upon him was still in the future.

Mark 14:46: The Roman soldiers 'laid hands upon' Jesus *(uslagidedun handuns)* as they arrested him prior to his crucifixion, certainly a fateful event not only for him but also for the broader sweep of history.

I think that the meaning of *uslagjan* as 'laying upon, laying hands upon' could have led to the idea of 'fate' as something that 'grabs hold of one, lays a weight upon one, takes possession of the path of one's life.' Ancient Greek depictions of Nemesis, a fate-bearing divine being, show him tapping or grasping the shoulder of his 'victim,' a way of designating the target of fate, laying hands upon them. Inherent in this word and its meaning is the action of 'laying upon,' tying back to the literal meaning of orlog as 'layers laid down.'

The second meaning of orlog in the non-Norse languages, namely 'war, battle, strife,' is also a situation that 'grabs' or lays hands or a heavy weight upon people as warriors required to participate in battle, whether they want to or not, as well as non-warriors who are 'grabbed' as victims of attack, rape, and slavery during wartime: all of these being extremely fateful events in their lives.

The History of Orlog

Professional warriors in a warband were under oath to follow the commands of their leader, leading them toward their fate in battle. Oathing taps into fate and is a fateful action that shapes one's life.

There seems to me to be a logical progression beginning with 'laying hands upon' and 'laying (obligations, necessity) upon' a person, and then progressing to the concepts of 'fate' and of the Norns or Wyrd / Wurð / Wurt whose hands shape our fates. Thus, the concept of 'laying upon / laying hands upon,' *uslagjan,* could lead to concepts of orlog and wyrd. However, my idea about the progression of meanings is speculative. Without written evidence of language usage, one can't be sure when and how the concept of orlog arose within the various Germanic cultures. Nevertheless, I am pursuing this topic as well as I can here, aiming to offer meaningful ideas about the concept of orlog and its potential role in the modern practice of Heathen philosophy, religion and spirituality.

I am using this as my current working hypothesis: that the clear-cut meaning of orlog = fate developed sometime *after* the Gothic translation of the Bible, and *before* the earliest writings in the other Germanic languages. In other words, based on this reasoning the orlog-concept may not have been present during Proto-Germanic-speaking times, but began its development after the branches of the Germanic languages began separating from each other, sometime after 350 CE. By around 650 CE the orlog-concept was well-developed as we see in the earliest non-Gothic Germanic writings beginning at that time-period. In Chapter 7, "The Curious Case of the Missing Wyrd-Word," I explore another perspective on the development of the fate-concept among the Goths.

The History of Orlog

Svartheiðrinn: Orlog as Fateful Inner Struggle

*Contributing author **Svartheiðrinn** adds the following thoughts about the meaningfulness of the connection between orlog as fate, and orlog as war, battle, strife.*

As Winifred noted, Anglo-Saxon, Old Saxon, and Old High German forms of the word orlog mean both 'fate' and 'battle, war, strife'. This is an interesting overlap, not only linguistically but also semantically. Fate is usually shaped through some form of battle, war, or strife, whether these take place on an actual battlefield or internally, within one's own psyche. As humans, we find ourselves torn between the desire to spring into action and fear, or other considerations, that hold us back from acting. As long as the inner struggle is ongoing, one side of our psyche fighting another without any of the sides prevailing, what lies ahead is still a blank page awaiting to be written. Then, the resolution of the inner conflict determines the content about to be laid on that page of our lives: will it be a heroic poem or scornful lines?

As an example, in the epic poem *Beowulf,* the young warrior Wiglaf, despite his youth and lack of experience, comes to Beowulf's aid while he fights the dragon. (Wiglaf's tale begins at l. 2602). All the other warriors are terrified: in their hearts, fear has won over loyalty, dignity, and the desire for fame. But young Wiglaf stills his fears in the face of danger. In his heart, love and loyalty for his king and kinsman Beowulf prevail. By contrast to the veteran troops and their commanders, Wiglaf resists the voices of fear and doubt. He summons up the courage to stab the dragon thus allowing Beowulf to deal it the final blow. By first winning his inner battle, Wiglaf then sets forth to write the next page in his life's book. His feelings steer his orlæg. Wiglaf becomes Beowulf's successor, and, as the new king, Wiglaf's orlæg is now intertwined with that of his own people.

Inner battles are orlog in seed-form: what happens on the actual battleground hinges on what will grow out of that seed. Then, confrontations on the battlefield further weave new strands of orlog. Outcomes of battles, internal and external ones, taken individually and cumulatively, become the foundation for new decisions to be made and new actions to be taken. The word *orlog* captures perfectly the blurriness between fate and battle, as a profound linguistic and semantic subtlety.

Orlog, Layers, and Laws

2. Orlog, Layers, and Laws

In the previous chapter we looked at meanings of orlog primarily in the non-Norse old Germanic languages, with the focus on 'laying layers' and on 'war, battle, strife.' Now we'll turn to a meaning of orlog that is derived from study of Norse literature, namely that *lǫg* refers not only to 'layers,' but also to 'laws': laws spoken by, and laid by, the Norns.

Comparing Roots of Orlog in Multiple Languages

Old Norse ørlǫg has been extensively studied and discussed; I'll turn here to Karen Bek-Pedersen's summary of its likely meanings from her book *The Norns in Old Norse Mythology*. She identifies two distinct but similar interpretations; both of them rest on the understanding that the Norse word *lǫg* refers to both 'laws' and 'layers'. The interpretation most often used is that ørlǫg refers to *ur-laws:* original laws, primal laws, laws laid down in ancient times at the beginning of things.

The other interpretation focuses on *ør-* as a form of the preposition *ur-* meaning 'out of, from,' rather than 'primal, ancient.' Thus the meaning becomes "that out of which something is laid down." (Bek-Pedersen, p. 170.) This

Orlog, Layers, and Laws

interpretation still leaves the idea of 'laws' in the picture; in Bek-Pedersen's words, it is "the stuff out of which laws can be derived" (p. 170). For this second interpretation Bek-Pedersen uses the analogy of woolen yarn being the material 'given' by ørlǫg; while one is free to make various items of clothing out of this yarn, there are many things that cannot be made from it (p. 170). In this view, ørlǫg 'conditions' or sets conditions upon what we can do with the circumstances dealt out to us by the Norns, exerting some control but leaving us some choice as well.

With respect to the Old Norse word ørlǫg, the connection with laws seems clear, whichever interpretation one uses. This is reinforced by the phrase used to describe the Norns' actions in *Völuspá* vs. 20 where they 'lay laws / layers' at Urð's well: 'there they lay laws, choose life for children of aldr, speak ørlög (*þær lög lögðu, þær líf kuru / alda börnum, ørlög seggja*).

The connection between 'layers' and 'laws' is a logical one when we look at systems of common-law. Common-law is generally based upon precedent: on past judgements, experiences, observations of what works and what doesn't in the particular society where it is practiced. Common-law depends on 'layers' of law and practice that preceded it, and is different from statutory law. Statutory law is 'made,' not 'laid': it is made by legislative bodies and by kingly decrees, rather than arising organically out of precedent and history. As a modern example the US Congress creates statutory laws, often called 'acts of Congress,' such as the Clean Air Act, whereas local municipalities develop their own interpretations of common-law matters such as those pertaining to nuisances, ordinances, permits, and property disputes.

Orlog, Layers, and Laws

Gothic has the word *ur-redan*, meaning 'to make ordinances.' It comes from *redan* (related to Anglo-Saxon *rede)* meaning 'to counsel, to provide for, to think of,' plus the prefix *us-*. (*Us-*, meaning 'out, out of, from, forth from,' changes to *ur-* before an initial letter R.) So *ur-redan* or ordinances and rules are what grow out of thinking about matters, using good counsel to provide rules that support an orderly community. *Ga-raideins* is the noun meaning 'ordinance, rule, authority'.

In *ur-redan* we see a word similar to the literal meaning of Old Norse *ørlǫg:* laws are 'what grow out of good counsel / rede' in Gothic, and 'what grow out of primal layers' in Old Norse. Yet in the Gothic word there is no implication of 'fate,' it is simply a practical word for ordinances and rules. In Old Norse, laws grow out of 'layers laid down in the past,' with an implication of otherworldly powers (the Norns) being involved, whereas in Gothic laws grow out of good counsel and good governance. (As an aside, this shows quite a difference in their perspectives on 'what laws are': Old Norse shows more of a common-law perspective, while Gothic shows more of a statutory-law perspective, perhaps influenced by Roman practices.)

The connection between 'layers' and laws' does not seem to be present in the non-Norse Germanic languages, except for the late (Danelaw period) Anglo-Saxon borrowing of Old Norse *lag* = law to form their word *lagu* meaning 'law'. Anglo-Saxon has older, more widely used, and linguistically unrelated words for 'law,' as is the case with the other Germanic languages. One Anglo-Saxon word related to law is *riht,* the root of our word 'right,' having to do with justice, rule, custom, 'the right / legal way to do things.' The same word and meaning occur in Gothic *raihts*, Old Saxon *rehts*,

Orlog, Layers, and Laws

Old High German *rihti, girihti,* and Proto-Germanic **raka, *rehta, *garihtija.*

Unlike with Old Norse *lagu,* none of the law-related words in the non-Norse languages were used to form a word relating to 'orlog' and 'fate.' Although law-related considerations may well play a role in 'fate' as it works its way through our individual lives and our societies, none of the words and concepts of 'law' in the non-Norse languages, such as *gesetnes, riht, folc-riht, æwe, ur-redan, domas, ælðeow,* and others, bear any etymological relationship to their words *orlæg, orlege, orlag, urlag.* In all the Germanic languages examined here, except for Old Norse, 'law' and 'fate' were not linguistically connected.

What was the real meaning of 'law' for widely-dispersed, small groups of people who had no written records and no powerful centralized authority-structure? They certainly had customs, traditions, expectations of behavior, that were taught during childhood and were enforced by the community. They generally had some authority-figure(s), both secular leaders such as king or goði, and priestly ones such as the law-speaker or law-warder (see deVries 1935, p. 262). What this leader spoke would have been 'law' for that specific time, location, and circumstance, not necessarily a forever-afterwards law broadly applied to everyone, everywhere. Germanic and many other ancient peoples were well aware that if they traveled to a foreign land, the law that they were subject to there might be very different than their traditions of law at home.

In general for the ancient Germanic peoples, 'laws' were laid down by ancestral traditions, by precedent, by learning from experience. Bek-Pedersen notes that the meanings and usage of the Old Norse words (a) *skǫp* = 'shaping;' (b) *siðr / forn siðr* = 'customs, practices, traditions, including religious practices;' and (c) *lagu* = 'law' are very similar: they refer to 'the way things should be, the customs and practices laid down by our ancestors' (p. 174).

This combination of patterns—customs and traditions, decisions shaped by leaders to fit specific circumstances— would have gradually laid layers of precedent, upon which more sophisticated law codes could be built as tribes and villages consolidated into larger and more powerful societies. This is indeed what happened in the Germanic lands and tribes, where their customary system of law was of great importance. They relied on trained 'law-speakers' to remember and recite them at the assemblies or Things. Both the 'law-speaker' and the 'law-warder' were considered priestly positions of authority (deVries 1935 p. 262). Each kingdom, tribe, village, etc. had its own tradition of laws.

Inner Law and Outer Law

Bek-Pedersen has an interesting point to make about the difference between 'law' and 'orlog'. Everyone must follow their community's laws or be outlawed, she notes, whereas ørlög operates on the individual level. She explains that:

Ørlög "is a person's individual 'law' which is given to them at birth and which they cannot go beyond. They may interpret this 'law' in a variety of ways, but they cannot 'break' it. Moreover, this 'law' is ruthless and adheres neither to social nor to human norms, although it does maintain order of a kind" (p. 172). The law is created by the community and made publicly known. "Fate is secret, unknown and internal, laid down for the individual by an unseen, uncontrolled and uncontrollable force" (p. 173).

Orlog, Layers, and Laws

These are important points, and to Bek-Pedersen these functions of law and fate have the same purpose: to keep order at different levels of existence (p. 173).

I would offer some additional nuances to this explanation. In Germanic thought, law is essentially, fundamentally, a defining feature of their community, including both the living and the ancestors. Everyone participates in it to some degree; it forms the substrate of community life and hence of normal human behavior. It also helps to define the identity of the community as a whole. I think it's fair to say that many ancient Heathens would consider their own law to be the defining feature of their community; people who transgressed it were outlawed, cast out of the community.

Ørlǫg, as Bek-Pedersen points out, is conversely a 'law' that is secret, inscrutable and individual, the exact opposite of an open system of laws created by generations of humans living in community. Consider this: in a great many instances seen in Norse and Germanic poems and sagas, the pressures of a grim orlog drive individuals *against* the patterns of laws and community customs. As I see it, while laws are made to keep order, orlog sometimes brings about *disorder* and lawless behavior, at least within the domain of Midgard. This is especially seen in the meaning of orlog as 'war, strife, conflict, adversity,' which are very common meanings in all the Germanic languages except Old Norse, where this meaning exists but is rarely used. Orlog, so often experienced as a 'dread blow of fate,' can be chaotic and disruptive.

Orlog, Layers, and Laws

Sigrun and Helgi II

One among many examples of this disruptive aspect of the Norns' shaping can be found in the Eddic poem *Helgakviða Hundingsbani II* or the *Second Poem of Helgi Hundingsbani*. It's a complicated tale, thought by some scholars to be mismatched fragments stuck together, but it's clear that *skǫp Norna,* the shapings of the Norns, play a role in it. The heroes of the poem, Helgi and the Valkyrie Sigrun, are said to have been lovers and spouses reborn from previous lives, and their efforts to reunite end up causing bloody slaughter (which was also caused by feuds and killing involving other characters—all layers from the past).

Both characters grieve the slaughter even though they were involved with causing it. Helgi calls Sigrun a 'strange wight'—*alvitr*—in verse 26, a clue that as a Valkyrie (though born of humans) she stands outside of human law. He has just killed Sigrun's father and kinfolk, partly due to past feuds, partly due to his and Sigrun's wish to marry even though she had already been betrothed to her father's ally Hodbrodd, who is now dying on the battlefield.

Helgi says to Sigrun that he realizes this death of her kinfolk is not all good fortune for her (it's good that they can now wed, but her family line is decimated) and he believes that the Norns have something to do with this. He continues in verse 28, saying that she did nothing to stop the battle, that it was 'shaped for her' *(var þér þat skapat)* to be the cause of strife among powerful men. Sigrun weeps over this outcome. Helgi comforts her, saying she is their battle-goddess *(Hildr)* and that warriors cannot escape what is shaped for them. Sigrun expresses her regrets over the situation: "I'd choose now that those who are gone could live again, and that I could still hold you in my arms" (v. 29).

25

Orlog, Layers, and Laws

All of these events involve past battles and deaths, vengeance for past deaths, betrothal, battle and slaughter to unmake the betrothal and bring about marriage to someone else. Orlog has been busy shaping events here, laying layers on top of complex layers, not paying much attention to 'law' and the aims of law to create social order and stability. The laws or shaping of the Norns came about, but bear little resemblance to human law as a method of ordering social life. If orlog has any cosmic-level ordering function—a question we will consider later—apparently that function is not always reflected in everyday community life, unlike laws.

A Common Denominator

Let's return now to this point: though all of the Germanic peoples had a great respect for and reliance upon their concepts of law, none of the non-Norse Germanic languages had a meaning associated with 'law' for their 'orlog' words. They used the meaning of 'layers,' not 'laws,' and unlike Old Norse, their words for 'layers' and 'laws' are not linguistically related. *Some concept other than 'laws' lies at the root of the orlog-phenomenon,* at least as conceived in the non-Norse branches of people and languages, writing centuries earlier than the Norse texts. I suggest that the meaning of 'layers = laws' and its connection with ørlög may have been a later evolution of the concept that occurred specifically in the Nordic lands. What was the earlier concept as it developed in other Germanic-speaking regions?

We're looking here for a common denominator in the meaning of orlog-words in the different Germanic language branches, one that we can use as a basis for further understanding in our modern world and world-view. The second interpretation summarized earlier by Bek-Pedersen comes close for our purposes: not 'ur-laws' exactly, but in Bek-Pedersen's words, "the stuff out of which laws can be derived" (p. 170). I see no reason why the two meanings of *or-* / *ur-* should not be combined in this context, so that we have not just "the stuff out of which laws can be derived," but the ancient stuff, the primal stuff, the original stuff, the stuff of greatest importance: *ur-stuff.*

    I would take these ideas further and suggest that it is not only 'laws' which arise from this *ur*-material or 'stuff.' I would call this stuff *'the layers which form a substrate out of which fateful patterns, events, and circumstances arise,'* including but not limited to laws and other patterns of human behavior and social life.

    Paul Bauschatz' brilliant book *The Well and the Tree: World and Time in Early Germanic Culture* is a doctoral dissertation that examines the early Germanic concepts of time and fate with special focus on the Beowulf poem. This book has had considerable influence on modern Heathen thought, including my own. In his chapter "Action, Space, and Time" Bauschatz uses the imagery of the Well and the Tree to picture how life is lived within Space, symbolized by the World-Tree, and Time, symbolized by the Well. Humans, living in Midgard upon the Tree, the fabric of Space, enact deeds which form like dew and drip down toward the Well below, the fabric of Time. Insignificant deeds and events fall outside the rim of the Well and are gone, while significant ones fall into the Well itself and form the basis of orlog. In turn, water / orlog from the Well is sucked into the roots of the Tree to nurture new layers of deeds in the life and worlds of the Tree. The Tree of Life, of

Orlog, Layers, and Laws

existence in Space, builds up in rings through this nourishing action: thus orlog underlies the structure of space-time.

Bauschatz also uses the image of constriction and containment of a spring or well-structure, which encloses the water of the well and forces it powerfully upward instead of letting it spread out weakly as a thin flood of water over the landscape. This illustrates the actions of constraint, necessity and orlog in powering the heroic life, a topic we will return to in discussing the relationship between orlog and ordeal. Heroes are powered by the pressure of orlog constraining their actions, creating the necessity that leads to heroic deeds. Without that force of necessity arising from orlog, there is little incentive for heroic action.

Defining Orlog

The definition of orlog that I'm using in this book is thus: *layers of significant deeds and events laid in the past which form a substrate out of which fateful patterns, events, and circumstances arise.* This meaning is entirely consistent with the etymologies of orlog-words in all the Germanic languages, not only the Norse meaning of 'ur-laws.' This definition certainly implies layers of laws: human-made laws, laws laid by the Great Powers, and natural laws such as those of cause and effect, but it is not limited to the formal concept of laws. Deeds, actions, decisions, words, choices, events, circumstances, natural processes: all can be laid as layers within the Well and in the growth-rings accreting around the Tree, as life continues through the ages.

Two modern German words can help our grasp of this idea. *Ursache* (OOR-sah-heh) means literally *ur*-matter, *ur*-thing. *Ursache* is the 'place, person, circumstance, thing, situation from which anything begins or comes; a cause, a source, something or someone that produces an effect or result.' *Ursprung* literally means the *ur*-spring, the *ur*-source. It is the 'source or origin, the originating time, place, point, or cause of an event or circumstance,' and its adjective *ursprünglich* includes the meaning of 'primal'. Both of these words work very nicely as descriptors for orlog, for Urð's Well, and for the work of Norns.

The influences within this primal, layered substrate of orlog 'condition' the circumstances of our lives, without necessarily being immutable laws. The interactions between ourselves and this substrate, in each generation, give rise to patterns including—but not limited to—the customs, laws, traditions, and practices that we create, individually and collectively, in order to deal with the results of these influential layers of orlog in our lives and our world.

A postage stamp celebrating the 1000-year anniversary of the Icelandic Althing, the gathering where laws were (and still are) made and acted upon, where deeds were judged, and fateful events decided upon.

3. The Shapings of the Norns

We've taken a look at the etymologies, histories, literal and symbolic meanings of the orlog-words; now let's expand our understanding by turning to another word that falls into the same general field of meaning when referring to the actions of the Norns. Bek-Pedersen points out that the two predominant words used in Old Norse to describe 'what the Norns do' are *ørlög* and *skǫp* (p. 172). *Skǫp* and its cognates in the other languages refer to 'shaping' and 'creating.' They are used to describe the Biblical creation in Christian writings. The meaning extends further; for example, the noun derived from the Anglo-Saxon word for shaping is used to mean the authoritative decree of a king or a Deity. Using the words of the decree, they shape the lives and actions of those who are subject to them, as the Norns 'speak orlog' and shape the lives of humans.

Having examined the word 'orlog' and its variants in some detail, let's take a look at this word 'shaping' as it appears in various old Germanic languages and earlier. It refers both to the action of shaping—the verb form, and to that which is shaped—the noun form of the word. In the older languages, the plural is often used as a noun: the 'shapings' of the Norns.

The Roots of Skǫp
(plural form of *skapa*)

Here are the roots and forms of the words for 'shape, shaping' in the various Germanic languages.

Table 3. The Roots of 'Shaping'

Proto-Indo-European (PIE): **skep* = "base of words with various technical meanings such as to cut, to scrape, to hack. 1a. shape, form, creation. 1b. *-ship* from Old English *-scipe* = state, condition" (e.g. friend-ship, relation-ship, apprentice-ship, etc.). (Watkins p. 80)
Proto-Germanic **skap(j)an* = 'to form, create'; …may be derived from *skapp / bon* = 'to shave, scrape'. (Kroonen p. 440)
Gothic *(ga-)skapjan, skaftjan,* = to shape, to shape one's course, to be about to do something. *Skafts* = a shaping, a making. *Gaskafts* = creation, creature.
Old Norse *skapa* = to shape, form, mould. *Skap* = shape, form, one's nature, sense, meaning, mood. Plural form *skǫp* = fate, destiny. deVries' dictionary proposes that this word comes from *skafa* = to shape something using methods of scraping, cutting or carving.

The Shapings of the Norns

Anglo-Saxon *ge-sceap* = shape, form, created being, creation, one's nature, decree, fate, destiny, dispensation, condition. *Ge-sceap-hwíl* = the time of death appointed or shaped by fate; *to gescæp-hwíle* = at the appointed time. *Ge-scieppan* = to create, form, shape, make, order, destine, arrange, adjudge, assign.
Old Saxon *gi-skaft* = 'state, condition, form, shape, one's nature.' *gi-skeppian* = 'to produce, accomplish, create.' *Gi-skapu* plural form = 'decrees of fate.'
Old High German *scepfen, skepfen* = to make, create, do.
Faroese *skapa* = to shape, form, mould, cause, bring about.

To summarize: the languages that use a 'shaping' word specifically with reference to 'fate' are Old Norse and Old Saxon, both using the plural form to mean 'fate', as well as Anglo-Saxon which uses the singular form. I have not found 'shaping' words that specifically refer to 'fate' in Old High German, Gothic, or Proto-Germanic, but the 'shaping' words in these languages cover meanings of 'creation / bringing into being,' 'causation / bringing about,' and 'shaping one's course' which for our Heathen mindset do point toward the fate-filled actions of the Norns or Wyrd. If not specifically referring to fate, these meanings are certainly related to orlog and fate.

As we can see from these linguistic roots, the general idea of *skapa / gesceaft* has its roots in carving, cutting, shaping something physical. The phrase in the *Völuspá* about the Norns 'scoring on slips of wood,' *skáru á skiði*,

The Shapings of the Norns

points directly toward their actions of 'shaping,' *skǫp,* in the same way that their 'laying of layers' points toward ørlög, the ur-layers, the primal layers:

Urð hétu eina, aðra Verðandi,
skáru á skíði, Skuld ina þriðju;
þær lög lögðu, þær líf kuru
alda börnum, ørlög seggja.

Urð one is called, another Verðandi,
Scoring on slips of wood, Skuld is third;
There they lay layers, there life choose,
For children of aldr (mortals), speak ørlög.
(Verses 20-21, my translation)

'Shaping' something gives it meaning, purpose, functionality. An uncarved piece of stone or wood, one that is not deliberately shaped, does not have the same meaning, purpose, functionality as a carved one. Something that is shaped by a conscious being retains a reflection of the shaper's intention; this is especially true when it comes to 'shaping words' such as the laws spoken by the Norns or by a king or Deity. 'Shaping' is much more direct, authoritative, more finalized than the 'laying of layers' that we see in the word 'orlog.' To shape something implies that there are 'shapers,' intentional and skillful beings who are doing the shaping. It also implies that whatever is shaped retains that shape while it remains in existence, as carved wood or stone does. Here are some quotations from the *Poetic Edda* illustrating the power of the Norns' shaping:

The Shapings of the Norns

"The Norns shaped the *aldr* of the young prince." *(Helgi I,* vs. 2, Poetic Edda.) Larrington translates *aldr* as 'fate' here; I translate it as 'lifespan, lifetime,' but the meaning of 'fate' is certainly implied, however the word is translated.

The dwarf Andvari, sometime-keeper of the cursed treasure-hoard of the Nibelungs, complains that "A wretched norn shaped us (me) *(skǫp oss)* in ancient days." Larrington translates *skǫp oss* as 'shaped my fate.' *(Reginsmal* / Lay of Regin v. 2, Poetic Edda)

"A descendant of Skjoldings may not break Sigrdrifa's sleep, because of *sköpum norna"* (because of the Norns' shapings). *(Fafnismal* / *Lay of Fafnir,* v. 44, Poetic Edda.)

Hallfreðr: Skǫp Norna as Heathen Troth

Interestingly, the phrase *skǫp Norna,* 'the shapings (plural) of the Norns,' was used to signify the Heathen faith or troth in general. An example of this usage is shown in the following quotation from *Hallfreðarsaga* (dated to approximately 996 CE). This saga describes, in part, the skald Hallfreðr's reluctant and resentful steps toward conversion to Christianity as pressed upon him by his patron king Olaf Tryggvason, the often-brutal converter of Norway to Christianity. In chapter 6 of the saga, Hallfreðr composed a series of verses; after each one, Olaf complained that it was too Heathen and said Hallfreðr must try again. The verse quoted below was the fifth and last of these attempts and apparently met the king's requirements. Even so, it is easy to detect the resentfulness that underlies Hallfreðr's words:

The Shapings of the Norns

So it is with Sygna-ruler (Norway's ruler):
(Old) customs and Blót-sacrifice are forbidden.
Most must shun
The time-honored shapings of the Norns *(fornhaldin sköp norna)*.
All must leave behind
Oðin's word for (the sake of) the rood (Christian cross).
Now I am forced (away) from Frey's
Kindred to worship Christ.
(my translation)

Sá er með Sygna ræsi
siðr að blót eru kviðjuð.
Verðum flest að forðast
fornhaldin **sköp norna.**
Láta allir ýtar
Óðins orð fyrir róða.
Nú em ek neyddr frá Freyju
niðjum Krist að biðja.
(Chapter 6, Hallfreðarsaga Vandræðaskálds, Möðruvallabok version.)

Here we see that the 'shapings of the Norns' apply not only to individual lives, but to the spiritual paths taken by folkdoms, tribes, peoples. Our Heathen faith itself is the 'shaping of the Norns,' an insight that holds profound significance for modern Heathens.

Examples of How the Word 'Shape' is Used

Here are more examples of how 'shape' is defined and used with respect to orlog and wyrd in various old Germanic languages. (All are my translations.)

The Shapings of the Norns

I wrote in Chapter 2, "Orlog, Layers and Laws," about the *Second Poem of Helgi Hundingsbani,* where Helgi and Sigrun bring about the death of her kinsmen in their effort to wed. 'Shaping' is several times used in this poem as an expression for fate, orlog. Helgi tells Sigrun that she did nothing to stop the battle, that it was 'shaped for her' *(var þér þat skapat)* to be the cause of strife among powerful men (v. 28). Sigrun weeps over the loss of her kin, and Helgi comforts her, saying that warriors cannot escape what is shaped *(sköpum)* for them (v. 29).

In the Old Saxon *Heliand* the word *wurde-giskapu,* meaning 'wyrd-shaping,' and the word *orlag-hwile* or 'orlag-while' meaning 'the time of fate and death' are used as synonyms for each other (ll. 3354-5).

In the Old Saxon *Heliand,* Jesus is shown entering Jerusalem and speaking a prophecy: "Woe to you, Jerusalem, that you know not what wyrd has shaped for you *(wurði-giskefti)* nor what shall become of you." (ll. 3691-2)

In the Gothic Bible there is a phrase describing Judas as the one who was 'shaping a betrayal toward Jesus' that would lead to his fated death. (John 12:4)

Here are some examples from Anglo-Saxon based on compound words using *gesceaft,* meaning 'a shaping, what is shaped,' and also refers to 'creation.'

Beowulf died fighting the dragon that was threatening his people. His death was described as the end of his *lif-gesceaft,* the shape of his life that included his fated death. (l. 3064)

The Shapings of the Norns

Similar to *lif-gesceaft* is *ealdor-gesceaft:* the shaping of one's ealdor or aldr, one's span of life and the conditions one experiences during that span. The *aldr / ealdor* is discussed further in Chapter 5.

Mæl-gesceaft refers to fate shaped by speech or decree (mæl = speech, talk*)*: "That which happens at its appointed time in accordance with the decrees of fate. *Ic bád mælgesceafta* I waited for that which in due time fate would assign me." (Bosworth-Toller dictionary.)

Metod-sceaft, metod-gesceaft, meaning 'metod-shaping': "Decree of fate, doom, fate after death." Metod is a poetic term that refers sometimes to Wyrd or 'fate,' sometimes to Heathen Gods or the Christian God. When used in a Christian context, *metodsceaft* often referred to a person's fate after death: their God's spoken judgement and assignment to hell or heaven. Cognate words with the same meaning are Old Saxon *metod* and Old Norse *mjötuðr*. Another poetic term is *metod-wang,* 'metod-field,' meaning a battlefield, a field where fate / orlog happens according to the decrees of the Powers. Beowulf says that "Wyrd swept all my kin to *metodsceafte,"* to their doom that was shaped by otherworldly powers. (l. 2815)

It's quite clear that the concept of 'shaping' was seen as something wyrd-ful, fateful, in the old Germanic languages, a power that lies in the hands of supernatural beings as well as those of humans in positions of power.

In contrast to deliberate shaping, the image of the Norns 'laying layers' is a more indirect action; it lays the foundations for what is to come but is more of a 'conditioning' force than a strict 'shaping' force as the image of carving or scoring offers. Implied in this distinction between 'shaping' and 'laying layers' is that orlog can be seen as either a deliberately directed process undertaken by conscious beings (shaping), or as a natural, organic process of cosmic ordering, of the action of cause and effect, that does not necessarily require the actions of supernatural beings (the laying of layers). Layers can be laid by natural processes, as one can see in layers of soil, sediment, and rock formations here in Midgard. We'll return to this point later when discussing the metaphysics and evolution of orlog.

Do Runes Play a Role?

Interestingly, no spinning or weaving actions are mentioned in the poetic descriptions of what the Norns do, as Bek-Pedersen discusses, even though spinning and weaving show up in imagery of other beings of Fate, such as the Greek *Moirai*. The Norns' work as described in the Völuspá verse quoted earlier involves scoring wood, laying layers, choosing life, and speaking ørlǫg. Some commentators on this Völuspá poem that I've read indicate that the phrase *skaru á skiði,* 'scoring on slips of wood,' may have been interpolated into the poem, but have not given references to support this statement. If it was interpolated presumably it came from some other description of the Norns extant at that time period.

Whether or not it was interpolated, I believe this phrase is of great importance—perhaps it was interpolated *because* of its significance. Our previous linguistic discussion shows that, in fact, scraping or cutting wood may well be the originating concept behind words for 'shaping' in all the Germanic languages. Thus, this 'scoring on wood' may be the *primal action* of the Norns, setting into motion and

The Shapings of the Norns

shaping their following actions of laying layers, choosing, and speaking. In effect, it is by their 'scoring on wood' that orlog is laid.

This is one of the few drawings I've found in the public domain where the Nornir are carving (presumably runes) on slips of wood and casting them, rather than 'spinning fate.' By Ludwig Pietsch.

Though I am not discussing runes directly in this book, something needs to be said about them in this context. It isn't stated clearly whether the Norns' 'scoring on slips of wood' involves runes or not, but honestly, what else would they be scoring? Perhaps not the specific runes we know about today, here in Midgard, but surely the shapes they score are runes of some kind: mysteries expressed as symbolic shapes, which channel magical, creative power according to the will of the rune-carver. From this

The Shapings of the Norns

perspective, the Norns' initial actions as they 'shape fate' are to generate and direct rune-power, which then provides the potency and impetus for their further actions of laying layers, choosing life, and speaking with power.

We are given clues to the degree of primal power that can be wielded by the runes in the well-known account of Odin's sacrifice of himself to himself, hanging on the Tree for nine nights to attain the runes. In the *Hávamál* of the *Poetic Edda,* verses 138 through 145 describe this self-sacrifice to gain runes and wisdom, its powerful results, and go on to challenge the knowledge and will of those who would attempt to follow this path.

The Shapings of the Norns

Odin was not the only one who engaged in a rune-quest; the founding runemasters of other powerful races of beings are also listed in *Hávamál* verse 143: "Odin among the Æsir, Dain among the Elves, Dvalinn among the Dwarves, Asvið among the Jotnar." Presumably all these mighty runemasters had to meet some great challenge in order to gain the runes for their respective tribes.

Verse 145 closes with "so Thund carved before the close of the nations' history, where he rose up, when he came back," Thund being one of Odin's many names or *heiti* (descriptive nicknames). An example of Odin's fateful use of the runes is shown in *Helgi Hundingsbani II,* where he is blamed for a kin-war: "Odin alone caused all the misfortune, for he cast hostile runes between kinsmen" (v. 34, Larrington translation of the *Poetic Edda*). I believe that all these lines about Odin describe his actions which shape 'fate,' orlog, by laying down layers that spread their shaping influence through time and space. I think there is little doubt that ancient Heathens believed runic magic can potentially shape orlog / wyrd. When wielded by humans, runes are not powerful enough to completely overcome the Norns' original shaping, but they hold some efficacious power of influencing matters during the course of our human lives, nonetheless.

So, to return to our original point, the idea that the Norns carve runes as part of their process of shaping orlog seems to me consistent with ancient Heathen beliefs about the fundamental shaping power of runes—power which is known to be used by Deities and other primal beings. I suspect that the Norns have their own runes, secret to themselves, and use them to empower and direct their shaping actions.

The Shapings of the Norns

Speaking Orlog

Urð's Well, the gathering-place of the Norns, is located under a root of the World-Tree that (somewhat paradoxically) reaches toward heaven. This is the same place where the doom-stead or formal assembly of the Æsir is located, where they gather daily to make decisions and pass judgement. *(Gylfaginning* 15, p. 19, in Sturluson.) The dooms or deemings—the judgements—of the Holy Ones take spoken form: they name the heavenly bodies and decree their courses, for example, in verses 5-6 of the *Völuspá*. The seats or 'stools'—*stola*—of the Deities here and in other verses of the *Völuspá* are called *rökstola*, where *rök* has the following meanings: "reason, ground, origin / wonder, sign, marvel," according to the Cleasby-Vigfusson dictionary. DeVries' dictionary offers the German equivalents of "exposition, reason, course, fate" for *rök,* and notes the cognate Old English word *racu* = "course, bed of a river, tale or account," as well as Old Saxon *raka* and Old High German *rahha*, both meaning "tale, story, account." Larrington's translation of the Poetic Edda renders *rökstola* as "thrones of fate." I suggest that as practicing Heathens, we understand that all of these definitions of *rök* are descriptors of these mighty *rök*-beings, the Æsir—their abilities and activities—and also suggest that each of the words defining *rök* offers fruitful threads for meditation.

So, these *rökstola* are the seats that the Deities take during their most formal meetings where they originate or provide a foundation for cosmic phenomena, consolidate their understanding of events, direct the course of events including war and peace, pronounce judgements and decrees. They do this by speaking—and this is fateful speaking, speaking that shapes the course of events in the

The Shapings of the Norns

Worlds. The *rökstola,* or 'thrones of fate' in Larrington's translation, are mentioned again in verses 24 and 26 about the events of the 'first war in the world,' where the Gods again 'speak doom' and lay out their plans for action.

Urð's Well and the Norns are also present there, at the same place by the root of Yggdrasil; presumably they are witnesses and perhaps participants in the deemings of the Gods. Both the Norns and the Deities are laying layers of orlog in the Well during these events, shaping the events and what springs from them by their words and actions. These acts of formal speech are not ordinary chatter; they have the power to lay orlog and set it in motion in the Worlds. In my understanding, it is the witness of the Norns which causes the deemings of the Deities to be laid in the Well as layers of orlog—the Norns facilitate the transformation from 'speech' into 'orlog' by their witness and participation at the doom-stead of the Gods, just as they 'speak orlog' themselves.

Do the Norns perform this 'speech-to-orlog' transformation only for themselves and the Gods? Or do they help us do it, too? They do help us shape our Will into deeds and then into orlog, which then shapes the overall course of our life and our life-ways. They do this in many ways, but the most profound way the Norns help us transform speech into orlog is through the Heathen sacrament of symbel or sumble.

4. The Ancient Role of Symbel

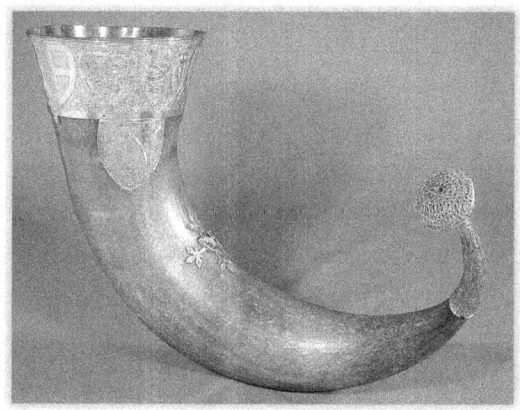

'Kongshornet,' a king's drinking horn beautifully decorated with filigree.

Orlog is shaped by speaking, as well as by the scoring of runes by the Norns, which I assume is accompanied by speech in the form of rune-galdor. Deeds may 'lay' orlog, but speech 'shapes' it. What gives 'speech' such power? Is it only Norns and Deities whose speech has such power, or do humans have some degree of this as well? What is the connection between speech, actions /deeds, and orlog: what weaves them together?

The Ancient Role of Symbel

The answers, I believe, lie most deeply in the Heathen sacrament of symbel or sumble, though we enact this connection in everyday words and deeds as well. Our words matter, our deeds matter, in every context of our lives when we realize how they are connected with orlog. When we speak in symbel in the company of the Gods and Goddesses, the Norns, and perhaps our fellow Heathens too, we have the opportunity to share most deeply in the shapings of the Norns, as they apply to our own lives and actions. Thus *skǫp Norna,* our Heathen troth itself, is—word by word, deed by deed—shaped into being as a living faith in Midgard today.

In old Heathen thought, it was not only the Norns, Deities, and powerful rulers whose words could shape the course of events. The speech of ordinary people, too, has power when spoken in the right way, under the right circumstances. Our deeds may 'lay' orlog, but speech 'shapes' it: this is a profound insight into the power of the symbel ceremony with its formal oaths, boasts, and toasts. "Speech is the means by which the fact of any action is made explicit and the way in which its continuing present is assured" (Bauschatz p. 109).

Shaping Speech in Symbel

Let's return here to Bauschatz' book *The Well and the Tree: World and Time in Early Germanic Culture.* Concerning the ceremony of symbel / sumble, a ceremonial feast that includes drinking, oaths, boasts, toasts, he offers an extensive list of references relating to this practice beginning with Tacitus' *Germania,* written about 98 CE. He continues with a list of references to Old Saxon *sittian at sumble,* Old Norse *gamban-sumbl* (glorious or mighty sumble), and Anglo-Saxon *symbel* or *symle* (pp. 72-3). The Norse also had the

The Ancient Role of Symbel

same or similar practice called the *Bragar-fulli*, pledging over the ale; I offer a 'case study' that features that term in the next section.

In Bauschatz' Chapter III on *"Beowulf* and the Nature of Events," he offers an in-depth analysis of scenes in the *Beowulf* poem where significant speeches are given in symbel, and examines their underlying implications relating to wyrd and orlog. These speeches link history and genealogies, past deeds and reputation, with current reputations, events, oaths, and intended future deeds. Bauschatz explains that there are formal structures to these speeches which have metaphysical links to the laying of orlog. "There seem to be at least two important kinds of 'fact-establishing' speech...the *bēot* or the *gilp* (speech that binds the present to the past) and, for want of a better term, the 'account' (speech by which the past is brought forward into the present)" (Bauschatz p. 109). The term *gilp* is also spelled *gielp* and *gylp*, pronounced 'yilp'.

Bauschatz is referring to the order of this formal speech, where first facts are established, such as Beowulf's descent, heritage, and his past deeds. Then that foundation from the past is carried forward into the present, accounting for the reputation or *gefrain* that he has earned. During the course of this speech Beowulf is challenged by one of King Hrothgar's advisors, called a *þyle,* as to whether he has truly earned his reputation. This type of challenge by a Thyle or other person in authority is part of the formalities, and must be answered in a satisfactory way that proves his understanding of wyrd / orlog, before Beowulf can continue on to actually speaking the oath that he is giving to the king and people of Heorot: to slay Grendel and deliver them from their ordeal. Bauschatz explains that:

The Ancient Role of Symbel

"The most important instances of both the account and the *bēot* in *Beowulf* occur in conjunction with the *symbel,* the ritual feast, in the poem (but, it needs to be stressed, not only there). A *symbel* proceeds first to whatever speaking is central to the occasion. The speech making takes the form of either *bēot* or 'account' or both (most frequently both). Relevant events from the past are reiterated and, through their being spoken, create a context in which advice or counsel can be given to those making the *bēot.* ...This having been done, he [Beowulf] can better and more credibly announce his intentions:

> *I oblige myself with grip*
> *To fight with the fiend [Grendel] and fight for my life..." (Beowulf* ll. 438-9.)

(Bauschatz p. 110, 111; parentheses are his.)

In other words, having used the right speech to establish his own reputation as a successful warrior and one who keeps his word, and having shown that he is aware of the workings of orlog, Beowulf is now prepared to swear his oath: that he binds himself to fight Grendel and either win or die fighting.

In this and analysis of other *Beowulf* passages, Bauschatz illustrates the art of speaking in symbel in such a way as to shape orlog by one's powerful and well-thought-out words, and by the orlog and intentions that underlie those words and are woven into them. "It is the nature of any *bēot* to place its action directly into this flow" of wyrd (p. 112).

For explanatory purposes I'll put these actions into the context of the Norns' work here, even though Beowulf was dealing in the cultural context of Wyrd, not the Norns. But the shapings of the three Norns can still be seen in the process I just discussed. In step one, Beowulf speaks of Urð's domain: his heritage, his history, the orlog he has laid in the past. In step two he announces his intention at this present moment, Verðandi's domain: to swear an oath to kill Grendel. As part of this oath, he acknowledges Skuld's domain by recognizing the shild, the consequences of his oath: he will either be victorious, or he will die, and he binds or 'grips' himself to these consequences by his oath. Throughout Beowulf's speech the word *sculan*, 'shall,' is used, placing the events under the power of scyld / shild or Skuld. The entire process that Beowulf has followed places his oath and the deed that follows from it into the flow of Wyrd, the shaping of the Norns.

This process of speaking in symbel, as shown and discussed at length by Bauschatz, ideally requires a deep understanding of orlog, Wyrd, shild or consequences, the Norns and their domains, as well as the skill to shape one's words to fit the requirements of symbel and succeed in laying the intended orlog in the Well. Having looked at this very formal context of oathing in *Beowulf*—as presented in the Late West Saxon language of England and located in the culture of the Geats, a Danish tribe—let's turn farther north now and look at an example of oaths and their consequences in a poem from the Poetic Edda.

The Fateful Oaths of Hedin, Helgi, and Svava

Here is an analysis, a case study of orlog if you will, based on the *Poem of Helgi Hjorvardsson* in the Poetic Edda, using Larrington's translation. It shows the power and complexity of orlog that results from oaths taken in symbel. We're beginning with a text-passage inserted into this poem and continuing in the verses afterwards (Larrington p. 125).

The Ancient Role of Symbel

Helgi's brother Hedin was going through the woods one evening to attend a Yule Blōt when he met a troll woman. She tried to seduce Hedin but he refused, whereupon she said: "You'll pay for this when it comes to drinking to pledges" *(bragar-fulli* in Old Norse, similar to *symbel* in Anglo-Saxon). The account continues: "In the evening pledges were made. The sacred boar was led out, men put their hands on it and then they made their vows with the pledging cup *(braga-full)*." Hedin had long been in love with Helgi's wife Svava, and apparently his honor and courage in resisting this illicit love were damaged by the curse of the troll-wife. Without intending to, under the influence of the troll-woman's curse Hedin swore an oath that he would have his brother's wife. Afterwards he bitterly repented of this oath and went to confess it to his brother.

The poem continues with Hedin confessing to Helgi that a "terrible crime has come upon me: I have chosen that royally-born bride of yours with the pledging-cup" (vs. 32). Helgi generously responds: "Don't reproach yourself! For both of us, Hedin, *what's said over ale must come true"* (italics mine). The Old Norse phrase here is *munu verða ölmól:* "ale-speech / ale-words must become"— must come into being. Helgi continues by telling his brother that he's been challenged to a duel and thinks that he may shortly be killed. It would be a good thing, he says, for Hedin to wed his brother's widow if that happens (vs. 33; ON original: Jonsson p. 203.)

The overall sense of this passage is that making oaths—'speaking over the ale' in the context of a formal ceremony like the Yule pledging, the bragar-fulli or symbel—sets in motion a course of events that cannot be altered. The same thing can be said about the challenge to a duel, made and

The Ancient Role of Symbel

accepted, that sets orlog in motion for Helgi. Apparently Helgi's duel-challenge occurred during a bragar-fulli or pledging ceremony as well, since he tells his brother: "for *both* of us, what's spoken over ale must come true."

This passage gives a very good example of the orlog-power that words have when spoken over ale in symbel. It's interesting to see how it turns out at the end of the poem, because although Hedin swore an oath that linked his wyrd with Svava's, Helgi's wife Svava was not a party to Hedin's oath. How does this play out for both Hedin and Svava?

Svava was a Valkyrie (though of human descent) and had, in fact, earlier sworn her own powerful oath. Apparently she felt that it conflicted with Hedin's oath to wed her. When Helgi, at the moment of death, urged her to wed Hedin, Svava responded that "I declared this in Munarhcim, when Helgi chose me, gave me rings, that I would not willingly, if my lord were gone, hold a man of no reputation in my arms" (vs. 42). Here Svava is laying down a challenge: she's implying that due to her own previous oath, she's not required to wed Hedin because she deems his reputation is not worthy of her. Hedin responds to this challenge: "Kiss me, Svava! Never will I come... (back) until I've avenged Hjorvard's son; he was the best of princes under the sun" (vs. 43).

This is the end of the poem; we don't know how things worked out after that. But if we follow the strands of orlog that were laid here, we can figure that Hedin eventually wins respect and honor in Svava's eyes and she agrees to wed him, thus fulfilling both their oaths—and reshaping both their lives. And regarding the context of Svava's oath, I think it likely that it was 'spoken over ale,' as well. It sounds like her oath was given during her bridal ceremony, the

The Ancient Role of Symbel

'bride-ale'—the formal feast that was required to mark a legal wedding, during which toasts, boasts and oaths would have been spoken.

For me, the take-home points from studying this poem are:

(1) that oaths sworn, words spoken in symbel are very powerful and affect orlog;

(2) they will work their way through our lives, but may do so in unexpected ways;

(3) our oaths, words and deeds may affect other people's orlogs, and theirs may affect our orlog, especially if there are close associations or bonds between us;

(4) nevertheless there are ways for people to work with, to shape, their orlogs around such oaths in ways that work to their benefit in the end.

There's another take-home point here: try not to get cursed by a troll woman! But in fact that 'curse' was part of the larger picture of orlog in this whole complex situation. In another text-interpolation in the poem, Helgi says he suspects that the troll-wife and the wolf she was riding were in fact his own *fylgjur,* his fetches, appearing to his brother as harbingers of his approaching doom in the duel (Larrington p. 126). Though it seemed that the troll-wife, Helgi's fylgja, was cursing both Hedin and Helgi by making Hedin swear to take Helgi's wife, in fact Helgi's fetch was setting matters in motion for widowed Svava to take a trustworthy new husband, her brother-in-law and a good man who wished to earn her love and respect by mighty deeds. This was, at a very deep level, no doubt a mystical expression of Helgi's love and care for Svava, expressed by his fylgja setting a good orlog in motion for Svava as his death approaches.

At the end of the poem we are told that "it is said that Helgi and Svava were *endrborin,*" reborn into Midgard. The next poem in the Poetic Edda, the *Second Poem of Helgi Hundingsbani,* tells how in the persons of Helgi Hundingsbani and the Valkyrie Sigrun, Helgi and Svava were reborn and loved again, though much disaster resulted from their union in that life. I discussed that poem in Chapter 2, in the context of 'shaping' orlog. Many of the old hero tales, poems, and sagas, including the *Völsungasaga* and the *Nibelungenlied,* can be 'mined' for insights into the complex workings of orlog, oaths, and their consequences, as I have done with these Helgi poems.

I've written at length in this and the previous chapters about the Norns carving, shaping, speaking orlog, and looked at some ways that we humans too can shape orlog by our deeds and words. But what is it, exactly, that the Norns shape: what is the 'substance' that they work with as they shape the orlog of our human lives in this world of Midgard? They are not shaping a vacuum, a nothingness; they are not creating something out of nothing. In my understanding, there is a very specific substance or entity that the Norns shape: our Aldr life-force, life-span, and life-soul.

The Ancient Role of Symbel

*Embla and Askr,
humans shaped from logs or trees by the Gods
and given orlog by the Norns.*

5. What Do the Norns Shape?

"These maids shape people's **aldrs** (*skapa mönnum aldr*); we call them Norns." (*Gylfaginning* in the prose *Edda*)

"In one day was my **aldr** shaped, and all my life laid down" (*Skirnismal* vs. 13, *Poetic Edda*).

"Helgi the Hugr-strong was born to Borghild in Bralund. Night fell on the settlement, then Norns came—those who shaped **aldr** for the young ætheling." (*Helgi Hundingsbani I, Poetic Edda*, vs. 1-2.)

"Urð one is called, Verðandi another – scoring on slips of wood – Skuld the third. There they lay layers, there choose life for **alda**-children, speak orlog." (*Völuspá* vs. 20, *Poetic Edda*)

(All are my translations.)

What do the Norns Shape?

Aldr: Lifespan and Life-Soul

Orlog, wyrd, fate, destiny, life: these are shaped by the Norns according to the elder lore. But what is it, exactly, that they use as the primal material for these shapings? When one shapes, one shapes something into something else, one shapes some thing or some circumstance into a different form that is deliberately designed. We are told in *Gylfaginning* of the prose Edda that the Norns "shape men's / humans' *aldrs" (skapa mönnum aldr)* (15:32). In the lines about the creation of humans from trees or logs, the Norns "choose life for the children of *aldr" (Völuspá vs. 20)*. What is *aldr,* and why do the Norns choose it for shaping mortal lives?

Aldr and its variants is a word in the old Germanic languages that pertains to one's age, span of life, and to the life-force or life-soul that supports us during that lifespan. It also is used in descriptions of death, the end of the lifespan. The usage of this word in various Germanic languages is closely related to the usage of orlog and can offer further understanding toward the meaning and significance of orlog; in this chapter we'll pursue that understanding. (I discuss the Aldr as a life-soul in more depth in Rose 2021, Chapter 7.)

Aldr in Old Norse (ON) means 'age,' both a person's age and an age of time, and lifetime or lifespan. *Aldar* in Old Saxon (OS) also means age and lifespan, as does Anglo-Saxon (A-S) *ealdor.* Both ON *aldr-lag* and A-S *ealdor-legu* mean 'destiny, death': the Aldr life-span and life-force is what the Aldr 'lays' or 'sets down' at the fated time, the end of our lifespan. There is a clear parallel between *ør-lög, or-læg, ur-lag,* on the one hand, and *aldr-lag, ealdor-legu,* and the like, on the other hand. Both can refer to one's death, the

What do the Norns Shape?

moment when orlog, 'what has been laid down by fate,' comes to pass, and the moment when one's *ealdor / aldr* life-force or life-soul is laid down, given up to death, and one's lifespan comes to an end. In these words, *aldrlag / ealdorlegu,* we see again the meaning of 'layers, laying down,' referring back to the actions of the Norns who lay layers of orlog in the Well, and plaster layers of mud upon the World-Tree to nourish and sustain it.

The word *aldr* comes from the Proto-Indo-European root **al,* 'to nourish,' related to *alan,* with the same meaning, a word found in Gothic, Anglo-Saxon and other Germanic languages. It also means 'to grow.' **Al* is the root for words relating to 'age' in the various Germanic languages, including English 'old' and 'elder.' The connection between nourishment, growth, and the ability to reach old age is clear, especially when we think about the circumstances all through the millennia of human existence, when the availability of food, or lack of it, determined a person's health and longevity.

Nourishment is very much a 'layering' activity: day by day the food we eat feeds our body, building its layers of bone, muscle, tissues, organs, and supporting all the activities of our lives—very much like the Norns nourishing the World-Tree by patting layers of white clay on it every day. Our bodies are literally formed from the food and drink we consume. If such nourishment is not forthcoming, the body wastes away and 'meets its fate,' the consequence of deprivation, at the time of *ealdor-legu,* of laying down and letting go of the *ealdor* life-soul and the body it supports. This time when death arrives, the 'fateful hour' is also known as *orlag-hwile,* orlog-while, in Old Saxon and Anglo-Saxon.

What do the Norns Shape?

The Anglo-Saxon language offers some useful words for understanding more about the nature of Aldr / Ealdor: there is a word for the physical body, *ealdorgeard,* which means 'yard or enclosure of the *ealdor.*' One of the words for 'murderer' or 'killer' in A-S is *ealdorbana* or ealdor-bane. These words give us a picture of the physical body as an enclosure which contains and protects the *ealdor,* the life-force. Someone who breaks in and destroys this body-enclosure is the bane or murderer of the *ealdor,* allowing the life-force to spill out of its protected boundary and be lost, and thus bringing about *ealdor-legu.*

Beowulf's companions fled in terror from the dragon in order to protect their *ealdors* (*ealdre burgon,* line 2599). During his fight with Grendel, Beowulf sought to rob Grendel of his *aldr* (*alder beneotan,* l. 680). There is a parallel expression in the *Reginsmal* poem of the *Poetic Edda,* where the sons of Hunding are described as Eylimi's "aldr-snatchers" (*aldrs synjuðu,* l. 15), that is, his killers. The relatively physical nature of the aldr life-soul shows up in a dramatic scene in *Beowulf,* where a Geatish spearman threw his spear at a sea-serpent and the spear actually "stood in the aldr" of the sea-serpent (*him on alder stod,* ll. 1433-5). This physicality of *aldr* links it with the phenomena of nourishment, body, and death of the body that comes about at the fated time, *orlag-hwile,* the time of orlog and ealdor-legu / aldr-lag.

Table 4. Examples of Anglo-Saxon Ealdor Words
relating to orlog and the work of the Norns.

Ealdor-leg, aldor-leg, -læg: Life-law, fate, death; **æfter ealdorlege:** after death. Also Old Saxon **aldar-lagu,** used in the same context as *orlag, orlegi.*
Ealdor-gesceaft: 'Condition of life, state of life.' Ealdor-gesceaft literally means 'ealdor-shaping, ealdor-creation.' I interpret it as the lifespan and its events, shaped for us by the Norns as they *skapa mönnum aldr,* shape people's lives.
Ealdor-ner, aldor-ner: ealdor-refuge, saving one's life, granting asylum.
Ealdor-gedal, aldor-gedal: separation from life, the time of death. *Gedal* means 'what is dealt out, apportioned, or separated from.'

Our Aldr life-force or life-soul nourishes us on both physical and spiritual levels. It is shaped and given to us by the Norns at our conception, and in turn it takes the orlog given to us by the Norns and uses it to shape and measure out the events of our lives and establish their timing. Our processes of growth, maturation, and decline, our life-experiences, the timing of life-events, and our ability to perceive our own lifetime as a whole, a meaningful phenomenon that is ours alone: all of these are gathered by our Aldr-soul and formed into our own personal world or 'werold.'

What do the Norns Shape?

World and Werold

Our word 'world' comes from the Anglo-Saxon *wer-old*, meaning 'man-age'. The same word was used in Old Saxon, and Old Norse had an equivalent word, probably borrowed from Anglo-Saxon: *ver-aldr*. These words derive from *aldr, ealdor,* as discussed in the previous section. Werold was used in a very personal way in these old languages. To us, the world is 'everything out there', but to elder Heathens each person had a world, their own world. The Old Saxon *Heliand*, a retelling of the Gospels in a very Germanic format and language, offers many examples of this personal use of *werold*. The poet said that John the Baptist "would never taste wine 'in his *weroldi*"(l. 252). Mary said that she had "never in my *weroldi*" been with a man (l. 541-2). An old widow was "four and eighty winters in her *weroldi*"(l. 1024).

A more modern example of this ancient usage appears in the novels of the Anglo-Saxon scholar J.R.R. Tolkien. He wrote of King Aragorn telling his wife Arwen, when his death was approaching, that "my world is fading." (*The Return of the King*, App. A(v), "The Tale of Aragorn and Arwen.") Even though Aragorn's health, strength, and kingly honors were still with him, he could tell it was time for him to go (the choice was his) because he perceived his Werold fading.

When the aged Beowulf set out to face the dragon, he was facing his *worulde-gedæl,* the end of his life in this world (l. 3068). *Gedæl*, on the one hand, means dealing out something, including dealing out one's portion of life. On the other hand, it means separation, cutting off. The word *gedæl* or *gedal* was often used poetically as a synonym for death-orlog, the timing and nature of one's death, the separation from life and the body and the blow of fate that is dealt by Wyrd or the Norns. *Gedæl,* in this sense, is like our modern English 'to deal'; it refers to the wyrd that is dealt out to a person and brings about the moment of death, the end of their world. In parallel phrasing, the poet speaks of the monster Grendel's death as his *aldor-gedal* (l. 805), showing the similarity between *werold* and Aldr: both are subject to the fate dealt out by Wyrd.

It is clear, when reading how *werold* / man-age was used in context, that it referred to the space-time each person occupies and shapes during their lifetime. Their world was measured in years and characterized by the events, deeds and experiences that shaped their lives. Another way to understand this is to recognize Aldr as a soul or aspect of ourselves which can see and grasp our life as a whole, our past, present, and possible futures in this world of Midgard: a soul which gives meaning and power to this lifespan, this Werold.

In my view, it is this Aldr—this metaphysical soul-being or power which controls our lifespan and weaves our personal Werold—that provides the substance for the Norns' shaping. I believe, also, that it provides the locus for our sense of time and our subjective experience of it, a topic I explore further in Chapter 19 on "Time and the Time-Body."

In closing this chapter, I'd like to share a little of my personal experience and sense of my Aldr soul and its life-activity. Ever since early childhood I've had the eerie and beautiful experience, when the wind blows past me, of perceiving the wind and the dust it carries as Time itself—Time, and traces of history laid in that dust. I seem to 'smell' or inhale them in some indescribable way—traces of memory, of Being and meaning, the history of people, of

What do the Norns Shape?

landscapes, of soil and stone, of ecosystems and the beings that inhabit them. I've traveled in many beautiful places around the world, during childhood and adulthood, and in each place I walked I picked up traces of something deep—a sense of the character and the deep history of the land, which I now believe were subconscious connections with the various landwights and ancestral spirits, the spirits and energies inhabiting the lands. I could not explain or demonstrate these experiences in any way, but they are and always have been deeply meaningful to me.

I believe now, after many years of Heathen spiritual practice, that this awareness arises within me from my Aldr soul, shaped for me by the Norns / Wyrd as the soul who understands Time and my attunement to life-in-Time. Traces of time and history are always blowing past us on subtle winds, everywhere we go. Even when we are not consciously aware of this, our Aldr soul knows, and feels itself linked to other beings, Time, and World, within this sacred space of Midgard.

Note:
For further reading about Aldr, see my article "Aldr and Orlay: Weaving a World" on my website:
HeathenSoulLore.net
https://heathensoullore.net/aldr-and-orlay-weaving-a-world/

6. Time, Tense, and the Norns

Any effort to understand orlog and the Norns requires a consideration of the nature of 'Time' and how it is perceived and experienced by humans. Generic images of 'The Fates,' influenced by Classical mythology, often represent them as 'past, present, and future.' This makes sense to our modern minds, which are shaped to understand Time as consisting of a linear arrangement of 'past, present, future.' We stand in the present, influenced by the past, moving toward the future. This is so obvious to us that it might not occur to us to view the influence or action of Time in any other way.

This is not exactly how the people who spoke the old Germanic languages viewed time, and actions in time. *The Well and the Tree: World and Time in Early Germanic Culture,* by Paul Bauschatz, is a brilliant and profound book, one that has greatly influenced my thoughts and those of many other modern Heathens. His whole book is based on the philosophical implications of Germanic linguistics, resulting in "the binary opposition inherent in the Germanic tense system between past and present, or, better, between past and nonpast events. This particular opposition of action presents events in a way that is significantly different from our own, and from other Indo-European peoples." (p. xvii)

The Names

Bauschatz's linguistic and grammatical analysis of the Norns' names, fleshed out with reference to Eddic poetry, *Beowulf,* and other sources, shows that they are not related in a linear fashion to any clear-cut perception of past-present-future. The names Verðandi and Urð both stem from Proto-Indo-European **uert* or **wert,* denoting the motion of twisting, spinning, rotating, which leads to words for 'becoming' in many Indo-European languages (p. 13). "When Verthandi and Urth are semantically related, Verthandi becomes that which is in process of 'turning' or 'becoming,' and Urth would be that which has 'turned' or 'become.' ...Verthandi clearly reflects the actually occurring process of all that Urth eventually expresses" (p. 14).

Here we see 'past' and 'present' or non-past in close relationship with each other: the present, moment by moment, 'turning into' or becoming the shaped fabric of the past, while the past is, moment by moment, 'turning into' or 'becoming' the shaping conditions of the present. When we use the simile of rotation or turning, this close mutual interaction between past and present in old Germanic thought becomes clearer. It is imagery worth meditating upon!

Here is another description of the process: "...*ørlǫg* is spoken continually and layers of action are accomplished upon layers of action...everything is growing, and in the process of its growth, connected with its origins. To speak the *ørlǫg,* then, is to take account of all that happens with respect to all that has happened already." (Bauschatz p. 7)

Time, Tense, and the Norns

The past has clearly happened; the present is clearly happening. We can testify to this from our own living experience. We cannot do so with 'the future.' By definition it does not exist in our living experience; it has not happened already, it is not happening now. The Norn Skuld does not reflect the idea of 'the future.' Her name comes from *skulu*, meaning 'should, shall,' but in Old Norse this is not consistently used as the auxiliary of the future tense, such as "I shall go to work tomorrow." Instead, "*Skulu* occurs most frequently in contexts that express a generalized, universal present...general statements about what happens continually" (Bauschatz p. 12).

Bauschatz gives the example of how Thor shall / must wade through the rivers Kormt, Ormt, and the Kerlaugs when he goes to meet with the other Gods at the doomstead at Yggdrasil every day: *'þær* **scal** *þorr vada hverian dag' (Grimnismal 29)*. This statement indicates an ongoing daily event, not simply something he intends to do in the future. Thor must do this because, unlike the other Gods, he is too heavy to walk upon Bifröst, the rainbow bridge, and must instead wade through the rivers that lie below it. The phrasing does imply that he shall wade tomorrow as well, but it is not specifically the future tense, it is a statement about an ongoing situation, the 'everlasting present.'

Likewise, *skulu* appears frequently in the *Hávamál*, but in the context of 'what someone *should* do or ought to do,' not necessarily what they 'will do' as a statement of the future. "All occurrences (of *skulu)* express constraint, obligation, necessary continual action...Such obligations imply a continuous 'present,' which logically extends into the 'future,' but *skulu* does not directly denote such temporal conditions" (Bauschatz p. 13).

Time, Tense, and the Norns

There is a well-known phrase from *Beowulf* that says: *gæð a wyrd swa hio **scel**,* (l. 455). Literally, the translation is "Wyrd goes ever as she shall," showing how the same word, *scel* or *sceal,* is used in Anglo-Saxon, just as it is used in the quotation from *Grimnismal* above about "Thor shall *(scal)* wade…" The *Beowulf* phrase, "Wyrd goes ever as she shall," sounds like a tautology if we read 'shall' as we do in modern English, as a way of denoting a future action. What the phrase means is "Wyrd goes ever as she *must,*" as it is *necessary* for her or it to go. It's talking about a continuous present, an 'ever-time,' not only about what she will do tomorrow.

A being such as Skuld does not appear in Anglo-Saxon lore, but with this phrase emphasizing 'what Wyrd *scel* do,' using the same word as *skulu* in Old Norse, the root of Skuld's name, we can see that Anglo-Saxon Wyrd includes Skuld's function within her own domains of action. If we wanted to liken Wyrd to the Norns, we could even regard this phrase as implying 'Wyrd / Urðr goes ever as Skuld indicates she must.' Bauschatz notes that Skuld "seems to make reference to actions felt as somehow obliged or known to occur; that is, the necessity of their 'becoming' is so strongly felt or clearly known that they present themselves as available to be incorporated into the realms of Verthandi and Urth" (p. 14). This description invites careful thought and meditation on how it differs from 'the future.'

Note that the phrase quoted above is not 'Wyrd goes ever as she *will,*' which would be another way of forming the future tense in modern English. Using 'will' would have a different connotation in an ancient context, implying that it is her own will she follows, rather than necessity. If the phrase were simply talking about what she would do in the future, either 'shall' or 'will' could be used interchangeably in modern English. Instead, both 'shall = I must' and 'will = my own intention' have very specific, and different, meanings in the old writings.

Past versus Non-Past

If you look closely at the *Völuspá,* a poem which deals with events of the past, present, and future, you will see that it shifts around unexpectedly among the tenses of past, present, and future—not necessarily applying them in any kind of temporal order to discuss the events of the Worlds. The same is even more true in the much longer, more complex *Beowulf* poem. The author frequently shifts into some tale from the past, right in the middle of some present action taking place, in ways that we might find very confusing. To his original listeners, though, it made sense: there was, to them, an obvious connection between these events occurring during widely separated time periods.

Bauschatz considers that it makes sense to categorize Time, in the old Heathen mindset, as 'past' and 'non-past' rather than past-present-future.

"The past, as collector of events, is clearly the most dominant, controlling portion of all time. Man's world stands at the juncture of this past and the non-past, that is, at that point, the present, in which events are in the process of becoming 'past.' The past is experienced, known, laid down, accomplished, sure, realized. The present, to the contrary, is in flux and confusion, mixed with irrelevant and significant details. What we nowadays call 'the future' is, within the structure of this Germanic system, just more of the nonpast, more flux, more confusion." (Bauschatz pp. 138-9)

In the midst of all the flux and confusion of present and future, for the forebears it was logical to rest their tales, their intentions, and even their philosophy, on the solid ground of the past. This was the place to start from and the place to continually check back in with, in order to really make sense of what was happening in the present and what was about to happen in the future.

Passing the Strands

Here I offer a rather poetic description of the roles of the three Norns with respect to arrangement in Time. Urð represents What-has-Become, what is completed and fulfilled, what we consider to be 'the past.' But she and her domain are far from static or 'finished.' Instead, she stands next to Verðandi, she who rules What-is-Becoming, and they hand strands of orlog back and forth between them. Urð hands over strands from the past to influence the present that Verðandi is spinning, while Verðandi feeds strands from her 'Becomings' back to Urð as those Becomings are completed so Urð can weave them into her web.

Standing somewhat to the side, Skuld attaches threads or leader-lines of necessity, of What-Should-Be, to the strands being handled by Urð and Verðandi. Skuld's threads may be thin and fine, representing only slight, weak effects of What-Should-Be that we may be able to overcome if we firmly set out to do so. Or they may be thick and strong, representing some insurmountable necessity that we will simply have to deal with. These leader-lines of Necessity pull all the strands into a web-like, multidimensional pattern

Time, Tense, and the Norns

laid by orlog and spoken or galdored into being by all the Norns as they work.

Time, Tense, and the Norns

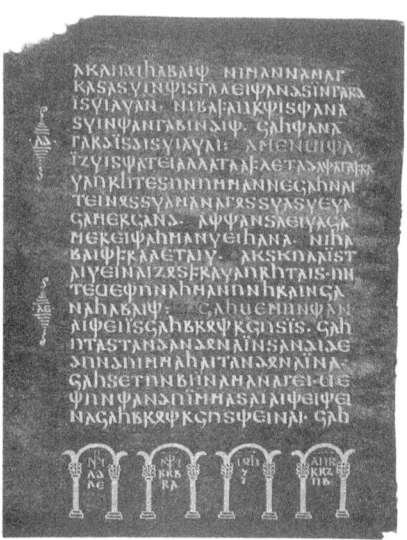

A page from the Codex Argenteus (the silver codex) version of the Gothic Bible, clearly showing the Gothic script developed by Bishop Wulfila (and probably others). The decorations on the left side, surrounding verse-numbers expressed as letters, look interestingly like spindles.

7. The Curious Case of the Missing Wyrd-Word

The Missing Word in Gothic

When I was researching the linguistics of the word 'orlog' I noticed something very curious to me in the Gothic Bible. I was looking for examples of the words and concepts of 'orlog' and of 'wyrd' to see how they were used in this oldest literary record we have of a Germanic language (not counting runic inscriptions). I did not find either word in any form that was similar to later usage of these words in other Germanic languages. In Chapter 1, I explained my thoughts about how the meaning of 'orlog' might have evolved from the Gothic form of the word, *uslagjan,* 'to lay upon, lay hands upon.' Though not used in the context of 'fate,' there is still the indication of 'layers laid' here, as well as the idea of 'grasping, laying hands upon us' as Fate tends to do. The use of Gothic *uslagjan* makes it clear that 'orlog' did exist as a word in Gothic, but it had not developed into the meaning of orlog that appears later in the other old Germanic languages.

But I looked in vain for any mention of wyrd, other than forms of the root-word it comes from, *wairþan,* 'to become, to happen' which of course are frequently used. Since the Gothic Bible was translated from a Greek-language text, I looked to see whether the word with equivalent meaning in Greek, *μοίρα* or *moira*, 'fate,' appeared in the original text. Since it does not appear there, that might explain the absence of any Gothic word for *wyrd* in the translation: there was no word in the Greek original that would be translated as 'wyrd' in the Gothic version.

As my next step in pursuing this mystery, I looked at how the term / concept of 'predestination' was translated from Greek into Gothic, as a concept similar to wyrd. Perhaps that would offer some clues. I found one instance in the Gothic Bible, which in English reads, "He predestined us to be adopted as his sons through Jesus Christ" (Ephesians 1:5). The Gothic word used for predestination in this passage is *faura-garairoþ* meaning 'a fore-speaking, a foretelling, a prophecy.' It is used to translate Greek προορίσας, *pro-orisas,* translated as 'predestination' in English. The root Greek word is ὁρίζω, *horizō:* meaning 'to ordain, determine, lay down, define, appoint.' The latter words sound very much like activities that the Norns undertake, and the prefix 'pro' means doing those things in advance, beforehand—ordaining, determining, laying down what will happen in the future.

What I find odd is that apparently the only way to express the biblical God's power of predestination in Gothic was to call it 'foretelling,' *faura-ga-rairoþ* or fore-speaking, 'fore-rede.' This implies that their God *knows* what will happen, but it does not necessarily imply that he *causes* it to happen, as the word in Greek does imply: he fore-ordains what will happen. It's the reverse of what we see with Odin's abilities: he and other Deities can order the placement and paths of the Sun and Moon in the sky and shape a World from the body of Ymir: these are God-powers, certainly. But if Odin wants a really accurate prophecy he doesn't try to do this himself, he goes to a seeress. (See the *Völuspá,* and *Baldr's Dreams,* in the *Poetic Edda.)*

In effect, when it comes to the power of predestination this biblical God as presented in Gothic is acting as a prophet or a seer by foretelling the future, rather than acting as a Deity who controls what will happen in the future. Unless, of course, we liken his action to that of the Norns, who bring about orlog and wyrd by 'speaking it' and thus laying it into the Well.

I think that this peculiar—to me anyway—translation from Greek 'fore-ordain, determine, predestine' to Gothic 'foretell' offers clues to Germanic ideas about how the power of Wyrd matches the role and power of Deities. In this particular event in the Gothic Gospels, the Christian God is acting as a prophet or seer, using powers similar to the way Wyrd's powers and the Norns' powers were conceived in other Germanic cultures.

Admittedly, none of these obscure threads of evidence gives us anything solid about Gothic beliefs about wyrd and beings who deal with wyrd. Did they in fact have the concept of Wyrd as understood in other Germanic cultures, and it just didn't make it into the Gothic Bible because the original Greek version did not refer to that concept? Or did they, in fact, not have that concept at all? There's no way for us to know for sure, since the Gothic Bible, which is not complete, is the only extensive document we have that's written in the Gothic language.

The Old Saxon *Heliand*, a retelling of the Christian Gospels, is littered with references to *orlag* and *wurt* / wyrd, but that is a looser, more interpretive retelling of the material while the Gothic Bible is a stricter translation. And, significantly, the *Heliand* was written around half a millennium later than the Gothic Bible—time during which the concepts of orlog and wyrd may have developed and become established in the Germanic cultures.

Haliurunnae

This half-millennium of time for word-development seems a likely explanation for the missing word-meanings, and I speculate that at least when it comes to orlog this is what happened. And yet...clues about concepts of 'fate' and beings who control or influence fate are present in so many early Germanic cultures, as well as other related Indo-European cultures, that I find it difficult to believe that this concept never occurred to the Goths. And if it did, presumably they had a word for it.

Indeed, there is a clue to the existence of 'beings of fate' in the Gothic culture. The following account is given in Jordanes' 6th century CE *Origins and Deeds of the Goths,* telling of the *Haliurunnae,* the 'witches,' who are here claimed to be the ancestresses of the Huns. Jordanes writes that Gothic king Filimer:

"...found among his people certain witches, whom he called in his native tongue *Haliurunnae.* Suspecting these women, he expelled them from the midst of his race and compelled them to wander in solitary exile afar from his army. There the unclean spirits, who beheld them as they wandered through the wilderness, bestowed their embraces upon them and begat this savage race... Such was the descent of the

The Curious Case of the Missing Wyrd-Word

Huns who came to the country of the Goths." (Jordanes, Ch. XXIV.)

To put this tale into historical context, the Goths first encountered the Huns around 372 CE, when they were living in what is now Ukraine. So according to the logic of this tale, the Gothic Haliurunnae must have been cast out of their tribe sometime considerably earlier than the late 4th century CE, if they were the supposed ancestresses of the multitude of Huns who attacked the Goths in 372.

Vala: The Norse Seeress.
Sculpture by Søren Lexow-Hansen.

The Curious Case of the Missing Wyrd-Word

Grimm mentions an instance that may refer to the same Haliurunnae, though perhaps in a different place: "Attila at the passage of the Lech is said to have been scared away by a rune-maiden calling out three times 'back, Attila!' (vol. 1, p. 404, note.)

Dowden notes that "Women and divination are frequent partners. Gothic women, the *haliurunnae* or 'Hell-runers' (where runes are still magical song and not yet a writing system), communed with the world of the dead." (p. 253; parenthetical text is his.) Generally speaking, seers and diviners communed with the dead in order to receive prophecies, like Odin calling up the dead *völva* of the *Völuspá*. Prophecies involve wyrd, fate, that is spoken of in words; surely Gothic had some native, historic term for this phenomenon since they reportedly had women who worked with it.

There are many other accounts of prophetesses and seeresses influencing the actions of armies in old Germanic lore from the time of the Roman empire and later. Dowden relates that:

"In 58 BC Caesar was puzzled that Ariovistus, King of the Suebi, would not engage in battle until he discovered the following from prisoners: 'Among the Germans there was a custom that their *matres familia* [the wives of the heads of household] declared on the basis of lots and prophecies whether battle might usefully be joined or not; and they had said that it was not fated for the Germans to win if they joined battle before the new moon.' Caesar, *Gallic war,* 1.50." (quoted in Dowden p. 253, brackets his.)

The Curious Case of the Missing Wyrd-Word

Gothic is not the only language where the word *haliurunnae* appears. The Old High German word *Hellirune* is listed in an old glossary, translated into Latin as *necromantia* or necromancy. DeVries states that it comes from *halja* = Hel, and *runa* = mysteries. "The *Hellirunen* are therefore women who search out the mysteries of the dead." (deVries 1935, p. 264.)

The word appears in Anglo-Saxon, too, as *helruna.* In old vocabulary lists this word is equated with *wælcyrige* (valkyrie), *hægtesse* (often translated as 'witch'), *pythonissa* (oracle, seeress, prophetess), and *parcae* (the Latin name for the Fates). (Cited in Damico p. 212 note 50, referring to Wright's *Anglo-Saxon and Old English Vocabularies.*) Without knowing for sure what the Gothic *haliurunnae* were involved with, it seems a reasonable assumption that it did include forays into the realms of wyrd and fate.

Seeresses, prophetesses, wise-women, Matronae, Disir, Idisi: women playing such roles showed up widely across the times and places occupied by Germanic tribes and cultures. Foresight and divination—understanding wyrd—were among their major roles. It seems unlikely to me that the Goths—a very large group of peoples spread across regions from what are now Ukraine, Romania, the Balkans into Italy, Spain, and southern France, and influential in the Byzantine and Roman Empires—had no concept of anything like 'wyrd,' even if that word does not show up in the Gothic texts we have. Their neighbors, allies, and opponents certainly had such concepts, and the Goths were far from isolated. My conclusion is that they must have had some word like 'wyrd' and that it simply was not used in their translation of the Bible.

The Curious Case of the Missing Wyrd-Word

For modern Heathen usage, 'wyrd' has been reconstructed as *waurþs (feminine noun) in Gothic. *(Himma Daga* English to Gothic Dictionary).

Part II: The Work of the Norns

"The Norns spin beneath Yggdrasil."
By L.B. Hansen, 1893

A drawing of a traditionally-garbed seeress by Louis Moe, from an 1898 edition of Saxo Grammaticus' History of the Danes.

8. Orlog and Wyrd

Etymology of wyrd:
Proto-Indo-European (PIE): *wert* = to twist / vertere = to rotate.
Proto-Germanic: *wurðiz*, from *werðan* = to come to pass, to be, to be due.
Old Saxon: *wurð, wurd*
Old High German: *wurt*
Anglo-Saxon: *wyrd*
Old Norse: *urð*

A great deal of useful writing about wyrd exists: scholarly and academic writing that extends over several centuries and across multiple languages, as well as writings pertaining to the meaning of wyrd in the present-day practice of Heathenry and Paganism. As Aaron Hostetter writes, regarding wyrd: "few words in any language have so much ethical and ideological power impacted into four tiny letters." The corpus of writing about wyrd is extensive, interpretations differ quite profoundly, insights abound, and so do confusions! The focus of this book is on 'orlog' rather than 'wyrd,' and an in-depth discussion of the meaning of 'wyrd' in all its permutations is far beyond our scope. But it is necessary here to touch on some salient points showing similarities and contrasts between them, in order to further refine our understanding of orlog.

Personification and De-Personification of Wyrd

The question of wyrd versus orlog is another instance where languages and their similarities and differences come into play. In Old Norse, there's little need for discussion about the differences between ørlög and wyrd: the chief Norn, Urð (the same word as 'wyrd') is a person, and ørlög is what she does / lays / speaks / shapes. Urðr is a being, ørlög is a phenomenon or a process. The noun *urð* exists in Old Norse but is rarely used; almost all instances of the word *Urð / Urðr* refer to the Norn herself, a personified being. 'Norn' describes the kind of being she is, a word that does not exist in the other Germanic languages. In the other Germanic languages it's more ambiguous: the words *wyrd / wurð / wurt* in Anglo-Saxon, Old Saxon, and Old High German can be used both for a being named Wyrd / Wurð / Wurt and for the phenomenon or process of wyrd; the latter would be called *ørlög* in this context in Old Norse. Jacob Grimm wrote, concerning the distinction between orlog and wyrd, that "it was only when the heathen goddesses had been cast off, that the meanings of the words (wyrd versus orlog) came to be confounded, and the old flesh-and-blood *wurt, wurð, wyrd* to pale into a mere impersonal *urlac*" (Vol. 1, p. 410, my parentheses).

It's clear from reading old texts in the non-Norse languages that orlog and wyrd were often used as poetic synonyms for each other, indicating that there was not much conceptual difference between them at the time these texts

Orlog and Wyrd

were written. Part of the reason for this may be that textual writing only came in with Christianity, mainly done by monks or those who were taught by monks, and it was necessary for Christian writers not to imply that there was a being, Wyrd, who had equal or greater power than the Christian God, the one who implements divine providence, judgement, and predestination in Christian thought.

There were, indeed, occasional implications that Wyrd has power independent of 'God's will,' even in early Christian times. One example is found in the Old English *Maxims II, 4-5:* "Christ's majesty is great, Wyrd is strongest" *(þrymmas syndan Cristes myccle, wyrd byð swiðost.)* Another example is from the Anglo-Saxon poem *The Seafarer:* "Wyrd is stronger, Metod mightier, than anyone's *gehygd,"* the workings of their Hyge or Hugr. (l. 150-1.) 'Metod' is ambiguous, often meaning the Christian God, but other times meaning something like fate.

Comparing the power of Wyrd to the power of Deities does seem to show a less-Christian, more-Heathen perspective, but it is still not clear whether wyrd here is a personal being, or simply a fate-like phenomenon outside of even Christ's control.

In general, early Anglo-Saxon, Old Saxon, and Old High German writers did not ignore the existence of wyrd, but often downgraded it / her from a great Power to an impersonal phenomenon—'divine providence' or 'God's will'—that is under the control of the Christian God, an expression of his will rather than an independent being. Even so, in the old poetry, using the word *wyrd* is both a poetic device and a signal that fateful action is taking place even when the Christian God is nowhere evident.

Orlog and Wyrd

As Bauschatz describes, "The influence and control of the past over the present are expressed directly by the term *wyrd* in Old English, and its mention in any text brings the power of all past actions explicitly to bear on the material presented" (p. 87). This action of wyrd is so powerful that the distinction between wyrd-as-phenomenon and Wyrd-as-personal-being perhaps becomes moot: her or its effects shape and direct the action that is occurring, regardless.

So, the personification of Urðr in Old Norse is clear, the personification of Wyrd / Wurt / Wurð in other old Germanic languages is ambiguous. Some of the ambiguity for modern readers comes from Old English grammar, which uses masculine, feminine, and neuter nouns as do modern German, French, and many other languages. We are unused to this in modern English where the pronouns 'she' and 'he' are normally only used for persons or personifications. So when we read a phrase such as *gæð a wyrd swa hio scel,* 'wyrd goes ever as she must,' it certainly sounds like the 'she' here refers to a personified being (Beowulf l. 455). Perhaps it was originally so intended, perhaps not; modern translators I've read render the word *hio* (she) as 'it' in this phrase, but for myself as a practicing Heathen, I prefer to regard this as a statement about a personified being, Wyrd herself, 'going ever as she must.'

If Wyrd was subtly de-personified due to Christian influence, that would result in conflating wyrd with orlog, both of them apparently being only processes or phenomena, rather than orlog being a process while Wyrd is a personal being. But there are certainly some clues about ways that wyrd may indeed differ subtly from orlog in the non-Norse writings.

Orlog and Wyrd

Anglo-Saxon *Wyrd*

Anglo-Saxon *wyrd* has additional meanings and connotations which are different from meanings of A-S *orlæg* or orlay. Wyrd comes from the root meaning 'to become, to come to pass.' Something is fulfilled, comes to fruition, which is rather different imagery than 'layers laid down.'

Unlike *orlæg* which refers to strife and battle as well as to 'fate,' I find no wyrd-words directly associated with war in Anglo-Saxon. Instead, there are wyrd-based words that relate to speech, eloquence, conversation, and history. *Gewyrdlic* means 'historical,' and a *gewyrd-writere* is a chronicler or historian. In other words, we use words, speech, writing, chronicles, to record and examine the workings of Wyrd, asking questions like: what exactly is the situation? What is happening? Why is it happening this way? Who is involved, and why? What events led up to the situation? We try to discern and analyze the strands to get a full picture of what-has-been, how it relates to what-is, and what-is-becoming.

With this concept of *gewyrd* as history, as the account of how wyrd played out in events of the past, we have a significant point of contact with the idea of 'shaping' in the sense of spoken decrees of Norns, Gods, kings, chieftains, religious leaders, and the ways that those fateful decrees and decisions play out in human history, including wars. These powers shape wyrd, and the historian uses words to describe and analyze how that wyrd played out—including words for 'shaping.' Then, that spoken / written / 'shaped' history, told through songs, tales, chronicles and books, influences the attitudes and actions of future generations. These activities imply a Being who speaks, utters decrees, consciously shapes

Orlog and Wyrd

or influences the events of history as Urð does in the Norse tradition. To my mind, this points toward Wyrd herself in personal form.

Take a look at the Anglo-Saxon word *wyrd-gesceap,* literally 'a Wyrd-shaping, what Wyrd has shaped', translated as 'decrees of fate.' Old Saxon has the same word, *wurdi-giskapu / wurði-giskefti:* what Wurð or Wyrd shapes. These are used as synonym for *urlag / orlag* in the Old Saxon *Heliand,* and to me it seems clear that in this usage Wyrd-the-Being is consciously shaping orlog. Wyrd is a sentient being, speaking decrees that should be followed and shaping events of history, just as the personified Norns 'speak ørlög.'

Here's another phrase where Wyrd could be interpreted as a person, found in *Beowulf* ll. 572-73: *Wyrd oft nereþ unfægne eorl, þonne his ellen deah.* In Chickering's translation: "Wyrd often saves an undoomed eorl when his courage holds." It's hard to picture wyrd as a non-personified phenomenon here: how would it 'know' whether the eorl's courage holds or not, and how would it then 'save' him, if it is not a sentient being? (I'll return to an in-depth analysis of this sentence at the end of this chapter in "Wyrd: A Case Study.") The online Bosworth-Toller Anglo-Saxon Dictionary, under section *"wyrd IIIa: wyrd as personification, fate, fortune,"* lists many examples of personification usage from Anglo-Saxon texts.

The word *wyrdæ, wyrde*—wyrd in the plural form—also occurs in Anglo-Saxon. It was used in several Latin-to-Anglo-Saxon glossaries as a translation for the Parcae, the Fates as they were known in Roman culture (Bauschatz p. 8). The plural form obviously implies that these are actual beings, not simply an impersonal phenomenon, but did the plural form *wyrdæ* exist natively in Anglo-Saxon, or was it

Orlog and Wyrd

coined in order to translate the Latin word? The Fates in classical Latin (Parcae) and Greek (Moirai) mythology appeared in threes, as of course do the Norns, and all of this imagery was known in early Christian Anglo-Saxon culture.

There are a few instances in A-S texts where 'wyrde' might be considered a plural form, but they are rare and ambiguous. The Anglo-Saxons may not generally have pictured Wyrd in plural form themselves, but when they encountered the "Fates" as plural persons in Classical mythology, they knew that in their terms these were *wyrdæ* or *wyrde*. Seeing wyrd in the plural form at all, even just when translating foreign words for 'The Fates,' indicates to me that Wyrd in Anglo-Saxon could be pictured as a sentient being, a being who in other cultures appears as a threesome. If they understood wyrd solely as an impersonal phenomenon, not as a person, then they would not have translated a Latin term for personified beings using that word.

We do see the plural concept turning up much later: the dramatist and poet William Shakespeare (1564-1616) includes the three Weird Sisters in his play Macbeth, stirring their cauldron of spells and bringing the decrees of fate onto Macbeth and those associated with him. It's likely that Shakespeare's portrayal of the three Weird Sisters was influenced by Norse mythology about the three Norns as well as Classical myths about the Fates, but the English word and concept of wyrd or weird was still in existence then, as it is now, and was used to name supernatural beings.

Synthesis

Here is the way that I presently understand the relationship of Wyrd and orlog, though it's a deep and complex subject

Orlog and Wyrd

that I find is gradually evolving in my mind. I think of Wyrd as a being, a singularity who expresses what the Norns express in their triplicity. In some ways, I see Wyrd as being the same thing as the Norns collectively are; in other ways she seems to stand on her own, possessing her own mysterious nature.

I might note one real mythological difference: as far as I know, Wyrd / Wurð / Wurt is never mentioned in connection with a Well in the non-Norse literature, though the German Goddess Frau Holle with her Pond / Well is, I believe, a resonance of the Norns and their Well. This is especially clear because Frau Holle draws babies out of her Pond—this is well-known folklore about where babies come from—and fairy tales about children falling into Frau Holle's Well and returning from her green meadows back to earth after a time with her are metaphors for death and rebirth. As the Norns 'choose life' and choose the time of death, Frau Holle's Pond gives forth babies, carried by the stork to their parents, and welcomes kindly the worthy ones who die into her realm through her Well. But as regards Wyrd, specifically, I don't know of her association with a well or water.

Certainly, in personal terms, I experience Wyrd and each of the Norns as individual beings. It's as though these views, Three or One, are different facets of the full Being that is Wyrd, and I move around, viewing one facet or another at different times. To add to the ambiguity, Wyrd herself, in my perception, seems to have no issue with sometimes appearing as a person, other times as a phenomenon. To me, it seems as though she is presenting us with an existential riddle, challenging us to plunge more deeply in our efforts to understand who and what she / it is.

Orlog and Wyrd

As one contributor to this book, Svartheiðrinn, notes, Wyrd is rather like the quantum phenomenon of light being both a wave and a particle, depending on the method one uses to observe it: sometimes she appears as a personal being, other times as an impersonal phenomenon.

Orlog is clearly not a person, but it is a presence that is so all-pervading and influential in the world and in our lives that in some ways it seems to act as a being. If 'Wyrd goes always as she must,' if the Norns 'lay layers and speak orlog,' if those layers of orlog and actions of Wyrd form a substrate of necessity that shapes our lives, then their effects upon us and the world are in fact very similar, whether those effects are caused by personal beings or by an impersonal phenomenon.

Wyrd: A Case Study

Here's an analysis of a line from *Beowulf* that provides context for many questions that we might have about Wyrd and the Norns as persons, and their roles in determining our fate. Though this example is based on a sentence about Wyrd, I think the implications apply as well to the Norns. Beowulf ll. 572-73 reads: *Wyrd oft nereð unfægne eorl, ðonne his ellen deah.* In a general sense, this says that "Wyrd often saves an undoomed eorl when his courage holds" (Chickering translation). It's hard to picture wyrd as a non-personified phenomenon here: how would it 'know' whether the eorl's courage holds or not, and how would it thus 'save' him, if it is not a sentient being?

In important phrases like this one that I use myself for Heathen meditation, I always like to look at the specific words that are used in more depth, which I offer here for your consideration. *Nereð* is translated as 'saves': "Wyrd

Orlog and Wyrd

often saves..." which has a rather Christian connotation of salvation. And yes, the *Beowulf* poet was Christian and chose his words accordingly, but let's go a little deeper. *Nereð* from *ge-nerian* means 'to save, rescue, liberate, preserve, defend, protect' in Anglo-Saxon. It is cognate to Old Saxon *nerian*, meaning 'to heal, rescue, or nourish.' Old High German has the same word and meaning, which is related to modern German *nähren,* to nourish (Berr p. 296).

I like to read the word *nereð* in this context as Wyrd in a sense 'feeding' or 'nourishing' the man's courage and strength, giving the meaning: "Wyrd often nourishes the unfey earl's courage...". Bauschatz writes much about the nourishing and sustaining nature of the Norns: "The Norns represent a powerful, continuing, regenerative force in the universe. ...and they regularly influence the lives of men" (p. 7).

One of the ways the Norns use their power is to nourish and protect the World-Tree by patting layers of white mud onto its trunk, taken from the sacred Wellspring that lies at its foot, to heal and regenerate the Tree from all the harms that befall it (*Gylfaginning* in the Prose Edda, [16-17], p. 19 in Faulkes). These layers represent layers of orlog, of continuing, ongoing life as reflected in the actions of all Beings.

The word *ellen* in our passage is usually translated as 'courage': "if his courage holds." It has other meanings as well: strength, power, vigor, valor, fortitude. As I see it, in this *Beowulf* passage Wyrd is nourishing the strength, power, vigor, courage of the man so that he can use it on his own behalf, to *save himself,* in fact.

The word *deah* implies the worthy use of something: here, the worthy use of his power, his courage, on his own

Orlog and Wyrd

behalf. Poetically, I might translate it as 'avails' here: 'if his courage *avails* him.' My interpretation of this passage is that for an unfey / undoomed person, Wyrd or the Norns will often nourish that person's powers and courage so that they are capable of overcoming the peril or challenge of their circumstances themselves.

My (unpoetic!) translation of the full meaning would thus be: "Wyrd often nourishes / supports the unfey person if their courage and power are used for a worthy purpose / used to save their life." I suggest that a Heathen view of this passage does not imply that the Norns 'save' people in some vague, undefined way, nor in any way that 'saving' would be understood in a Christian context. Instead, in true Heathen manner, Wyrd offers what we need so that we can save or help ourselves.

That aspect of the meaning seems clear to me, but the stipulation that this applies only to someone who is *'unfæg,* un-fey, undoomed' is more perplexing. If Wyrd has already doomed someone, then clearly she can't save him, which would go against her own spoken word or doom. But if she has *not* doomed him to death at that place and time, then he would not die in any case, so how exactly does she 'save' him, or help him save himself?

It's almost as though she 'pre-saved' him at that place and time, by her spoken word in the past which presumably doomed him to death at a *different* time and place, thus sparing him at the time that is referred to in this phrase. And there's clearly an implication that the eorl's choice of action influences the outcome: 'if his courage is used.' If his courage isn't brought into play, might he then die in that battle? But in that case, was the rising of his courage also predetermined by Wyrd so that he would be able to save himself? Or was his death actually not predetermined at all, and depended fully on his choice of action in that battle? But the word *unfæg,* undoomed, does point to the likelihood of predestination playing a role.

So is this situation an example of (a) predestination, (b) determinism, and / or (c) free will? One short sentence offers both enlightenment and confusion here! The matter of the Norns and their influence on determinism, free will, and predestination is the subject of the next three chapters, but I'll say up front that I find it a confusing subject, as full of questions as it may be of answers!

9. Causality and Determinism

Modern Heathens have pursued interesting and in-depth discussions about the relationships between wyrd / orlog, and determinism, predestination, and causation. Are the Norns / Wyrd deterministic? That is, do they determine our actions and the events of our lives directly? Does orlog determine our actions in the sense of causing—even forcing—them to happen? Do the Norns, Wyrd, or orlog predestine specific things in our life, such as our luck or unluck, or the circumstances of our death? In what sense do the Norns or Wyrd 'cause' something to happen? Do the Norns 'speak orlog' as it says in the Völuspá, and then orlog takes over and directs what happens? How does all this work? How was it understood in the past, and do we see things differently today?

These are subjects that many branches of formal philosophy have pursued for ages with regard to 'fate'; a great deal has been said and written about them, including by modern Heathens with backgrounds in philosophy. Here are some of my thoughts, beginning with musings on 'causation,' which seems to me the fundamental phenomenon upon which any discussion of determinism must rest. Without the phenomenon of causation, determinism could not exist.

The Norns as Caretakers of Causality

I consider causation to be a force or impetus similar to momentum in physics. It links one action or phenomenon with another into a cascading series or network of events, leading off in multidimensional directions. In the material world, causes and effects can be complex and multivariate, but are considered to be, at least in theory, predictable if one has a clear understanding of all the parameters (easier said than done!). In the 'inner worlds' of sentient beings—our thoughts, emotions, reactions, motivations, worldview— some believe that the same assertion holds true: if we understood all the parameters involved, we could predict the choices, decisions, actions and reactions of humans and other sentient beings. This is the basis for a deterministic view of human action as well as of the physical world. In this worldview, from a Heathen standpoint the Norns / Wyrd / orlog appear as the ultimate force that drives all events, all cause-and-effect that plays out in this world.

My view is subtly different from this. I see a difference between causality as a phenomenon, versus specific causes and effects that play out in our lives here in Midgard. I view the Norns as the *caretakers of the* **phenomenon** *of causality*. They ensure that causality *works*, that it operates, in the physical world and the metaphysical worlds of inner thoughts and feelings, as well as in other Worlds upon the Tree. They keep us and the Worlds from the chaos that would ensue if there were no such thing as cause and effect: a universe of random and meaningless phenomena. But I don't think the Norns or Wyrd necessarily determine the

Causality and Determinism

content, the specific details, of every choice, decision, action, and deed.

Let's compare this to the laws of physics. For example, the law of gravity says that here on Earth if we drop something it will fall to the ground. That's determined; it's a 'law' of the space-time where we exist in Midgard. But the law of gravity says nothing about whether we decide to drop something and why, what we decide to drop, where we decide to drop it from, how we react to the thing having been dropped, how other people react to us dropping the thing, etc. That is a list of subjective causes and effects that arise from that specific instance of the workings of gravity, but none of those things are 'determined' by gravity itself. The only thing that is determined is that if a thing is dropped, it falls to the ground. The rest of what I just listed are what people make of it.

So it is with the Norns: under their charge, 'causes' have 'effects.' They are attending to the right functioning of cosmological processes, in particular the process of orlog which is the foundation of continuity in Time, and of the way that Time influences all life in Midgard. The Norns / Wyrd direct the process of weaving Time and Space together, maintaining a cosmological environment where Midgard life can thrive.

Without the phenomenon of orlog, of cause and effect that take place in Time and Space, there would be no processes that depend on a series of phenomena occurring in any particular order: nothing happening that we would recognize as chemistry, biology, life, history, evolution, growth and development of living beings. In a 'causeless' universe, either there would be nothing at all, because no primal cause brought anything into existence, or everything would exist perpetually in an unchanging state, or else there would be a chaotic situation of random events, actions, and phenomena popping up and disappearing, bearing no relationship to one another in space or in time.

Some philosophers and physicists contend that this is how reality is: a situation of completely random events that only the human mind sees as being connected to each other through causality. I can't wrap my mind around this idea: for example, how would biology work, if the complex processes that make our bodies function occurred totally randomly? If the nerves that make our heart beat sometimes worked, sometimes not, sometimes went very fast, other times extremely slowly, flipped around randomly…that's heart-attack country, when the complex neurology and biochemistry that regulate the heartbeat within carefully controlled parameters cease to follow their own signals, their own processes of cause and effect.

If there were no cause and effect and everything was random, then eating a large amount of a deadly poison would be like Russian roulette: sometimes it would kill us, other times have no effect. Really? I have my doubts, and I doubt that those who claim there is no such thing as cause and effect would want to try that experiment! At least when it comes to living beings, I simply can't concede that causation does not exist: no complex living beings could function without minutely ordered systems of cause and effect maintaining their life-functions.

But let's pursue a hypothetical situation for a moment as an interesting thought-experiment: how might a scenario where reality consists entirely of random events affect how we experience our lives? In terms related to our subject matter here: what if we were orlog-less?

Causality and Determinism

What if we were Orlog-less?

Verses 17-21 of the *Völuspá* (Poetic Edda) tell us that three Æsir 'find on land' Ask and Embla (elsewhere they are called 'trees / logs' although here we simply have their names) who are without orlog and without other gifts that add up to life and human-ness. I find this lack of orlog fascinating, because it implies that having orlog is an essential part of what it is to be human. After the Gods give Ask and Embla the gifts of human life, the next verses tell us about the Norns and their action of 'speaking orlog' for children of Aldr: human beings. I think this is all part of the same event: the Gods give their gifts of spirit, breath, speech, behavior, appearance, but the transformation into humans is not complete until the Norns 'speak orlog' for them. *Orlog is an essential part of what it is to be fully human.*

What would it mean for us to be without orlog? Being without orlog would mean that there is no such thing as a meaningful sequence of events, layer building on layer, that leads to the existence of 'history,' 'experience,' 'precedent,' and all that derive from them. Cause and effect would only be understood in an immediate sense, not in terms of long, complex patterns.

If we did not each possess orlog as a dynamic force shaping our lives, then our lives and deeds would be random. There would be no pattern to our lives, no history, no non-random impacts on the world and on each other. *Any significance associated with a deed would evaporate after it was done, because it would be left behind in time, not stored as a layer within the substance of orlog.* There would be no reasons for our deeds and choices other than the impulses of the moment: neither past nor future would matter.

Causality and Determinism

For example, let's say you got so mad you punched a hole in the wall. Your fist would hurt, the hole would have to be repaired at a cost of time and money, but you would not realize any connections between these events. Even less would you understand any connections between whatever event made you mad and all your personal characteristics and personal history that made you likely to get so mad about that event, and then how that is linked with the hole in the wall and the pain in your fist. From a psychological standpoint, the experience of cause-and-effect would be missing, depriving you of self-awareness, awareness of the world outside you, the opportunity to learn from your experience, and the spiritual strength—the might and main—that an understanding of personal responsibility would give you.

This is a condition of psychological disorder that mirrors the physical disorder which would occur in the outside world under a situation where cause-and-effect did not exist. As another example: the process of digestion in living beings who consume material substances as food depends on a highly complex, ordered cascade of enzymes, biochemicals, autonomic muscular actions, microbial activities, all of them facilitated by other things such as neurotransmitters, nervous system activity, pH values, and much more: each of these are the result of certain causes and the cause of certain effects. If that minutely ordered process became random and unrelated to causes triggering effects and then those effects becoming the causes of following effects, digestion simply would not happen...and I flinch from imagining the results!

How much of what we know as 'civilization' would even develop without the primal layers of knowledge, experience, learning, crafts, arts, sciences, technology, engineering, and all the rest forming the foundation for the next layer of culture, generation after generation over centuries? Civilization itself can be understood as an accumulation of layers, building upon itself over time, just as orlog is. Culture is orlog in action, civilization is orlog in action, and we participate in these collective orlogs as well as in our own personal and familial orlogs. All of these accumulations that are the foundations of human life, along with analogous processes in Nature, are expressions of orlog, and they depend on the phenomenon of causality.

But how does this relate to determinism and free will as we humans experience these things? Does orlog control everything? Or does it, instead, *create the conditions under which we ourselves can learn to use causality to enact our own Will?*

Free Will *and* Determinism

Orlog is the necessary cosmic process upon which causality is based. As I view it, the Norns oversee the process of causality, in particular the phenomenon of causes and effects following each other in sequence—not always necessarily in linear sequence, but in multidimensional networks of relationship to one another. By the Norns' establishment of cause and effect, they create *the conditions under which we humans can be effective* in our own lives. We can make choices, form intentions, take actions, perform deeds, be aware of the results and their causes, and take responsibility for them—and we can do this *because* causality exists.

Because causality exists, we can learn about how actions and choices have results, have consequences. When we have little life-experience, those consequences are frequently not the ones we wanted or expected. As our experience and

Causality and Determinism

wisdom grows, the links between our choices and actions and their consequences begin to clarify. Life in Midgard is so complex that we never gain full understanding of consequences and their connection to our actions and choices, but gradually we approach some approximation of this. And more: we grow the moral and spiritual strength to take responsibility for our actions and choices, even when the consequences are not what we expected or intended.

Causality—and our understanding, however partial, of how it works—allows us to have real effects on our world. It allows our actions to have power and efficacy, and it gives us the essential opportunity to learn from experience: without these things we would go precisely nowhere!

The Norns are not programming us to do specific things, to make specific choices and decisions, except perhaps those that are most life-changing—the major turning points of our lives. On an everyday level they are making it possible for *us* to do these things ourselves by providing the Worlds with the phenomenon of orlog, the structure of cause and effect that makes life in Midgard possible and gives it meaning.

When we are conceived, they 'score on slips of wood, lay layers, choose life, speak orlog' for each of us, which weaves us each into the Web of Wyrd, the multidimensional field of orlog that they maintain. They attach to us the threads of orlog that arise from the history of our kin, our genes and heritage, the culture and circumstances we are born into, perhaps our past lives, too. The past is part of who we are and has an ongoing influence on us, but what we do with these threads in the present time depends upon our own choices and actions as well as the tuggings of these strands of orlog from the past and from our surroundings.

Causality and Determinism

This leads us back to questions of determinism and free will. It is probably clear from what I just wrote that in my view *both* determinism, in the form of orlog, *and* free will play important roles in who we are and what we become as we live our lives. Complete, 'pure' free will would lead, I believe, to a state of inner and outer chaos. Our Will itself is shaped by our experiences, circumstances, our thoughts, emotions and reactions, and by our consideration of consequences, of cause and effect: in other words, by an understanding of orlog to the best of our ability.

If our Will guides our actions when that Will is unconstrained by any considerations of orlog in the world and in our own lives, that would indeed lead to chaos. Free will that is unshaped by considerations of orlog is simply 'impulse,' with no impulse control. In 'considerations of orlog' I include an understanding of cause and effect upon ourselves and others around us, an understanding of our motivations and where they come from, an understanding, and acceptance, of the consequences of acting according to our Will and taking responsibility for this.

For wisdom to rule in our lives, we need to blend the actions of our Will with the understanding of orlog that life experience and participation in Midgard matters gives us. Some of our circumstances, and certain constraints upon our actions, are indeed determined for us, and so is the fact that death will happen. In other ways we have choices about how to act, what course to take, what to think, what stance to take. Our lives are not purely determined, nor purely free; they are a complex, shifting combination of both, and wisdom lies in understanding that and charting the best course possible each day as we live our lives and make our choices. By doing so, we lay our share of good orlog to shape our next day's actions, and the next generation's courses. We participate in our own small way with the shapings of the Norns in Midgard.

Significance: Making it Personal

In my studies I've seen plenty of evidence of various kinds for an ancient Heathen belief that Wyrd or the Norns shape the general course of people's lives and predestine their deaths, but as I've discussed, I've seen no evidence in ancient Heathen belief that this 'shaping' or influence applies to every tiny detail of our lives. Rather, the focus of the Norns' work is on the significant events and major turning points of our lives. Significant events have the power to shape our lives; insignificant events pass by with little impact on the overall pattern and shape of our lives.

As Jacob Grimm insightfully pointed out, the fairy godmothers and similar figures in fairy tales of European cultures are the 'descendants' of the ancient Norns. We see these fairy godmothers 'shaping' the lives of newborns during their naming or christening ceremonies through the gifts or curses that they give the babies. And sure enough, the words of the fairies come true: the princess is beautiful and sweet and loved by everyone per the gifts, and pricks her finger on a spindle on her 16th birthday and falls asleep so no one can wake her for years, per the curse, etc. But the fairy godmothers certainly didn't control how many times the child sneezed on the first day of February when she was five years old, or whether she got a pebble in her shoe when she went out to play on June fourteenth, or whatever. The godmothers shaped the significant events of her life but did not affect the daily details.

Causality and Determinism

As another example, I'm guessing that if you were taking a walk with an ancient Heathen and he stumbled and stubbed his toe, and you asked him 'did the Norns make you stumble just now?' he would look at you rather blankly. (Though he might easily say that his Fylgja or Hamingja, or someone else's Fylgja or Hugr, or an 'onflyer' or a wight or a hag or other unluck-causing being made him stumble...but I don't believe he would blame the Norns or Wyrd.) He might well agree that the Norns 'shaped' him to be a rather clumsy person who frequently stumbles, but that they reached out just now to make him stumble, or that they predestined him to stumble at that very minute in that exact place–I think this ancient Heathen would find that idea very unlikely. Unless, of course, that stumble led to some significant outcome: he dropped his weapon just at the moment that a lurker leaped out to attack and badly injure him, or the arrow that was shot at him out of hiding passed harmlessly over him as he was bent over his stubbed toe. That, obviously, *would* show the Norns' involvement!

But not every tiny, meaningless action or event of every minute of one's life is so significant, and it's the *significance,* not the event itself, that tells a Heathen that the Norns are involved. 'Significance' is the cue, the significator, of the Norns' involvement in our lives: their involvement is shown not just by any 'event' happening, but by a significant event. And that significance can be internal, personal, idiosyncratic, known and meaningful only to ourselves, or it can be something that is externally obvious to others as well as to ourselves. It might, at the time it happens, be significant only to the Norns, but in hindsight we may realize its significance ourselves.

Causality and Determinism

I would add that the more aware we are of the Norns and their influence in our lives, the more clearly we see significance in the events and actions of our lives. Eventually we might reach a sort of mystical state where we perceive almost everything as significant, and at that point, the deterministic conception of the Norns might make a lot of sense based on this experience. But I'd add a caveat: in this scenario, it seems to me that the 'significance' we're detecting is due to our perception of the Norns' involvement in the details of our life: *we feel that the Norns' attention to us is the significant thing,* not the minor and otherwise meaningless event itself.

In this 'mystical' scenario, is every meaningless event (such as dropping the toothbrush as we start to put toothpaste on it, or for that matter, *not* dropping the toothbrush) something that really was programmed by the Norns from the moment we were born? Or was the real programming by the Norns our own state of mind that pursues this sense of significance through the details of our lives and thus perceives our connection with the Norns?

In this mystical or devotional state of mind, I would say that the nature of each little event doesn't matter, to us or to the Norns; it only matters because of the interpretation and significance we place on it as evidence of the Norns' attention to us and what that means for us. In a case like this, the Norns might have 'shaped' us generally as a person who perceives such significance in daily events and connects it with the Norns, rather than the Norns deliberately causing every tiny event and action of our lives.

For each of us (mystics or not), when we are born and the Norns 'lay layers, choose life, speak orlog' for us, I do not believe they are determining every detail of our lives.

Causality and Determinism

Fundamentally, they are weaving us into the already existing web of wyrd, the orlog of our place and time in this world. They are shaping a space for us to fill, but the details of that space, its color, shape, texture, sounds, its personalization into the unique being that is our Self—*this work is ours.*

The Norns give us a place to belong in time and space and social context. They link us to the past, maintain the orderly processes of cause and effect in Midgard, and—essentially—they offer possibilities for us to take effective action and thus influence what is coming into being. They also shape the most significant events and turning points of our lives. All this provides context for our own work of laying worthy orlog throughout our lives and using our understanding of this process to live wisely and well.

Causality and Determinism

"Study for Destiny" by Beatrice Offor

10. The Norns as Beings of Fate

Modern Heathens with a religious sense more rooted in past tradition might hold the view that the Norns / Wyrd and orlog predestine the circumstances of our death, and may determine the more significant events of our lives as well. Certainly, in terms of the Norns predestining our death, this is a matter more of faith or belief than something which can be philosophically examined. Those with a less religious, more philosophical bent might also lean toward a deterministic view, but base it on orlog as a phenomenon, on cause-and-effect laying out a deterministic path of life for us. In the beliefs of some, the Norns lay out that path for us from the beginning of our lives; in the view of others, our own past actions and perhaps transpersonal past lay out that path for us and we must follow it. Or one might see it as a combination of both: the Norns' / Wyrd's actions plus our own actions laying out a deterministic path for us. The influence of modern Western ideas of karma may also play a role in how one understands these matters. One way or another, with a belief in the Norns / Wyrd / orlog as real influences in the cosmos, questions about fate and predestination must arise.

The Norns as Beings of Fate

Tending Causality, Shaping Fate

If the Norns are, so to speak, the caretakers or supervisors of causality, is that all that they do? Do they simply tend this cosmic process, weaving the countless strands spun by beings and their actions into the multidimensional Web of Wyrd? Or do the Norns also *intervene* in this process, bringing about events that are caused by their own independent will, choices, and decisions rather than simply arising out of orlog-as-causation?

Urð one is called, another Verðandi,
Scoring on slips of wood, Skuld is third;
There they lay layers, there life choose,
For children of aldr (mortals), speak ørlög.
(Völuspá, vs. 20-21, my translation)

This verse from the *Völuspá* that we've encountered before certainly implies that they do intervene: the Norns 'carve on slips of wood, choose life, and speak orlog,' as well as 'laying layers' of orlog. 'Laying layers' equates to 'tending causality,' in my view. 'Speaking orlog' may do this too: the Norns are marking the layers of orlog as 'official' by formally pronouncing their meaning, their significance, as the layers are laid in the Well. *Perhaps orlog is not orlog, does not function as orlog, unless and until the Norns speak it?* This would go along with Bauschatz's description of significant deeds and events falling as drops of dew from the Tree into the Well, and from the Well are drawn up to nourish the Tree again, whereas insignificant deeds and events fall outside the Well and are lost (see Bauschatz Chapter IV, "Action, Space, and Time"). I believe that this 'speaking orlog into reality' is one of the major things the Norns are doing, and I find it profoundly meaningful for Heathen spirituality. We are mirroring this action, at the human level, when we speak our boasts in symbel.

But is this all that 'speaking orlog' involves, or is there more to it? Do the Norns actually *create* orlog by speaking it, as opposed to acknowledging and empowering the orlog laid by the deeds of others? The other two actions they are described as doing, 'scoring on slips of wood,' and 'choosing life,' imply this greater sense of agency, of intentional actions and choices on their parts.

I wrote in Chapter 3 that I believe the first of this series of actions by the Norns involves scoring runestaves, and runework is without question something that is intended to bring about a willed action, a result or effect of some kind—something new, that would not necessarily occur without the runework causing it. 'Choosing life,' perplexing as this phrase may seem, clearly speaks of choice, of willed action that brings something new into existence, as runework does. It isn't clear whether 'choosing life' simply means choosing for a new being to come into existence, or whether more specifics are implied. Do they also choose the life-circumstances, the major influences on that life, and the duration of it? It's my impression that ancient Heathens did believe this: that the Norns choose for beings to come into existence, into specific circumstances that shape that existence, and that they choose the duration of that life.

Nornir / Valkyrja: Choosing Life / Choosing Death

I think, too, that the Norns 'choose life' in direct contrast to the Valkyries or *valkyrja,* fate-bearing beings who 'choose death' for warriors in the midst of battle, usually at the behest of Odin who gathers some of the slain as his

The Norns as Beings of Fate

Einherjar, his chosen warriors in Valhalla. I have no way of knowing the poet's intention in the *Völuspá* verse, of course, but I believe the contrast is deliberate in the poet's choice of words here. The words *val-kyrja* (Old Norse) and *wæl-cyrge* (Anglo-Saxon) mean 'slain-choosers,' the choosers of those who will die. The Norns, conversely, are first and foremost choosers of those who will live.

"Valkyrie," by Peter Nicolai Arbo.

The Norns as Beings of Fate

Odin and Freya have their chosen ones, the warriors they have selected for afterlife in their God-Halls. The Norns have their own chosen ones: all of us who enter into life in Midgard, into the realms where orlog and wyrd operate. There are 'lesser norns' who help in childbirth, as well as the three great ones who "choose life." These lesser norns are referred to in the *Lay of Fafnir:* "Which are those norns who go to help those in need, and bring children forth from their mothers?" (v. 13, Larrington's translation).

After choosing each of us for life, however, the Norns also choose the time of our death, our *orleg-hwile* or orlog-while. To summarize the Norns' choices with respect to human life, they choose:

1) our life in the sense of being born into Midgard,

2) our life-span which includes our time of death,

3) our Aldr / Ealdor life-soul which is connected to them and serves as their 'agent' in our life and in Midgard, and

4) they influence the shape of our Werold, the fabric of our total life-experience.

Looking at it this way, what I see is not that the Norns are specifically focused on bringing about death, as might be implied by the frequent use of 'orlog' to mean 'death,' but rather that they choose our *life-span* in Midgard, which is then necessarily brought to a close by our death. But it is life that is important; death is simply a necessary consequence of mortal life. It is perhaps significant that Skuld, the Norn governing 'what must be,' is also named as a valkyrja in *Gylfaginning* of the prose *Edda,* where she "always rides to choose the slain" (Sturlason p. 31). Skuld herself is the link between the Powers who choose life and life-span, and those who choose death, the ultimate necessity for mortal beings.

'Fate' versus Causality

Now we approach the question of 'fate,' if fate is understood to be something that lies *outside* the workings of causality: fate as brought about by the deliberate action of some powerful force or Being. The word 'fate' comes from Latin *fari,* 'to speak,' leading to *fatum,* 'that which has been spoken.' This is remarkably similar to the speaking or the decrees of the Norns. One set of definitions for 'fate' is "the development of events beyond a person's control, regarded as determined by a supernatural power. The course of someone's life, or the outcome of a particular situation for someone or something, seen as beyond their control. The inescapable death of a person." (Oxford Languages Dictionary online.)

Causality in a way is the antithesis of fate: it occurs as a natural, explicable process that humans can, to some extent, understand and control, whereas fate comes from outside the human and material world; it is inexplicable, uncontrollable, unpredictable, and apparently lies outside the realm of natural causality. So, how does this work, if the Norns are on the one hand the caretakers of causality, but on the other hand are beings of fate who impose their own decisions *outside* of the workings of causality? Isn't that contradictory?

Wyrd and Will Together

I suggest that these apparently contradictory roles work, for the Norns, in somewhat the same way that the contradictory roles of free will versus determinism work for us as humans, as discussed in the previous chapter. The Norns work with causality, with orlog laid as layers by the actions of many beings over eons of time, as we humans work with aspects of

The Norns as Beings of Fate

our lives that are determined—that lie outside of our options for free will. Both we and the Norns (and the Gods) deal with what has already been laid down as orlog, by ourselves and by others. These layers of orlog condition or shape the circumstances we deal with today. But in this moment of time, as it is coming into being, we can often choose among the paths that lie ahead of us: choose to follow our own will, which is free to an extent, and conditioned or constrained to an extent.

Beowulf provides a good example of this in his actions on the day of his death. First is an episode of reflection: Beowulf has heard about the dragon and has decided he must slay it to protect his kingdom. He and his thanes reach the cliff where the dragon's cave is, but before proceeding Beowulf wants to ponder on his life. He knows that "Wyrd is immeasurably close;" his time of death is near. His Sefa-soul mourns, restless, ready to depart. He knows that his Feorh-soul "will not be wrapped in flesh for much longer." *(Beowulf* ll. 2417-2424). Beowulf is well aware, in other words, that wyrded death waits for him in the dragon's cave, but he continues on this path.

Beowulf then goes into the dragon's cave, braving the flames which foreshadow his own balefire. He bears his famous shield and sword, which have never failed him before, but they do now. For the first time in his life "Wyrd did not grant him glory in battle" (l. 2574-5). Nevertheless Beowulf *wealdan moste,* wielded as he must. The word *wealdan* can mean 'to have power over, to control, to rule or govern, to have the power to choose or decide, to have power to do, to be able' (Bosworth Toller dictionary). This is the power of the Will, and he wields his Will *both* as he 'chooses', *and* as he 'must.' Collapsing under the flaming

The Norns as Beings of Fate

attack of the dragon, Beowulf uses the utmost power of his will for his final strokes. He breaks his sword on the dragon, wounding but not killing it. Then after his young thane Wiglaf weakens the dragon further, dying Beowulf draws his knife and gives the fatal blow. *(Beowulf lines 2545ff.)*

Here is the point. Wyrd laid out the time and events leading to Beowulf's death; Beowulf knew this and followed it as he must. But he had a choice at the very end: to collapse in failure under the deadly attack of the dragon, or to rise for one final moment and wield his knife and his will against the dragon. The Norns ordained his death at that time and place, but the final blow he dealt the dragon, with his shattered shield and sword in pieces around him, was Beowulf's choice. (An interesting exercise is to look at orlog from the dragon's point of view…I leave that for the interested reader to explore!)

This is what I mean by 'Wyrd and Will together.' Wyrd / the Norns lay out conditions that constrain our lives, but within those conditions there is always a place for our own will to act. This is a great mystery of Wyrd and the Norns:

*Even when we must deal with necessity, with a determined situation that we can't get out of, we can **merge** our free will with that necessity, accepting the reality of what orlog has already laid down. We thereby **choose** to walk our necessary path with greater power, achieving and learning far more than we would if we dragged ourselves whining and moaning along that path because of necessity alone, unwillingly, without bringing the full power of our Will to bear on it.*

The Norns as Beings of Fate

This mystery of wyrd and will together is one that I believe Odin models for us very profoundly with his choices and deeds, as well as other Deities, heroes, and unsung wise folk living everyday lives. The stronger our Will, the might and main of our spirit and character, our wisdom and understanding of the operations of orlog, the more able we are to expand the field of options for our free will—even within the layers of necessity that constrain us. When faced with necessity, adding the power of our Will to the actions we *must* take raises us to greater heights of achievement and of Being.

This is the situation of the Norns as well: their wills, their might and main, their wisdom and understanding, their power overall, far exceed our own. While they work continually with causality and orlog, they are also able to find or create opportunities for the exercise of their will, their choices, their designs, and work them organically into the layers of orlog that are coming into being.

The 'workings of fate' that the Norns engage in are, for them, comparable to the 'free will' that we humans can operate under to some extent in our lives. Orlog is there, it exists, and the Norns, like everyone else, have to work with 'what is there' unless they decide to, and are capable of, tearing it all up and starting over! (Even Ragnarök doesn't completely do that....) Orlog places conditions on what can and cannot be done by the Norns, the Deities, humans, and everyone else, though it may be that orlog can only do this once the Norns have 'spoken it.' That's the deterministic side of things. On the other side, humans have some free will and we choose how to use it. Norns apparently do this too: they carve runes, they 'choose lives,' they speak decrees that lay out new elements to be woven into orlog that is now coming into being. This seems, to me, like actions of free will on their part.

Their 'free will' actions of carving and choosing and speaking, however, have the opposite effect on humans and other beings. When they exercise their 'free will' and set fate or wyrd in motion, it sets boundaries around the exercise of our own free will. We have some ability to lay orlog of our own: some of the orlog we lay by our actions results in shaping our lives the way we want. But if the Norns have spoken otherwise, have decreed something to happen or not happen in our lives, then our free will is overridden by their decisions. When this happens I believe, as I wrote earlier, that we gain by adding the power of our own Will to the impetus of necessity laid by the Norns, and trust that this path will ultimately take us in a worthwhile direction.

When the Norns are simply 'tending the processes of causality' and nothing more, then there is some room for us to shape things our own way by using those processes in our favor. The Norns do not arrange every detail and event of our lives. They leave us a good deal of space to forge our own paths, and to work with our Holy Ones to shape our paths as truly worthy ones.

Foresight and Predestination

❦ O ❧

11. Foresight and Predestination

Foresight

As I discussed in Chapter 6, Bauschatz argues that the concept of 'the future' was ambiguous in old Heathen understanding of how the world works. It had less of a grip on their thoughts than did 'the past' and 'the present,' and its significance was of a lesser order, largely because the future is less known than the past is and has less 'weight' to it in terms of shaping the present. Even so, it's clear that the ability to foresee the future played an important role both in everyday life and in dramatic moments captured in sagas, tales, and myths, showing that the concept of 'the future' had its own significant place in ancient Heathen worldviews.

Both in real life and in tales, sagas, and myths, the wise-woman, seeress, *völva,* or *spákona* played an important role in Heathen society with her ability to discern and foretell the future (there were men who practiced this skill as well, though fewer). Our contributing author Svartheiðrinn discusses this in more depth in the next chapter.

The *Völuspá* is a prime example: the dead seeress in this Old Norse poem is called forth temporarily from her afterlife by Odin's command. She begins her account at the very

Foresight and Predestination

beginning of the Worlds, before anything exists, and continues into the future, to Ragnarök and past it into Worlds reconfigured after the Muspell-conflagration. Implied in Norse poetry and myth is that Odin is influenced by this foreknowledge and shapes his deeds accordingly.

Vala, the Norse Seeress.
Sculpture by Søren Lexow-Hansen.

The same is true for deeds of Frigg. In *Baldr's Dreams,* included in the Poetic Edda, the Æsir learn about Baldr's forthcoming death from another seeress. In response to this foreknowledge, Frigg fared about the Worlds and "received solemn promises so that Baldr should not be harmed by fire and water, iron and all kinds of metal, stones, the earth, trees, diseases, the animals, the birds, poison, snakes," except, unfortunately, she missed getting a promise from the mistletoe (Sturlason, prose *Edda,* p. 48). Odin responded differently: he took steps to father another son who would avenge Baldr's death *(Baldr's Dreams* v. 10-11.)

Foresight and Predestination

Foreknowledge spurred Odin and Frigg to undertake mighty deeds in an attempt to forestall or mitigate the dire orlog that was impending, but as we know from the myths, what was foreseen did indeed come to pass, in the case of Baldr's death. In the case of Ragnarök, perhaps it has already happened as some modern Heathens believe, and / or perhaps it is still pending, but it looms there, a vast presence on the horizon of 'the future.'

Looking at foresight from a human perspective, here is a description from Chapter 4 of *The Saga of Erik the Red*, which provides a wonderfully detailed description of an itinerant Icelandic spákona or seeress and her work of foretelling. The seeress Thorbjorg has come to a neighborhood that has been suffering from both epidemic illness and dearth, or lack of sufficient food and other resources needed for survival. The worried residents all gather at the farmstead where Thorbjorg is hosted for a traditional oracular ceremony. After elaborately detailed preliminaries, including preparing a high seat for her, she speaks with the local spirits during the ceremony and then announces: "now are many things clear to me which before were hidden both from me and others. And I am able this to say, that the dearth will last no longer, the season improving as spring advances. The epidemic of fever which has long oppressed us will disappear quicker than we could have hoped." Thorbjorg next foresees for the woman who has helped with the ceremony, saying "…there shall arise from thee a line of descendants both numerous and goodly, and over the branches of thy family shall shine a bright ray." And "afterwards the men went to the wise-woman, and each enquired after what he was most curious to know. She was also liberal of her replies, and what she said proved true."

Foresight and Predestination

Divination about the future as well as other hidden matters was so widely practiced among all the Germanic peoples, both during Heathen times and after official conversion, that I won't attempt to describe it in any detail, just mention it as evidence that 'the future' was certainly of interest to them. In Chapter 7 I quoted a reference to divination in Caesar's writing, dating from 53 BCE. Divination was practiced in numerous ways, using rune-casting, dreams, oracular work, and innumerable folk-customs like washing one's face in the morning dew on May Day to see the face of one's future husband.

A good way to seek for traces of Heathen customs is to look at the old laws and 'penitentials' of the early Christian churches in Heathen lands, which give lists of Heathen practices that should be punished. For example, here is a quotation from the *Paenitentiale Theodori,* attributed to Theodore of Tarsus, who held the position of Archbishop of Canterbury from 667 to 690. In chapter I. XV, *De Cultura Idolorum* ('Concerning the worship of idols'), it states the punishments due for working divination and other Heathen-like spiritual activities: "If a woman has performed incantations or diabolical divinations, let her do penance for one year. About which it says in the canon: Those who observe auguries or auspices or dreams or any kind of divinations according to the customs of the heathens…(lists their punishments)."
https://en.wikipedia.org/wiki/Magic_in_Anglo-Saxon_England#:~

Foresight and Predestination

The Influence of 'the Future'

In many cases, especially when it comes to actions of the Gods, foresight or knowledge of the future has an impact on actions of the present, just as orlog from the past does, but it functions in a different way. The past has an existential influence on the present: that is, the past has existence, presence, weight, primal layers that have been spoken and laid, and cannot fail to shape the present. Does 'the future' have that same degree of weight, of influence, on what happens in the present?

When we look at this question closely, as it involves foresight, the role of 'time' becomes quite complex. Here are the steps that I see happening as the time-dynamics of foresight play out.

1) A future scenario is revealed to a person who is concerned with it. Let's take Odin as an example: he is told about Ragnarök, and about Baldr's death. These are events that 'must be,' that are wyrded to happen: they lie in Skuld's domain.

2) Odin acquires this knowledge in his own 'present time' as the seeresses speak to him. He is becoming aware of what will happen in 'the future' but he obtains this knowledge during the present moment as he listens to the seeress. This is Verðandi's domain of Becoming, of knowledge and awareness coming into being in Odin's mind.

3) Once this knowledge becomes his, it 'has-become,' it is a completed fact. The knowledge has taken on existence in his awareness and has become layered within Odin's personal orlog, along with its layering in the larger orlog of the Worlds. This is Urð's domain of completed fact: the knowledge is embedded in Odin's awareness and his orlog

Foresight and Predestination

and is thereby influencing his choices and deeds, laying new layers of orlog.

4) Odin proceeds to take action in response to this awareness: he undertakes complex deeds and decisions to prepare for and respond to these events.

And here is my point: it is, in fact, Odin's already completed knowledge, layered into orlog by that completion, which is driving his actions. His knowledge-hoard about the future now lies in his personal past and present, layered in his orlog, and his responses are being enacted in the present. The future itself is still not there, has not happened, and cannot—it seems to me—directly influence his deeds because it does not yet exist. The only link that lies between 'the future' and 'Odin's actions' is the knowledge gained from foresight. The future here has no weight, no actuality or completeness, as 'the past' laid into orlog has. What is influencing Odin's deeds is his knowledge, the way he has processed that knowledge and reacted to it, all of which has already been done and laid in the well of his mind and Urð's Well.

So, back to the question: does 'the future' as revealed by foresight have the same weight, the same influence, on our choices and deeds as 'the past' does? In my view, it cannot, though I know there are others who believe that 'the future' does exist as objective fact, or perceive that 'time does not exist.' If these are true, then perhaps the future does have a comparable degree of influence...or perhaps the question becomes meaningless if 'time does not exist.' But as I see things, 'the future' can only influence us if we know, or think we know, what that future will be and react accordingly, and that knowledge is gained and processed in our 'present' and stored in our 'past.' Only then does it truly

Foresight and Predestination

become part of our orlog, and grow forth from that orlog into our present deeds that will, eventually, shape our unknown future. 'The future' does not shape our present. The past shapes our present, and the present, as it reaches completion and becomes the past, simultaneously shapes the future through the layers of orlog that are laid.

Predestination

What I've spoken of so far relates to foresight, to a view of the future that a sentient being, like a human or a Deity, has achieved and its influence on their actions. What about actual predestination? Foresight sees 'a future;' there's no absolute guarantee that this is the exact future that will happen, nor exactly when or how it will happen. Foresight, and even more the interpretation of foresight, can be mistaken. Predestination is pretty much solid: the Norns, Wyrd, or a Deity has said or arranged that something will happen, and it has to happen whether we're aware of this looming event or not. Ancient Heathens generally believed that the time and circumstances of their death were predestined, whether they were foreseen or not.

A person might have a 'destiny' not directly related to their death, as well. The *First Poem of Helgi Hundingsbani* in the Poetic Edda foretells, in stirring poetry, the power and success of Helgi from the moment of his birth. Eagles scream and sacred waters pour down from heaven as Helgi is born. The Norns attach strands of fate, *ørlögþöttu*, across the lands that Helgi will rule, weaving them into his orlog, while ravens foretell his heroic life. This is clearly intended as a portrayal of predestination, and the rest of the poem shows how that predestination played out in Helgi's life and deeds.

Foresight and Predestination

The difference I see between foresight and predestination seems to me a significant one from a philosophical standpoint. Foresight, and prophecy, simply means seeing what will happen; it does not necessarily imply control over those events. The seeress or *völva* who narrates the *Völuspá* isn't making Ragnarök happen—she's just foreseeing and foretelling it. It's true that people in Germanic and other cultures often 'blamed the messenger' when a foreseeing or prophecy was unfavorable, imagining that the speaker of the prophecy was actually causing it to happen. Svartheiðrinn discusses in the next chapter how seeresses, völur, and spákonur—people skilled at working with orlog—can to some extent influence the shaping of orlog that they foresee.

I agree that one can, to an extent, work with the strands of orlog that are coming into being, adding one's influence to the multiplicity of whirling orlog-strands to nudge things in the direction one wants to go. But this involves 'influence;' it is not full-blown 'causation.' There is no certainty that all the details of one's foreseeing are absolutely true, nor that one can fully shape the future as the Norns do. Even the Deities find that difficult or impossible, as we can see in the examples of Baldr's death and Ragnarök that I discussed in the previous sections. What we, and the Deities, do is use whatever knowledge of the future we can gain to plan the best ways of meeting and dealing with that future, and nudge things in the direction that we want.

As opposed to foreseeing, which is descriptive, predestination is causative: it is causing something to happen in the future, which is not something that humans can do with full certainty. We can often cause something to happen in the present according to our intention: that is within our power. And we can schedule and plan things for the future that may well happen just as we had previously planned...but they may not. We may be able to predict how certain things will happen in the future if we have enough information to do so, but again that is not controlling the future.

Even when we undertake something with a completely predictable outcome, such as a well-understood scientific experiment or an engineering project, that outcome will happen in accordance with the laws of nature rather than being created out of our own will alone—that's why it's predictable. Predestination is done by the Norns / Wyrd / Deities purely by the exercise of their Will. Prediction is done by a good understanding of natural laws and other relevant factors.

For example, we can correctly predict that if we tip a glass of water upside down, the water will pour out. We control the experiment by tipping the glass, but the water poured out according to natural law: we do not create or control that law of gravity. We might hold up the glass and 'foretell' that "This water is destined to fall out when I tip this glass," and then we do so, and it does. We are the *proximate* cause of the water spilling, by tipping the glass, but not the *ultimate* cause of the water falling, which is the law of gravity. We could not do the reverse and say "This water is destined to rise up out of this glass and fly around the room in the shape of a bird at 6pm this evening;" it wouldn't happen simply by our will and declaration, because it contravenes natural laws.

We are often able to intend something and do much to make it happen, working with natural laws, human skill and will—and with esoteric and magical skills, too—to reach results that we intended and designed. We obviously influence the future by our deeds in the present—every one of us, in all kinds of ways—but we don't have the ultimate, precise, willed control over future events that predestination implies, though some humans do have the ability to foresee what will happen. True predestination as the Norns and sometimes Deities enact it lies outside of human ability.

The Ambiguity of Time

Looking closely at predestination leads us again toward the ambiguity of the time element. The Norns ordain something to happen in the future, they predestine it. But 'where,' in time, is that action of theirs actually placed? They speak the words, carve the runes, that will bring into being a certain future act or situation, and they do that at a time that is 'present' at that moment of shaping. Then, having been spoken, been shaped, this act of predestination was laid into orlog: the substance of What-Is, what has been accomplished, otherwise known as 'the past.' From there, from its position in orlog and the past, it shapes events that are coming into being; this eventually results in the event that has been predestined. *It is still the past,* the layers of orlog working their way through the present like yeast fermenting in bread, which controls or conditions what happens in the present and leads to the predestined future.

In a way, we can see that the ancient concept of wyrd or orlog works *backwards* in time: orlog needs to arrange our life in such a way that we arrive at the time and circumstances of our death, our 'orlog-while,' according to a schedule that was laid in the past—or arrive at whatever other event was predestined. We can see this in the lore, because *both* 'what has been laid in the past,' *and* 'the

Foresight and Predestination

predestined future event' are called by the same terms, orlog and wyrd, in the ancient writings. And both those words mean, linguistically, 'what has been laid, what has become' in terms of the past: orlog is 'the primal, original layers;' wyrd is 'what has become, what is, what exists.' Both of those shape or condition Verðandi's 'What-Is-Becoming' and Skuld's 'What-Should-Be,' the present and aspects of what we conceptualize as the future. But the impetus, the shaping power, is established in Urð's or Wyrd's 'What-Is, which today we call 'the past.'

This way of perceiving time and what occurs in time is, I believe, at least part of what Bauschatz was referring to when he wrote about "the binary opposition inherent in the Germanic tense system between past and present, or, better, between past and nonpast events. This particular opposition of action presents events in a way that is significantly different from our own, and from other Indo-European peoples" (p. xvii).

The assumption that 'the future' has great power over the present, inherent in our idea of 'destiny' that leads us into the future, is not clearly reflected in Germanic mythology and in ancient concepts of how time, actions, and events unfold. It is not that they had no idea of, nor interest in, what might happen in the future—of course they shared this common human concern. What is different, I believe, is the question of the *agency* of the future over the present.

Getting back to the question I asked earlier: does 'the future' have the same degree of weight, of influence, on what happens in the present as the past has, in old Germanic thought? I believe, based on the discussion here, that it does not. Both in the situation where foresight influences our present actions, and in the situation where the Norns secretly predetermine or predestine events yet to come, the effective agency that drives the actions in the present, leading toward the future, *still lies in 'the past.'* It lies in What-Is, which exists because it has been accomplished, has happened, and has entered into reality thereby—has been laid in the Well, and incorporated into the Tree. 'The future' has not done this and never will, until it becomes 'the present' and then 'the past.' By which time, of course, it is no longer 'the future.'

Destiny: A Pull or a Push?

Here are a few thoughts of mine that compare the influence of the future, specifically 'Destiny,' to the influence of the past. This is a personal viewpoint, and many readers may feel it does not agree with their own perceptions. I share it just to provoke thoughts about the role of Time and orlog in our lives—wherever those thoughts might take you!

  To put it simplistically, the idea of 'Destiny' is that it lies in 'the future' and pulls us toward it: it is a destination we are purposefully headed toward, whether that purpose is defined by us or by predestining entities: Norns, Wyrd, or Deities. We imagine that it has been placed somewhere ahead of us in Time, and that we are inevitably drawn into the future to catch up with it and 'meet our destiny.' By contrast, the idea of 'Wyrd,' of the power of predestination that the Norns have, is that it lies in the past, in orlog, and it *pushes us from the past,* rather than pulling us toward something that actually lies in the future.

  Here is what I find meaningful about this distinction. If we are pulled toward a future destiny, then it seems to me there is only one way forward for us: the one that leads to 'our destiny.' The road is laid out for us ahead of time—it's

Foresight and Predestination

not laid by us, and we may be clueless about it—and we are drawn toward our 'destiny' like a nail to a magnet. If the Norns do predestine our death, then this acts as a given 'destiny' for us, of course, but what I'm talking about here is some specific life event or deed or role laid out as 'our destiny,' as is often represented in hero-tales or doom-filled narratives.

If, instead of being pulled from 'ahead,' we are being pushed from 'behind,' that influence is still very powerful, it conditions our present options, but there's a difference: the specific path ahead of us has not yet been set. We're being pushed in a general direction, yes, but we may have considerable freedom in choosing the details of how we get there. We can forge our own path, make our own mistakes, gain our own unique life-experience along the way. That life-experience includes working with our Deities as we go, both they, and we, exercising our free will within the conditions orlog has laid, and learning much along the way. To me, there's more room for initiative, choice, freedom of action, autonomy, in the 'push' model of orlog as opposed to the 'pull' model of 'Destiny.' In Chapter 32, I offer a different image of destiny: 'unfolding' rather than pushing or pulling.

I realize there are different views that can be taken about the existence, and thus influence, of 'the future' and of Time itself. Whether you agree or disagree with my arguments in this chapter, I hope they have stimulated your own thinking on these subjects. What I've laid out in these chapters about the work of the Norns is what I understand from working with the old Germanic languages, myths, poetry, and ancient views of how the world works: views which I find both profound and inspiring, and which have shaped my Heathen path.

Foresight and Predestination

Spákonur and seeresses often sat on a 'high seat' or seiðhjallar to do their formal oracular speakings. This photo shows my own high seat, made by a Heathen craftsman to my design more than thirty years ago. It includes carved images of Huginn and Muninn overseeing the high seat, as well as many other incised carvings not visible here. The black linen apron that I embroidered with the Tree and the Well is used for my spaeworking ceremonies.

12. *Svartheiðrinn:* The Nornir Walk Among Us

By Daniela Svartheiðrinn Simina

Nornir, the Norns: the word conjures, usually and stereotypically, the image of three old women sitting together and spinning. A cliché born from the influence exercised by the image of the Moirai, the Goddesses of fate in Greek mythology? Maybe. Or maybe the image of the spinning Nornir is rooted into something so deeply ingrained in human thought that the simple mentioning of fate and destiny brings to mind the act of spinning. Like their Greek counterparts, the Norns influence fate, albeit differently:

"Urð one is called, Verðandi another –
they carved on a wooden slip – Skuld is the third;
they laid down laws, they chose lives
for the sons of men, the fates of men."
(Völuspá v. 20-21, *Poetic Edda,* Larrington translation)

While the Greek Goddesses of Fate spin, measure and cut the thread allotted for a person's lifespan, the Norns lay out fate by 'spinning' words. The words the Norns speak are laden with power. Speaking words of power is spinning magic with words. The Norns spin and string words into sentences which are then woven into the fabric of events.

The Roles of the Nornir

The three Nornir's names are indicative of their roles. Urð, Verðandi and Skuld are often translated as Past, Present and Future which is simplistic. More accurately, Urð and Verðandi are related to the verb *verða,* to be, reflecting a specific nuance—to become, rather than generically existing or finding oneself in a certain state. Skuld literally means debt. Skuld is cognate to the English word 'should.' These suggest that the name Skuld does not indicate random future events but, by analogy with paying a debt, it refers specifically to events that occur as results of actions already completed. (See Waggoner 2021, p.512; Bek-Pedersen 2011, pp. 78-79.)

Nornir lay out the various premises for things to happen. They call into being the protagonists who will engender the fates crafted by them. And as the Norse myth tells, protagonists' actions lay the foundation for future events to unfold, which is, according to the myths, a new layer of fate sunk into *Urðabrunnr,* the Well of Urð. The name Urð has the additional meaning 'fate' and is cognate to Anglo-Saxon *wyrd,* which means that Urðabrunnr is not any mythical well but a repository of fate with its multiple layers of causality and projected futures. The Old Norse word for fate is ørlög. The Nornir lay into the Well slips of wood on which they inscribed people's fates. In the utterances of the

Norns, words are the pieces of fibers to be spun and woven into what becomes yet another layer of orlog into the Well.

Lesser Nornir

While Urð, Verðandi, and Skuld are the best-known ones, they are not the only Norns in Norse myth. In the Prose Edda, Snorri Sturluson mentions two categories: the greater Norns whose actions reverberate at a cosmic level, and the lesser Norns who apparently visit every child when it is born and speak its destiny. There is great diversity among Nornir:

"Which are those norns who go to help those in need
And bring forth children from their mothers?"

"From very different tribes I think the norns come,
They are not of the same kin;
Some come from the Æsir, some from the elves,
Some are daughters of Dvalin"
(Fafnismál v.12-13, Poetic Edda, Larrington translation)

The Valkyrja of Darraðarljoð

When determining the fate of warriors on battlefields, the Valkyries or Valkyrja act in the capacity of Norns. *Darraðarljoð,* a poem included in Njál's Saga, gives us a glimpse of how Valkyrja act to shape the outcome of a battle, by weaving the fate of combatants. *Darraðarljoð* tells about Valkyries deciding the outcome in the battle of Clontarf which took place in 1014 CE near Dublin, Ireland. 'Warp, weft, and woof' are terms relating to the threads and fabric on the loom.

The Nornir Walk Among Us

See! warp is stretched
For warriors fall,
Lo! weft in loom
Tis wet with blood;
Now fight foreboding,
'Neath friends' swift fingers,
Our grey woof waxeth
With war's alarms,
Our warp bloodred,
Our weft corpse blue.
This woof is y-woven
With entrails of men,
This warp is hard weighted
With heads of the slain,
Spears blood-besprinkled
For spindles we use,
Our loom ironbound,
And arrows our reels;
With swords for our shuttles
This war-woof we work;
So weave we, weird sisters,
Our war-winning woof.
Now mount we our horses,
Now bare we our brands,
Now haste we hard, maidens,
Hence far, far away.
Then they plucked down the
Woof and tore it asunder,
And each kept what she had hold of."
(Darraðarljoð, Njál's Saga, Ch. 157)

Human Deeds

It is largely agreed that the Norns decide upon the circumstances of one's birth and death and to a certain extent about milestones on one's life path. However, the human protagonists are not helpless marionettes at the hands of invisible powers pulling strings. Individuals have agency and they must play to the best of their abilities the hand dealt them by the Norns. Norse myth, and the Heathen ethos rooted in it, encourage people to make the most out of life in Midgard. Even for the incapacitated, life is worth living: an industrious person is appreciated and can make an honorable living.

"A lame man rides a horse, a handless man drives a herd,
a deaf man fights effectively;
a blind man is better than a burned one would be;
no one has use for a corpse."
(Hávamál v. 71, Waggoner translation.)

One's fate being laid out by Norns does not prompt a fatalistic outlook on life. It is rather an invitation to live fearlessly and build a good reputation to be remembered by. Reputation is the direct result of one's deeds. Warriors, for example, would oftentimes go to extremes to earn a reputation because good reputation held huge value in Norse societies.

"Cattle die, relatives die,
you yourself die likewise;
but glorious reputation never dies
for anyone who gets a good one for himself."
(Hávamál v. 76, Waggoner translation)

The deeds that make a person's reputation also contribute to the shaping of orlog and so, in the greater scheme of things, one does not leave footprints only through the immediate outcome of their actions. Such a footprint makes a person a direct contributor to the sacred Well whose waters feed and nourish Yggdrasill. The future of the Worlds, all ecosystems aggregating around Yggdrasill, depend on what kind of layers are laid in the Well's waters: footprints feed into orlog. Based on their quality, such footprints will foster growth and healing or fuel conflict and destruction.

Orlog Influences the Gods

Norns' actions touch upon all levels of reality across all the planes of existence. They measure the length and also decide upon the quality and type of thread for everyone's destiny, including the Gods' destinies. Worried about a recurring dream that troubles his son, Baldr, Oðinn goes to the gates of Helheim where an ancient *völva,* a seeress, is buried. Oðinn uses his magic to awaken the woman from her long sleep and questions her about the past, the future and about Baldr's fate. Oðinn finds out that his beloved son is destined to die.

"I saw for Baldr, for the bloody god,
Odin's child, his fate in store;"
(Völuspá v. 32, Poetic Edda, Larrington translation)

But the prophecy also talks about a younger brother of Baldr avenging him. The prophecy appears to be set in stone while at the same time it isn't. If Oðinn wants the death of Baldr avenged, he must father another son.

"Baldr's brother was born quickly;
Odin's son started killing at one night old.
He never washed his hands nor combed his hair,
until he brought Baldr's adversary to the funeral pyre;"
(Völuspá v. 33-34, Poetic Edda, Larrington translation)

Seeresses, Spákonur, Völur

A tale in the Icelandic *Flateyjarbók* mentions the itinerant seeresses known as *spákonur* and *völur*. The involvement with prophesying fate casts the *spákonur* as the Nornir's human counterparts.

"In those days, seeresses travelled through the land, who were called spákonur [spae-wives] and prophesied about the lives of men."
(from *Flateyjarbók,* vol 1, pp. 345-359, as translated in Waggoner 2021, p. 516.)

In Midgard, seeresses can foretell what lays ahead while also being able to influence the outcome to a larger or lesser extent. Völur and spákonur are Midgard reflections of the Norns. They speak the word-thread of what is, of what has been already spun by the Norns while also having the capabilities to weave additional fate-fabric when speaking their prophecies. The thread that is already spun by the Greater Norns cannot be changed, but there are several patterns to choose amongst, for weaving. Spákonur and völur embody the Nornir by masterfully weaving new patterns through ritualized action, speaking and chanting words of power. In the act of prophesying spákonur and völur can actively contribute to the shaping of fate.

Beyond acknowledging what is already predetermined, seeresses are expected to promote positive outcomes. They are expected to ritually and/or magically support people in a community to overcome adversity. Failing to do so made völur and spákonur subject to threats and harsh action against them from the people they prophesied for.

In *Nornagests þattr,* a tale told in the *Flateyjarbók,* Nornagest tells his own story involving seeresses. When Nornagest was born, his father invited three spaewives to both foretell and favorably influence the baby's future. Two among the spaewives predict the baby will become a handsome, brave and lucky man, a very pleasing prophecy. The third seeress, probably envious that she was not invited to speak, prophesies that the baby will only live as long as the candle burning by his cradle lasts. This seeress gets pushed out of her seat and the older among the three mitigates the outcome by snuffing out the candle and giving it to the mother to preserve it carefully and never light it again. The parallel between the spaewives and Norns is explicit in the conclusion of the story:

"After that the seeresses went away and tied up the youngest Norn and took her away, and my father gave them good gifts when they left."
(from *Flateyjarbók,* vol 1, pp. 345-359, as translated in Waggoner 2021, p. 516.)

A Co-Creative Process

But fate-shaping, adding layers to the orlog inside Urðabrunnr, is a co-creative process. Nornir, Gods, spákonur, and the very humans for whom the fate is being laid out through prophecies, all play active roles. In the *Saga*

The Nornir Walk Among Us

of Erik the Red, Chapter 4, a woman called Thorbjorg Little Völva, a ritual specialist, is invited to prophesy for a Greenlandic community. But, for the endeavor to be successful, Little Völva needs support. It is a collective effort in which everyone contributes from setting up the special high-seat to preparing the ritual meal and singing the sacred songs. Little Völva, the members of the household and indirectly the animals sacrificed to prepare the feast, all contribute to bring forth the best possible outcome: a prophecy that besides hope, yields tangible outcomes for those present. The ritual and the völva's words shape destinies, the equivalent of the Norns weaving new layers that go into the Well of Urð. This passage illustrates how in her own way, Little Völva acts in ways not dissimilar to those of Norns as described in the Eddaic material.

Spákonur emulate the Nornir in that they can act upon fate by both predicting outcomes and influencing them, at least to some extent. Whether made by Nornir or spákonur, prophecies' fulfillment involves collective effort. Oðinn must father a son, who in turn, must commit to avenge Baldr. The Nornir weaving the fate of a battle can only work that out if the opponents will actually do battle. Little Völva can consult the spirits and assist the people who asked for her help, only if someone in the audience can sing the *varðlökkur,* the sacred songs.

Fate laid out by Nornir is not a life, or death, sentence to be accepted with passivity. This holds true at both cosmic levels and here in Midgard. At a cosmic level, Gods must do their part to either fulfill or mitigate the outcome of Nornir's decisions. Here in Midgard, people known as spákonur, völur, spaewives, spámaðr / spae-men, seers and seeresses, and by many other names, engage in the dynamic process of foretelling and shaping of fate by prompting people to take concrete action.

In molding orlog, spákonur emulate the Nornir's actions and make the Nornir relatable to a modern Heathen population. Without them, the spákonur, völur, and the many other kinds of seers, the Nornir would be nothing but abstract and mysterious powers. Spákonur act as bridges between this World and the Other, connecting cosmic and mundane levels. Through speaking fate into being and by prompting others to act, seeresses perpetuate the cycles of orlog-making, as a balancing act, while acting between what is fated and the free will of the individual.

"Völva," by Vangland.

Part III. Orlog Manifesting in Human Life

13. Dealing with Orlog: Yesterday

"Belief in fate did not encourage resignation or passivity—indeed, almost the contrary is the case." (Winterbourne p. 109).

" 'If there's anything more powerful than fate, / then it's courage, which bears fate unshaken.' This human defiance—and dignity—in the face of the inevitable (was) one positive characteristic (of Heathens) that would give way after the conversion in favor of something with very different psychological contours, viz. Christian humilitas." (Winterbourne p. 163, note 51.)

In Chapter 5 I wrote about the Aldr soul and our Werold—the tapestry of our life-experiences and life-span in Time that is woven by our Aldr. There, I introduced the Anglo-Saxon word *gedal* or *gedæl,* meaning 'that which is dealt out, apportioned, separated into parts.' This comes from the verb *dælan,* 'to deal.' *Ealdor-gedal* is an Anglo-Saxon synonym for death: it refers to both to the life-span we are dealt by the Norns, and to the end of that life-span and Werold, the separation from life in the world, that happens at death. How did people in the past deal with their sense of *aldr-gedal* / orlog impacting their lives? What attitude did they have toward this daunting knowledge?

There is an old word that is often used to describe the attitude that people took toward their orlog or wyrd, whether it involved fateful events during life, or the approach of fated death. This word is even carried over into a saying from today's Scots and northern English dialects, derived from Old English: "to dree one's weird," meaning to endure / accept / submit to one's fate. This verb 'dree' has cognates in the old Germanic languages as shown below, which expand our understanding of its meaning.

Table 5. Roots of Dreogan / Drýgja / Dree

Proto-Germanic **dreuga* = 'enduring'; **dreugan* = 'to do a duty' (Kroonen). **Driugijana* from **dreugaz = long-lasting' in the sense of 'eking out' (Wiktionary)
Gothic *driugan* = 'doing a duty, to serve in military draft.' *Ga-drauhts* = soldier.
Anglo-Saxon *dreogan* = to work, suffer, endure. Middle English *drien* = 'to perform, to experience, to put up with, to endure.' Also: to do, to work, perform, to pass life, to fight; to bear, suffer, dree, endure.
Old Saxon *driogan* = to carry out, accomplish, suffer, undergo, endure.

Dealing with Orlog: Yesterday

Old Norse *drýgja* = 'to commit, perpetrate, carry out, accomplish, to make go far, to suffer hardship.' *Drjugr* = substantial, lasting, enough. 'To commit' is used in a negative sense, such as committing a crime or a sin.
West Frisian *dreech* = strong, enduring, long-lasting.

Let's look at a few in-depth examples of how this word *drýgja* is used in Old Norse, to get a sense of its meaning in relation to orlog. Although most usage in the elder lore implies that orlog is synonymous with one's time and mode of death, established by outside forces, there are instances and associated verbs that offer more complex and nuanced interpretations of orlog. Here are a couple of the strongest examples.

Odin and Loki 'Ørlög Drýgðuð'

In *Lokasenna* of the Poetic Edda, verses 22 through 24 show Odin and Loki insulting each other, dragging up old history about incidents when they behaved in a so-called 'perverted' manner. In verse 25 Frigg scolds the two of them, saying that:

"The ørlögs of both of you should never be told in front of others, what you two Æsir *drýgðuð (carried out / fulfilled / endured / aligned with)* in days of yore…"

The word *drýgðuð*, used in the Old Norse text here, can be translated into any of the words I listed in parentheses. I usually assume when reading Old Norse poetry that the poet intends for more than one meaning to be carried by a word or kenning whenever possible. On this assumption, Odin and Loki:

(a) *'carried out, fulfilled, accomplished'* (active sense) their orlog of 'perverted' deeds;

(b) *'endured'* (passive sense) the orlog that forced them into 'perverted' deeds, and

(c) *'aligned'* their actions with orlog, presumably done deliberately to accomplish something important in spite of having to undertake so-called 'perverted' deeds to do so.

This shows some of the complexity of orlog: it is not only a simple, unidimensional phenomenon of predestination. It is something that we can react to and work with in a nuanced way, based on our own motives, attitudes, understanding, our own philosophy of life.

Völund and the Swan Maidens

There is another passage that uses the same interesting word *drýgja* with reference to orlog. The first verse of *Völundarkvida* or the *Lay of Völund* (Poetic Edda) describes three Valkyries in swan-maiden form flying over Myrkwood and arriving at Wolfdales where Völund and his brothers live. The verse says that the Valkyries *ørlög drýgja:* they come to fulfill ørlög, or to align people and events with orlog. This is certainly the case in the poem: after some years of marriage with the swan-maidens / Valkyries and then their mysterious departure, Völund's two brothers take off to seek their wives and continue on to many other adventures told in Germanic legends. Völund is captured by brutal king

Dealing with Orlog: Yesterday

Nidud or Nidhad because he is alone, despondent and unwary, waiting for his swan-maiden wife to return.

"The Swan Maidens," by Walter Crane. It's interesting to note that swans swim in Urð's Well, hinting at their connection with wyrd and fate (Gylfaginning p. 19, Prose Edda). Perhaps this is where the swan maidens go when they are 'off duty'?

As Nidud's captive, Völund bears a heavy, doom-filled orlog, brings orlog-death to Nidud's sons, and impregnates Nidud's daughter with a son who goes on to play a role in later Germanic heroic legends as Widia, Wittich, Vidigoia. It is clear from the context that the orlog borne by the Valkyries

Dealing with Orlog: Yesterday

to Wolfdales was not primarily their own orlog; it was the orlog of Völund and his brothers, as well as Nidud's offspring and Völund's son. The swan-maidens were the ones who set all these fateful events in motion: *ørlög drýgja*.

The front of the Franks Casket, carved from whale's bone, showing a complicated scene from the Völund / Weyland myth in the panel on the left.

These two examples with Odin and Völund show that even in ancient writings there is some indication that orlog was more than simply the fated time and manner of death. There is still a strong implication that other beings—the Norns— are the source of the orlog, and that third parties like swan maidens or Valkyrja may play a role in bringing orlog to pass, but the 'orlog' that occurs in both these examples is neither 'death' nor 'battle, war.' It is a complex, cascading series of events, especially in the Völund example, which becomes more clear when we follow the long, twining Völund / Weland / Wayland saga—before, during and after Völund himself—throughout the Germanic hero-tales spanning many lands, languages and centuries. The same can be said of the *Nibelungenlied* and the *Völsungasaga,* involving a series of complex oaths, deceptions, and betrayals that lead inexorably from one disaster to another. The careful study of these sagas can show much about the concept of *ørlög drýgja:* enduring, fulfilling, aligning with orlog.

Dreeing our Wyrd

As I wrote earlier, there is a phrase used in Scots and northern English dialect, descending from Old English: to 'dree one's weird.' It means to endure it, to tread the path of its fulfillment, however difficult. Here is a quotation that uses this term:

"Where she waits, there must I go, surrendering all else, forgetting all else, to **dree my weird** and hers."
(1898, G Firth Scott, *The Last Lemurian*, Ayer, published 1978, page 81. https://en.wiktionary.org/wiki/dree_one%27s_weird)

The verb 'to dree' descends from Anglo-Saxon *dreógan.* Here is a phrase in Anglo-Saxon quoted in the online Bosworth-Toller dictionary about the word *dreógeþ:* "*Ðeós woruld gesceap dreógeþ:* this world fulfills its destiny." We can translate this phrase literally as "this world drees what has been shaped *(gesceap)* for it." Depending on our own attitude, world-view, philosophy of life, we can understand this word *dreógan* and its cognates in other languages to mean 'endure, struggle with, work at, fight for, fight against, find fulfillment in, suffer through' and more.

Gesceap / skǫp / orlog exists, whether laid out by the Norns, by our own deeds, or by natural processes of cause and effect. It is a 'big deal,' and it is our choice how we deal with it. In a nutshell, *drýgja / dreógan / dree* is what we choose to do with the *gesceap / skǫp / orlog* that has been dealt to us and to the world around us.

Or-deal

I've been using the word 'deal' when speaking of portioning out orlog, dealing out orlog, and also when referring to what we do with orlog: we *deal with it,* one way or another, successfully or unsuccessfully. This leads us to another relevant word: *ordeal.* As we've discussed here, orlog refers to the primal or originating layers of events and actions, out of which present causes and effects arise. *Or-deal,* in this context, is literally what is 'originally dealt out to us,' our portion of orlog, the ur-deal, like the hand each person is originally dealt in a card game, out of which each player tries to shape a win as the game proceeds. It's an ancient word, stemming from Proto-Germanic **uzdailiją,* meaning 'that which is dealt out,' (from Wikipedia on Ordeal) and **uzdailijam* = apportioning out, judgement (Watkins p. 14). In Chapter 28 I present some ideas for how one might deal with / dree one's orlog today.

14. The Role of Luck

I've written, in Chapters 13 and 28, about dealing with orlog and ordeals. There's another phenomenon in Midgard life that is, or seems to be, closely related: luck, good and bad. What role does luck play in our orlog and in dealing with it? Some people today firmly believe luck is a factor in the events of our lives, some firmly don't believe that, and others are somewhere in the middle. There's no question that it played an important role in the beliefs and actions of Heathens in the past. In this chapter I'll explore some connections and contrasts between luck, orlog, and ordeal.

The word 'luck' did not come into English (from Middle Dutch) until the 15th century, probably as a gambling term: 'to chance, to happen by good fortune' (Wiktionary etymology). The way 'luck' is used in modern English often pertains to something happening by random chance, or by the intervention of some kind of Great Power. Many people believe in good luck coming from blessings and good wishes, and bad luck coming from curses or phenomena like the 'evil eye.' Magical and folklore practices are and were believed to influence luck.

The Role of Luck

Some Differences Between Orlog and Luck

Orlog was in ancient times understood primarily as being the circumstances and timing of one's death, set by the Norns or Wyrd when one was born. We can see that, at least in this conception of orlog, there is not much room for the ebb and flow of luck and unluck in our lives to have a great deal of impact on our actual orlog, if it is already set in motion at the beginning of our life. It is more likely to work the other way around. If the orlog laid down for us by the Norns calls for us to be afflicted by bad luck or blessed by good luck at a given point in our life, then wyrd will nudge the flow of circumstances to bring this about.

Orlog or wyrd in the sense of an individual's death, as the ancients saw it, is 'assigned' to us; it is 100% certain and comes upon us in the time and way established by the Norns at the beginning of our lives. The circumstances of the life lived between the two points of birth and death was the domain of luck, and generally not as heavily influenced by the great powers. Rather, it was the smaller powers, the spirit beings such as the *hamingja, fylgja, disir, alfar,* and so forth, that guided the actions of luck and unluck in their lives. While they saw orlog as being certain and fixed, luck is complex, variable; the outcome of the luck or unluck is not entirely certain in any given circumstance. There are many influences upon each person's luck or unluck, including the luck or unluck of other people with whom one interacts, which can have a strong impact on one's own luck.

In older understandings, luck is something that can be gained or lost, and it is 'contagious'. It acted as a kind of power that could be transferred between persons, for example by a luck-filled king or chieftain to his followers. This was a great source of the power and respect

The Role of Luck

that a leader held: the power of their luck, their *hamingja* in Old Norse or *'spēd* / speed' in Anglo-Saxon, and the ability to share it and spread it around. Hence the word 'Godspeed' as a wish or prayer for luck from the Deity.

Many modern Heathens believe that we have a good deal more power and influence over our own orlog than was generally the case in ancient times, when the Norns or Wyrd were mostly the ones driving the train. Orlog is now seen not only as the time and manner of our death, and the crucial events that lead up to this, but also as a phenomenon that shapes our whole life-time, our Werold. As the idea of orlog has evolved in modern Heathen times, it seems to me it has converged more closely with the idea of luck than it originally stood. In the past, orlog was mainly the 'big picture,' the beginning and end with a few major events in between, while the various forms of luck flowed around in the middle, influencing the daily details of our lives. Now, with the more modern idea of we ourselves 'laying orlog' during the course of our lifetime, orlog becomes more easily confused with the luck whose playground is the details of our everyday lives.

An ancient Heathen would definitely strive to gather all the luck that he or she could: by associating with those who have greater luck; by obtaining lucky objects, land, etc.; by participating in fortunate enterprises; by listening to the rede, the good counsel, of humans, Gods, or spirits to guide them into the path of luck; by cultivating and propitiating spirit beings who could give luck or unluck. Though it was recognized that luck was given to each person — greater or lesser degrees and types of luck – yet there was always the effort to increase luck and avoid unluck.

The Role of Luck

Varieties of Luck

Ancient Heathens had more than one word for 'luck', and many compound words to show the different types and domains of luck. *Sael, saell, saeld, sælig* appeared widely in the old Germanic languages, and meant 'luck, good fortune, prosperity, blessing, happiness,' and related concepts. The Gothic word *selei* meant 'goodness, kindness,' and *unselei* was 'evil, wickedness.' These words are related to the *seelie / unseelie* terms that are used in Scots folklore for the 'good' and 'harmful' tribes of fae or elves, who may bring good or bad luck to humans they encounter. These Scots words derive from Old English *sælig*, and they reinforce the connections between 'goodness / good luck' and 'evil / bad luck.' Here are some examples of different kinds of *saell* luck that a person might have, based on Old Norse terms, as discussed in Grønbech's chapters about luck:

Arsæll = luck with fertility of land, crops, and livestock.
Byrsæll = luck with seafaring and sailing weather.
Kinsæll = luck in one's kindred: numerous, prosperous, frithful, of good reputation.
Sigrsæll = victory luck, battle luck.
Vinsæll = luck with friendships and patronage.

Heill was another Old Norse word for luck, and included the concepts of health, wholeness, haleness, luck, good fortune, blessing. An important type of *heill* one might possess is *ordheill*, the luck or power of using words to cause either good or harm, as in blessing or cursing. Grønbech describes *ordheill* as a "wish charged with power," expressed verbally (p. 147, vol. 1). Another meaning for *ordheill* is that people speak well of the person who has it; he or she has the good

The Role of Luck

luck of an excellent reputation. *Mannheill* is the good fortune of getting along well with others (*mann* means 'person' of any gender). *Illa heill* is bad luck generally.

Old English had the word *spēd* (pronounced 'speed'), still used occasionally in old-fashioned phrases such as 'Godspeed' or 'God speed the work / journey, etc.,' meaning good fortune and success in one's endeavor: literally God's luck or blessing on the work. 'Speed' meant luck, success, prosperity, wealth, abundance, opportunity. Its opposite, *wanspēd* ('waning-speed') meant poverty, misfortune, failure, lack. Of great importance was the King's Speed and the good it could bring to battle success, land, fertility, prosperity, fortunate opportunities and so forth. The Germanic tribal king held an enormous amount of luck within himself, and could spread it around into many domains of action; this was, in fact, the basis for his power of kingship, and if his luck failed, his kingship might too. (Grønbech vol. 1, p. 138.) Other types of 'speed' that one might have include *freondspēd* or friend-speed, and *tuddorspēd*, which is good fortune with one's offspring: many healthy children blessed with prosperity, good luck, and offspring of their own. And there are other terms related to luck in all the Germanic languages; these are just some examples.

Cat Heath in her book *Elves, Witches & Gods* provides a useful discussion of Heathen concepts of luck. She writes that there are "intrinsic lucks," listed as *gæfa, gipta,* and *heill* in their Norse versions. The first two terms are derived from 'gift.' These lucks (or lack of them) are inborn as 'gifts;' in modern English we might use a similar concept and say 'he has a gift for music; she has a gift for languages.' These seem to me like 'gifts' from the Norns and orlog—or lack of gifts,

The Role of Luck

if they are not laid in one's orlog. The second category that Cat discusses is 'extrinsic luck,' *hamingja* and *fylgja*, lucks which can take on spiritual embodiment as separate beings closely connected with a person throughout their life. (Heath, pp. 92-95.) I discuss hamingja and fylgja in more depth in the next section.

The whole Germanic concept of 'luck' was complex, nuanced, many-faceted, with many words used to express these facets. There was no single word, like modern English 'luck,' that would have covered all these facets. In fact, Grønbech suggests it makes more sense to use the term 'lucks,' plural, because of the many types and characteristics of luck that were referred to in ancient sources, folklore and folk practices. His view was that these lucks were indeed of different kinds and sources, not all expressions of one single thing (p. 171-2).

The 'luck' I've described here is not at all random, nor does it come and go at the whim of some great power distant from earthly life. Instead, in this old Heathen understanding luck—both good and bad—is generated for us and by us through the processes of life, of actions and deeds, of relationships with other people, objects, land, places. It is also generated and given by the smaller spirits who inhabit the world around us: landwights, housewights, ancestral spirits, other types of spirits, and may arise from our relationships with our closest Deities. This form of luck is shaped within us along with our life and deeds: it's the opposite of random chance, and shows much similarity to the process of orlog itself. Luck and orlog are not the same thing, but they are linked in complex ways, and much of that linkage operates through luck-bearing spirits. There are a multitude of luck-bearing spirits in the folklore of all the

The Role of Luck

Germanic lands and peoples, as well as many others. To describe the meaning of luck as an outgrowth of life and action, rather than random chance or the whim of a Power, let's turn to the Norse concepts of the *hamingja* and *fylgja*.

Hamingja and Other Luck-Bearing Spirits

Norse *hamingja* is a complex concept. It can refer to an out-of-body spirit-shape that some people can take on—often an animal form—to engage in magical or shamanistic activities such as fighting with an enemy in similar form, or scouting ahead during a journey. As Winterbourne describes, *"hamingja* carries three main characteristics—shape-shifting abilities, 'fortune' as such, and the guardian spirit" (pp. 38-9). It is sometimes considered part of one's own soul, other times as a more independent spirit attached to one. The term is used in similar ways to other terms for spirit-beings or shape-functions such as *fylgja, kinfylgja, hamr, hugr, hugham, vörðr.* It can be challenging, and perhaps fruitless, to attempt to consistently distinguish one from the other among these various spirit-forms as they are described at different times and places in Scandinavian lore and folklore; we'll focus here on the hamingja and fylgja and their connections with personal luck.

As the scholar Jan DeVries describes, the *hamingja* is the indwelling luck, in the form of a protective spirit that accompanies a person life-long. It also takes the form of a power or energy that can radiate out from a person or other kind of being, as well as from features of the land. When someone had a lot of this kind of power, for example a chieftain or war-leader, they could lend it, send it, or spread it around among their followers. The *hamr*—the afterbirth, caul, and the metaphysical 'shape' of a person—contains a

The Role of Luck

soul or a soul-like being, that gestates along with a child, is born with them, and accompanies them throughout life as a protective and luck-bearing spirit, called the Hamingja and / or the Fylgja (meaning 'follower'). These beliefs are widespread, and likely go back to Proto-Germanic times, before the Germanic peoples split off from each other, if not even earlier times. (deVries 1956, pp. 222ff.)

DeVries also notes the difference between this pattern of everyday luck versus the impacts of larger matters of orlog / wyrd in one's life. He suggests that ancient Heathens would not assume that the details of their entire lives were controlled by fate set by the Gods. Rather, from the beginning to the end of life, there is an 'inner lawfulness' *(innere Gesetzlichkeit)* which determines its course, that lies in the inner being of the person. Here, deVries says, we can think of the *hamingja* and the *fylgja,* spirits attached to each person whose guidance leads to an inner consistency or logical course of life. But, outside of this realm, catastrophes and disasters can occur, breaking into this pattern of normal life, that were attributed to outside forces, to the powers of fate. (DeVries 1956, p. 268.)

This idea of an 'inner lawfulness' points us back toward Chapter 2 about Orlog, Layers, and Laws, and the differences I discussed between 'community laws' versus 'inner orlog.' Rather than 'inner lawfulness' *per se,* I would call the phenomenon deVries describes an 'inner pattern'—a pattern that comes from the hamingja's / fylgja's rootedness in both orlog and luck. The 'ground of orlog and luck' that hamingja is rooted in comes from the larger environment of collective and ancestral orlog and luck, beginning with the environment of the womb and the child's genetic structure—this is why it's understood that the hamingja / fylgja is associated with the womb, placenta and caul.

If you search Wikimedia Commons for images of 'fylgja' you'll find lots of photos of placentas. Note that a word for 'womb' in Anglo-Saxon was *hama*. In Germany there was sometimes a custom of burying the afterbirth and planting a tree over it, which then became the 'life-tree' or 'fate-tree' of the child. There were numerous afterbirth-related folk-customs in all the Germanic lands which indicated the belief that the afterbirth is connected with luck, fate, and soul. (See my chapter on the Hama soul in Rose 2021.)

The personal, inner pattern of luck, having been established and attached to a person in the womb, continues to develop throughout their life. We are surrounded by patterns that shape us: inner and outer patterns, individual and collective patterns. DeVries's suggestion is that the hamingja constellates the inner pattern that corresponds to our personal 'luck,' while major intrusions, disruptions, upheavals of that pattern are due to 'fate' or the Deities interrupting that pattern. Of course, such interruptions can be beneficial and 'lucky,' as well as 'fateful' in negative ways.

The Fylgja spirit gives not only luck, but can also offer intuitions that help protect and guide a person, enhancing their ability to take advantage of good luck and avoid bad luck. There are many small spirits of land, home, fields and crops, workshops, mines, spirits dwelling in land formations such as rocks, water bodies, certain trees, etc., and all of them are capable of giving one good luck when well-treated, and bad luck if they are not treated well. They are also known for giving advice, and important warnings or foretellings on occasion, to those with whom they've developed a relationship of trust. For example, they might warn of a forthcoming drought, or of an enemy's intentions.

Similarities between Hamingja and Orlog

Grønbech, in his chapters on Luck, describes in much detail how hamingja and luck work. Possessions absorb hamingja (spiritual energy and character) and luck from their owners, though they do not lessen the owner's hamingja and luck thereby—rather, they increase them, as long as the objects remain in good condition and in the possession of their owner. If the possessions are passed down in the family line, their hamingja and luck are enhanced by each generation, and can reach legendary proportions thereby.

If the possessions are stolen or damaged, the owner loses proportionally from his or her own store of hamingja and luck. If the loss is severe enough, it can even portend disaster or death. If hamingja-filled objects are shared as part of founding a relationship—marriage, friendship, alliance, partnership, patronage—then the relationship is strengthened and deepened proportionally to the hamingja and luck of the objects shared as gifts. Grønbech explains further about how hamingja works:

"Treasures and man are one; but the man has his time, and that done, another succeeds him; the treasure remains, handing on the luck to his successor. Man comes to his appointed day; by virtue of his luck he makes his way across into the other existence; but he does not take the whole sum with him; part, and that no insignificant part, remains in the things he leaves behind him, there to await the man who follows. With very good reason, then, weapons, clothes, household implements may be called bearers of life; not only is the sword a lasting thing, it is a well of life, whence a man may renew his store, through which he can draw up power from the primeval source. The settler struck his axe into the new soil to mark it as his property, and it (the axe) has hamingja enough to bring the whole piece of land under its will, making it (the land) to serve its owner, and guard him against aggression." (Grønbech Vol. II p. 108)

Here we can clearly see imagery that leads us back to orlog. Through the process of worthy actions and a worthy life, we lay hamingja and luck as layers within heirlooms, land, possessions, and the intangibles we pass on to others. These layers of luck build upon each other, influence each other, and enhance the hamingja thereby.

Here is another example of the similarity between processes of hamingja and of orlog. The ancients considered it possible to give, sell or exchange a material object but fail to give the intangibles associated with it. Often such trickery was attempted, and many customs arose which had the purpose of ensuring that the new owner received all that they had bargained for, both the tangibles and intangibles. "It was demanded that the owner should lay his whole mind in the transfer, and give the soul as well as the externals; care was taken to prevent his sucking up the luck himself, before handing over the property." (Grønbech Vol. II p. 78)

Thus, in an agreement based on trust and goodwill, the giver / seller would speak words that showed the intent to transfer the whole possession over. Examples are: "May you use this in good health," or "I give you this sword, and I think it bears great luck with it." This additional, spiritual value inherent in the object was laid into it in layers because of the

The Role of Luck

worth of its owner and the owner's use of it in worthy actions.

"The soul surrendered in the thing was...an individual actual mind or, as we should say, a psychological state, *backed up by the whole, past and present and future power and responsibility of the hamingja.* And in handing over his pledge, the giver could and would state in words what were the attitude of his mind in giving, if only he understood the—by no means easy—art of *guiding words aright* and driving the right hamingja into them. All that is said and promised, reserved and required, is *'laid upon'...the thing* and thus handed over to the opposite party." (Grønbech Vol. II p. 80-81, italics mine.)

In this quotation from Grønbech I have emphasized phrases that apply equally well to orlog, hamingja, the actions of humans, and the work of the Norns. Orlog is spoken and laid by the Norns, and shapes what comes next. Hamingja is spoken—promised or pledged—and laid within the item being given or sold. In both cases, the significance, the value inherent in its totality of being and interconnectedness, is 'fastened' into the object or the layers of orlog by being spoken of in well-shaped words.

My thought is that hamingja-luck is more involved with the smaller events of our daily lives, outside of the broad scope of major orlog-events, and is more subject to change due to outside influences. Metaphysically, our luck is guided and influenced by smaller, more personal luck-bearing spirits like the *hamingja, fylgja,* and *kin-fylgja,* as well as by wights in our environment like house-wights and land-wights. Orlog is presided over by the great Powers, the

Norns and Deities, though the luck-spirits are surely influenced by the great Powers and the orlog they mediate. The Norns might specifically shape episodes of good or bad luck to occur in our lives as part of our orlog or the ordeals they lay out for us, but those episodes are likely to involve the lesser spirit-beings as well. Luck and orlog are intertwined and have some influence over each other, but they are not identical, and orlog is unquestionably the greater, more overriding power.

Between Fire and Ice

Winterbourne suggests that "fate could be seen as what intervenes between chance and necessity" (p. 55). 'Chance' is the gamble, the toss of the dice; it happens, but it is random and has no intrinsic meaningfulness. 'Necessity' in this context equates to death, the end that must, in some way and some time, come to us all: the ultimate necessity of mortal life. Its occurrence is entirely fixed; there is no changing it. Fate or Wyrd, in contrast to chance, "orders events that would otherwise be random, and perhaps chaotic" (Winterbourne p. 55).

This idea shapes a vision for me: the view of a metaphysical spectrum where one end is totally random—call it Fire—while the other end is completely fixed—let's say Ice. In between the two is the place where Life itself exists, and all that Life can be and do. This is where humans and all other life-forms, physical and spiritual, have their Being, and also where the Gods and Norns preside. Fate / Wyrd / orlog intervenes between the random chances generated by Fire on one end, and the fixed Ice of the necessary end of Midgard life on the other. The Norns influence the processes that cause events to occur in this space where Life is. Their influence creates an overarching order amidst all the seeming mess and confusion of Life: an ordering process which takes shape as the World-Tree, the shape of all that is, watered and nourished by the Well of Wyrd that lies at its roots and stores the orlog laid down over millennia of time.

Within this ever-evolving flow and mass of orlog, this subtle process of ordering what Life brings into being, luck and unluck have their own roles to play, as do ordeals. From our limited human perspective random luck and unluck may at times loom large in our lives. From where the Norns sit, the ordeals that form as knots within the weaves of wyrd are truly significant, while the small lucks and unlucks of our lives are insignificant threads amidst the multitude of strands that make up the great tapestry of orlog.

The Insignificance of Random Luck

Let's explore that idea a bit further: that *random* luck and unluck are in essence insignificant when compared with orlog and true ordeals that are rooted in orlog. What is it that makes orlog and ordeals significant, and luck / unluck insignificant? I am not speaking of hamingja and luck-bearing spirits here, but rather 'luck as random chance.' The Norns are focused on what is significant, and their focus enhances, even defines, the significance of whatever they focus upon. If luck is a matter of 'chance,' then its origin is random, meaning that it does not arise from any significant workings of orlog. Its randomness distinguishes it from orlog, which is not random. Luck / unluck in the form of 'chance' comes from the Fire end of the spectrum that lies outside of orlog's workings.

The Role of Luck

Now, once this random event of luck or unluck occurs in our lives, does it then take on significance? Does it help us grow our character, our wisdom, strength, our might and main, our moral fiber? Does it lead us to enact significant deeds, whether of good or of harm? Does it lead us to fall away from an ethical or productive path? Does it lead us to grow in good ways or turn to bad ways? Does it change our life in truly significant ways? Then this random luck is significant because of its *outcome*, because of what we do with it, not because of what it is in itself, sheer random chance.

Luck / unluck takes on significance by what it causes us to do or not do, not because of what it is: a random or chaotic 'blip' erupting into the relatively ordered systems of the Lifeworlds embedded in layers of orlog. Something can't be defined as 'lucky / unlucky' unless it happens to, or affects, someone who *experiences* it as 'lucky / unlucky.' Thus, its nature as luck / unluck is not significant until it interacts with beings or events that possess significance, and thereby the luck is swept up by those beings or events into the workings of orlog. How does this work?

The Mediating Role of Luck-Spirits

I'm suggesting that some random event that we call 'lucky' or 'unlucky' gets swept into the flow of orlog by humans who experience or interpret it as 'luck,' thereby perhaps becoming an event of significance. How does this happen? Based on my understanding of old Heathen ways of thinking, I'd say that personal luck-spirits—a long list including the hamingja, fylgja, housewights, landwights, and often ancestral spirits (especially Disir) as well—have the role of helping us weave strands of good luck into our lives

The Role of Luck

in meaningful ways, ways that increase the good in our lives. They may also alert us to bad luck that is hovering about, and ward us from it to some extent, especially if the bad luck comes from ill-intentioned beings, whether human or spirits.

Without their help, we might not notice or realize the luck that comes our way, nor deal with it in good ways. We might waste it or fail to use it to best advantage. We might become greedy, exploitative, short-sighted, abuse the good luck that comes to us, 'pushing our luck' and turning it into bad luck for ourselves and others. Our luck-spirits weave our own small, personal lucks into our orlog the way that the Norns weave greater events and deeds into orlog of the Worlds. The luck itself may be a random event, but thanks to the luck-spirits we can use these random lucks to enhance our lives. Their work is part of the work that the Norns do: the wights hand the strands they weave over to the Norns, but those strands come through the hands of the wights first, reflecting their intentions, their will. Our luck is very much enhanced thereby, just as our responses to our luck give that luck significance it would otherwise not have. It's thanks to the luck-bearing spirits and our interactions with them, I believe, that luck becomes a part of orlog: operative within orlog, influential and significant in that context.

Luck versus Ordeal

Let's explore briefly the ancient belief that luck – the outcome of an event – demonstrates wyrd. This is the basis for the old practice of trial by ordeal in the form of a combat or contest between two or more people: whoever wins the ordeal proves that he or she is 'right' in the sense of being within the flow of both hamingja and orlog. Ordeals were

The Role of Luck

often used to prove guilt or innocence: if the accuser won, the accused was guilty. If the accused won, that proved they were innocent and that the accuser was guilty of defamation. The loser in the ordeal has gone against the flow of wyrd, and has no luck in the matter pertaining to the ordeal. A trial-ordeal stands outside the realm of law and ethics; the sole determinant of luck, wyrd, and 'right and wrong' in the situation is: who wins, and who loses?

An ordeal is very different from a gamble. A gamble, on a metaphysical level, is sort of like a wind-sock: it simply tests which way the luck is flowing at that point in time, though many people will try all sorts of tricks, wishes and curses to try to alter it! A true ordeal is not a gamble or a matter of luck; its reasons for happening and its outcome are not random. The ordeal is a showing-forth of the hidden shaping of the Norns, bringing orlog into manifestation through the challenge of the ordeal. Luck in the sense of random chance has nothing to do with the ordeal itself, but one's hamingja may shift later on, depending on what the outcome of the ordeal is. If one wins or succeeds in the ordeal, hamingja-luck is likely to change for the better, if one fails or loses, it likely changes for the worse.

This understanding of *an ordeal as an event that brings orlog into manifestation for us to deal with* can be applied to many of the difficulties and challenges in our own lives. When we are faced with a situation that feels like an ordeal to us, it's important to try to understand the layers of orlog that went into shaping this ordeal—both orlog that we might have laid, and orlog laid by others and by circumstances outside our control. There are likely to be things we can change ourselves, and other things we can't change but must respond or adapt to in the best way possible.

The Role of Luck

An ordeal calls forth our great inner powers and our wisdom, rooted in our own orlog: it is presented to us as a challenge so we can use these powers and grow them to be even greater.

Notes:
For further reading about how the sharing of hamingja lays good layers of orlog and establishes good luck in marriage you can read my article "Heathen Foundations of Marriage: Bargain, Gift, Hamingja," on my website HeathenSoulLore.net.
https://heathensoullore.net/heathen-foundations-of-marriage-bargain-gift-hamingja/

For a 'case study' analysis comparing the roles of luck and wyrd in the conversion of Norway to Christianity, see my article "Webs of Luck and Wyrd: Interplays and Impacts on Events," also included in my book Oaths, Shild, Frith, Luck & Wyrd.
https://heathensoullore.net/webs-of-luck-and-wyrd-interplays-and-impacts-on-events/

For more information about the nature of hamingja and its relationship to the complexities of our inner Self, see my article "The Shape of Being Human: The Hama Soul," also included in my book Heathen Soul Lore Foundations.
https://heathensoullore.net/the-shape-of-being-human-the-hama-soul/

15. Legacies

All of the topics I've discussed so far in this book can be viewed as legacies of wisdom from the Heathen past, woven into our understanding of our lives today. The Heathen ancestors figured out ways to understand and deal with orlog and wyrd, ways to handle luck both good and ill, how to face ordeals and grow from them. Some individuals were very successful in this, others were not. We can learn from all these experiences—successes and failures, experiments and explorations—all are worth considering for the lessons they offer us today.

I discuss in Chapter 19 the old concept of Time as relationship, as genealogy. The sequential aspect of Time where events follow one another in orderly, logical fashion is less meaningful, in this view, than the significant relationships between events and people that are created by orlog and wyrd, operating within 'time as a container of meaning,' as Bauschatz phrases it. This is the way that legacies are shaped, reaching from former generations to later ones with whom they are connected—sometimes skipping generations in the middle. These are gifts

Legacies

(sometimes curses) that are passed down through the operations of orlog.

In this chapter I'm rounding up a few of the specific legacies of wisdom that arise from Heathen orlog. The first section follows on from the previous chapter about luck-bearing spirits, discussing hamingja as a literal legacy, something that is passed down through generations of ancestors. The other two sections are focused on Heathen ethical legacies relating to ideas about 'predestined death,' and 'reputation versus karma.'

Hamingja as Legacy

I wrote about hamingja and its connection with luck in the previous chapter; here I'm returning to the subject to point out hamingja's role as a legacy, passed down from generation to generation within kindreds and occasionally from outside of kindreds too.

Hilda Ellis Davidson writes "as used in the sagas then, the *hamingja* stands for an abstract conception, that of something belonging to an outstanding person which is partly a matter of character and partly of personality, and partly something more than either—that strange quality of 'luck' or 'lucklessness'… It is something which can be handed on after death, and it usually remains within one family; it is usually connected with the name, so that if a child is called after a father or grandfather it is hoped he will inherit it automatically." (Ellis pp. 133-4)

There is an old Norse custom called the *nafnfestr,* a gift to mark the 'fastening of the name' of a deceased ancestor upon a newborn baby, or occasionally the re-naming of an

Legacies

individual if they had terrible luck and sought to change it by taking the name of a luckier, though deceased, person. The name "was intended to allow the child to share in the deceased individual's 'capacity for luck' *(máttr ok megin),"* their might and main (Lecouteux p. 162). I'm assuming that the *nafnfestr* gift would ideally have been an heirloom owned by the person whose name was being given. That way, both the name and the heirloom gift would bear the hamingja of the deceased person, thus amplifying the name-legacy and making more hamingja available to the baby.

The hamingja of a deceased person doesn't always go to a newborn baby; it can transfer to an adult much the same as the *kynfylgja* or kinfylgja does—the guardian-spirit of the family line. For example, in *Viga-Glum's Saga* Glum had a "great and remarkable dream" about a gigantic woman striding toward him:

"Vigfúss my grandfather must be dead, and the woman who was higher than the mountains as she walked must be his *hamingja,* for he was nearly always above other men in honour; his *hamingja* now must be seeking an abode where I am. (ix)" (quoted in Ellis p. 131).

This is an example of hamingja as a legacy, and there are other such examples in the sagas. Some of them indicate a transfer of ill-luck rather than good luck. (See Ellis's section on "The Guardian Hamingja and Dis," beginning p. 130).

In the previous chapter I talked about how hamingja is infused into material things: heirlooms, weapons, jewelry, land, tools, handmade items, etc., when they are made and used by people bearing strong hamingja. These objects can bring their hamingja with them when transferred in an appropriate way to another person. We can see a continuation of this idea in fantasy tales about mystically powerful swords that were forged by the greatest smiths or magical beings, and handed down from mighty heroes of the past to the present hero of the tale.

Hamingja is 'passed on' as a legacy from person to person, rather than being 'reborn' after going through an afterlife state, as a soul might do, even though hamingja does have soul-like qualities and carries aspects of personality with it. In a number of anecdotes, such as the one about Viga Glum, the hamingja, fyglja, kin-fylgja or other luck-spirit itself, in personified form, chooses where it will go after the death of its bearer.

I often wonder how much of the rebirth of Heathenry today is due to the hidden legacies of both reborn souls and of the hamingja / fylgja / other luck-spirits passed down from elder times, biding their time generation after generation until the conditions orlog has laid down are right for their re-emergence into our lives today. In this, I see again *sköp Norna,* the shapings of the Norns, as a deeply meaningful reference to our Heathen troth itself: their shapings yesterday, today, and beyond.

Ethical Implications of Predestination

"...the acknowledgement of the power of fate not only did not lead to spiritual and moral atrophy, but seemed in fact to act as a spur to man's religious sense of himself. Fate was a challenge, a force to be confronted—not a power to be meekly accepted in inaction and Stoic resignation. To know that one is fated to die in a particular battle, or in a particular place, did not make a man fight less hard, less bravely.

Legacies

*Instead it seemed to encourage in him a sense that human significance could be achieved **in spite of fate**."* (Winterbourne p. 58, emphasis is original. I might in fact say: 'human significance could be achieved *because* of fate.')

The old Heathen idea of predestination of the timing of death, as opposed to the deterministic idea of everything in life being predetermined for us, has important ethical implications. As discussed earlier, if we have no free will, if everything in our life has been predetermined, then ethical behavior becomes meaningless. Our choices don't matter; our actions are predetermined and out of our control, and there is no use learning from experience and modifying our behavior.

By contrast, a situation where we have predestined death, but otherwise have a measure of free will during our lifespan, can in some ways remove the factor of fear from our choices, promoting our ability to make the most ethical and courageous choices. This is how it worked for Heathen warriors in the past: they believed that the timing of their death was predetermined, that they could do nothing about it even if they fearfully guarded themselves from risky situations. So why hold back from what they considered right actions out of fear, when your death will come when it comes, regardless? Act as ethics and honor guide you, they would say, and don't worry about the outcome for yourself, which will come in its own time and its own way no matter what you do or refrain from doing. So you may as well do the right thing, the ethical action, and make your name and fame shine!

This ethical perspective worked particularly well for warriors, and for people who lived in physically difficult circumstances where death was a definite concern in many contexts: death from illness, infections, accidents, childbirth, delicate infants and children being at risk from harsh circumstances, dangerous work in fields and forests and smithies, bad weather, crop failure and famine, drought, fire, war and raids, etc. Being fatalistic about death helped them deal with such daily risks and the frequent loss of those dear to them.

Predestination as it applied to one's death supported a courageous attitude for them. But this did not imply that everything in their lives was predetermined and thus that they had neither freedom of choice, nor the ethical responsibility that accompanies that freedom. Ethical considerations were important to them, as they are to us today, and ethics requires that we have free will: the choice to engage in ethical action, and to refuse to engage in unethical action. Even when we face an inescapable situation that is locked in by orlog, we still have free-will ethical choices to make regarding how we face it and deal with it.

The general Heathen view today that we have more choice, more responsibility, over our actions and their outcomes has some implications that might have been less relevant in the past. Today we have many ways, both unavoidable and optional, to endanger our health and wellbeing—different ways than people in the past had to deal with. Sedentary lifestyle, unhealthy and non-nourishing food and drink, unhealthy habits, pollution everywhere including inside us, constant stress, vehicles and lots of other technology that can easily injure or kill us, irresponsible attitudes, etc....we all know what life today is like.

Being overly fatalistic, under these circumstances, can be a distinct disadvantage **if** it makes us think that we don't need to make any effort to live in a nurturing and healthy way, that we're free to indulge in unhealthy habits and irresponsible lifestyle because 'no matter what we do, orlog will get us in the end'! This is true, of course, but what that end is like, how long it drags on, the ways it impacts us and others, and how long and well we manage to live before it happens, may all be things that we can influence, positively or negatively, by the orlog we lay through our habits and lifestyle day by day.

Just as an example to consider: let's say that the Norns have predestined Person X to die at age 78. Perhaps that can't be changed. But will Person X live a difficult life for ten or fifteen years before that time, struggling with chronic illness or general debility? What effects will that have on the family and others, on finances, on resources? It may be that Person X's lifestyle choices, including the maintenance of spiritual health, during their adult life have considerable influence over their health or ill-health during later life. This is not always the case, of course; there are many factors beyond our control.

All I'm suggesting here is that we don't take the idea of predestined death as an excuse not to care for ourselves appropriately, as well as caring for others for whom we have responsibility, such as our children, our elders, and others unable to care for themselves.

'Reputation' versus 'Karma'

Many in modern Western culture have been influenced by Westernized ideas about the Eastern concept of 'karma.' (I am unqualified to discuss karma as it is understood in traditional Hindu and Buddhist philosophy; this discussion of the idea of 'karma' is based on modern Western interpretations of it.) The way 'karma' is understood in our present time and place seems like a very logical and fair way for the universe to work: good actions or deeds are rewarded by good circumstances, most likely in future lives but perhaps in this one, while evil deeds reap ill circumstances. Our present life circumstances are the fruit of our past deeds, good and ill, and we lay the layers of karma for our next life circumstances as we live this one. This seems to fit very well with the ancient Heathen concepts of wyrd and orlog, where the layers of the past give rise to events and circumstances of the present.

This point of view, however, is not reflected to any great extent in ancient Heathen views of orlog and wyrd, which they largely saw as fatalistic and under the control of the Norns or Wyrd. "Wyrd goes ever as she must," as the Beowulf poet puts it (l. 455), which doesn't leave a lot of room for human control, though the discussion in previous chapters shows some flexibility in that.

Modern Heathen ideas about our involvement in, and power over, our orlog tend to be much less fatalistic than ancient Heathen views. It seems to me that our modern views are more similar to the concept of 'karma,' and may well be influenced by it. I think that in general this is a benefit, since the ability to influence our own orlog / wyrd by our worthy or unworthy actions has important implications for modern Heathen ethics. If our fate is entirely out of our hands, then our deeds don't matter, they're just programmed actions, which means that our efforts to make ethical choices don't matter either. If our

Legacies

orlog and wyrd are indeed influenced by our actions, then our ethical choices matter, they shape our life and our orlog.

It's interesting that, as I understand it, these ethical considerations also influenced ancient Heathens very strongly, but not directly through any karma-like idea. Instead, their *reputation* both during and after their life was a major consideration, as Svartheiðrinn discusses in Chapter 12. They were motivated to perform worthy deeds, according to the values of their time and place, because they wanted to gain a great reputation that would enhance their quality of life and continue as a legacy after their death, benefiting their offspring and kinfolk as well.

In this context 'reputation' operates somewhat similarly to orlog. Orlog consists, in part, of 'what has been spoken,' layers that have been laid by words and thoughts. Reputation consists of what people say and think about us, what they have 'laid down' about us in their minds and their words to others. This process of laying 'reputation layers' goes on throughout our lives, as does orlog, and both reputation and orlog influence the quality of our life and motivate our deeds.

Orlog and reputation work in similar ways, except for an important difference: orlog is necessarily true, actually what happened or how we really experienced what happened. Reputation is not necessarily true: we may fool others into thinking more highly of us than we have truly earned, or conversely people may lie about us and harm our reputation in ways we don't deserve. While people may be fooled by lies, the Norns and the Holy Ones are not, however! Lies told by us or about us will not be laid in the Well; they are worthless, insignificant. We may indeed suffer, or cause suffering, because of lies, and that will affect

Legacies

those who lie. The suffering becomes part of orlog, and the act of lying becomes part of the orlog of the one who lies, because these acts and feelings are real. But the lies told, the words spoken that may influence human perceptions of our reputation—those lying words themselves have no substance in the Well because by definition they do not exist.

Lies are words that have no referents in reality, have no factuality to back them up, though they certainly do have consequences. Lies, by definition, refer to things that do not exist or do not have the shape or meaning that the lies imply. The *act* of lying, and its results, are laid as orlog in the Well, but the lie itself, the lying words, have no place within the Well. The Norns and the Holy Ones are well aware of the realities of our deeds and our inner selves, and it is those realities, not the lies, which they lay as orlog in the Well.

It's unfortunately, and unfairly, true that in human society it's much easier to turn a good reputation into a bad one, by our actions and / or by what people say about us, than it is to turn a bad reputation into a good one. People in the past, as today, were mindful of this and tried to build their good reputation by admirable deeds, and by making sure others knew about them! Hence the role of poets; everyone wanted to be worthy of mention in a song or saga, which would likely live on after they were gone as their legacy.

This is also an essential aspect of the various forms of 'boasting' in Heathen symbel, as Bauschatz discusses at length in his Chapter III, "Beowulf and the Nature of Events." We must speak truth in symbel—grow our reputations by speaking truthful boasts, toasts, and oaths, not lying boasts, not empty words that never lead to deeds, that

Legacies

fail to shape our lives with honor and spiritual might and main. The Holy Ones and the Norns hear us, especially when we speak in symbol, and it is much worse than useless to lie to them!

I'm suggesting that the desire for a good reputation in ancient Heathen times worked somewhat the same way that modern Westerners' understanding of karma works today—as long as one's reputation is built upon truth and not on lies or misinformation, and as long as we realize we are building our reputations in the eyes of the Great Powers of the Worlds, not just among humans. Whether one is 'building a good reputation in the eyes of all' or 'creating good karma for oneself,' either outlook promotes ethical action—action that we and others consider to be beneficial and worthy. And all deeds, including those motivated by wanting 'good karma' or 'good reputation' for oneself, involve laying layers of orlog in the Well.

I do see some subtle differences between karma and orlog, as I discuss in Chapter 25, "Beyond Individual Orlog." But if a modern Heathen considers that 'karma' and 'orlog' are similar and acts accordingly, I don't see that any harm is done by including this non-traditional concept in one's outlook. At the same time, I think that there is no need for a modern Heathen to consider 'karma' or make it part of their philosophy of life if they don't choose to, since both 'reputation' and 'orlog' can play the same ethical role as a belief in karma can when shaping a worthy life, and both are central to a traditional Heathen outlook. For those, like myself, who like to use words from old languages for important Heathen concepts, the Anglo-Saxon word for reputation is *gefrain,* pronounced yeh-FRAIN.

Legacies

As a final word on this topic, I note the importance of personal, face to face interactions with real people, as much as possible, as the foundation for building one's reputation. In-depth long-distance interactions matter, too: telephone, video, email, and forum conversations and discussions, publishing and discussing thoughtful works on websites, books, and video presentations, etc. We can't build real reputations via 'tweets' and 'likes,' sound bites and other tiny bites void of real meaning, much less by interacting with literally soul-less and heart-less AI bots. Though I'd say that it's easy enough to *destroy* reputations in those latter ways, unfortunately—our own, and others'. I think these considerations about the best ways to build, and avoid destroying, reputations should govern the relative amount of time and effort we spend on different forms of communication and interaction—face to face, and long-distance.

And always, we should keep in mind that our reputations are known, in their full truth, by all our Holy Ones, the Norns, ancestors, and other beings of the great Worlds. We should seek to shine in the eyes of our Holy Ones, as they shine in ours: this is our true legacy!

16. Orlog at the Time of Death

Orlog as Death, and the Question of 'Why?'

Orlog is the cosmic patterning which imbues events with meaning and significance, and intervenes between random, meaningless chance on one hand, and the 'end of events', or death, on the other hand. Because of orlog, our lives and the events of our time in the world have meaning, even after we die. We do not die because 'our time has run out.' We die because our orlog has reached its fulfillment, however short or long that may take in terms of earthly time. As Tolkien writes in his epic poem *The Legend of Sigurd and Gudrun:*

Whom Odin chooseth endeth not untimely,
Though ways of men he walk briefly.
In wide Valhöll he may wait feasting –
It is to ages after that Odin looks.
(vs. 14, pp. 70-71.)

It is this irrelevance of time, in contrast to the overwhelming relevance of orlog and wyrd, that leads to the old Heathen usage of the words 'orlog' and 'wyrd' as meaning 'death' itself: at the time of death, our orlog-while, our wyrd, has

Orlog at the Time of Death

come upon us. When we die, our orlog is 'fulfilled' because it is complete, it has fully entered into 'What-Is' and is sustained there by the work of the Norns and the Well.

This interpretation, however philosophically satisfying it might be in general, leaves unanswered the very painful questions that so often arise concerning deaths that feel to us so undeserved, so meaningless, so cruel. The untimely deaths of children and young people. Cruel and terrible modes of death that happen to people who certainly didn't 'deserve' such an ending, whatever age they were. Mass events like wars, disasters, genocides, that scoop up huge numbers of victims with no regard for their uniqueness, their individuality, for what each one might have 'deserved' from life and from death. And these questions come up not only in the context of death, but also in the context of physical and psychological injuries and disabilities that drastically affect people's lives.

All religions struggle with this question of 'why,' and ours is certainly no exception. If we look to ancient Heathen beliefs for answers, there's not any more clarity than there is in most other religions, other than straightforward fatalism: 'this happened because the Norns / Wyrd said so.' There's also not much information that we can find about old Heathen thoughts on these matters that is not influenced by Christianity. What I've found is material, mostly from folklore, that blames illnesses, accidents, misfortune, and death on spirit-beings: the lesser norns and 'fairy godmothers' giving people an evil fate; the family Disir who have 'taken against' a person; dwarves, trolls, evil spirits of many varieties causing illnesses, accidents, and loss of life-force; and occult actions by ill-intentioned living humans as well, affecting people's luck and well-being. I've written about some examples of these actions in various articles on my website and chapters in my books, as have other Heathens and academics.

All of these folklore explanations, however, focus more on the question of 'how' such ill-fortune happens and who causes it, but still do not really answer the question of 'why,' in a deeper philosophical sense. If we expand our search for 'why' to other philosophies, the most reasonable answer to this existential question that many people see, I believe, is the concept of 'karma.' Very simplistically stated: cruel and untimely ends happen because of ill deeds the person committed during previous lives. Once that karma is 'paid off' and they live further lives of good action, then death during those lives is kinder, as well as having better fortune during life.

The idea of karma would not be difficult to adapt to the context of orlog if one wanted to do so, though it is not a perfect fit—at least, as orlog was understood in the past. There are certain elements of belief that are needed for karma-type orlog to work, though, and those elements would need to be explored in more depth as they appear in Heathen belief in the past, and as they might develop in today's Heathenry. The most obvious belief-element needed is reincarnation and / or something similar like the hamingja-legacy that I wrote about in the previous chapter. Indications of reincarnation beliefs do show up in old Heathen lore, and also among some modern Heathens, as well as beliefs about hamingja and its ability to carry over luck and unluck into subsequent lives.

There is more work to be done in modern Heathenry along these lines, digging deeper into the 'why' of the connections between orlog, circumstances of life and death, and the Norns / Wyrd who influence or control them, as well as roles of the Deities. The direction of this work depends on what knowledge each of us feels we need, what we are drawn toward in terms of our beliefs about these matters. Does Heathen fatalism 'feel right / true' to us? Does reincarnation? Does a view of orlog modified by aspects of karma seem like the right philosophical approach? What about the roles of the Deities in these matters? What about beliefs about the soul(s) and their afterlife?

All of these beliefs and their potential relationships to orlog may play a role in our philosophical endeavors. I've developed some thoughts along these lines in my Heathen soul lore studies, and there is much more that can be explored in that direction as well as others. All of this effort goes beyond what we can cover in this book, however, and will need to fall under the category of 'unanswered questions' here!

Once death has occurred—however and why-ever it comes about, what comes next? Does orlog play a role in the transition between life and afterlife? Do orlog and the Norns operate directly in the Worlds where human souls have their afterlives? I don't—can't—have definitive answers to these and related questions, of course, but they are worthy questions to ask and to explore here.

Heathen Afterlife Beliefs

There is no question that the Germanic peoples had beliefs about the survival of 'somethings' after death—and I say 'somethings' because these beliefs indicated quite a variety of different kinds of afterlife beings. Some of them were reanimated physical corpses that would arise from their burial places. Others stayed in their burial mounds but were

Orlog at the Time of Death

spiritually available to provide luck and blessings to the surrounding land and to those who came with petitions to the mounds. Others were free-ranging spirits like the Disir, the female ancestral spirits of Norse lore, and the Alfar, a term for the male ancestral spirits. The Germanic (and Celtic) cult of the Matronae during the time of the Roman Empire included many ancestral female spirits as well as Land-Spirits, Goddesses, and demi-goddesses. Appearances of ghosts were relatively common, then as now.

There were beliefs about afterlife in Hel, Valhalla, Folkvang, and Frau Holle's green underworld domain, sometimes called the *Totenwiese,* the meadow of the dead. Anglo-Saxon had a word, *neorxna wang,* that also meant the meadow or field of the dead. It was translated as 'paradise,' indicating that it was a pleasant place for afterlife souls. German Goddesses, including Frau Holle, Berchte, Frick (Frigg) and others were known to gather and care for the spirits of the dead, especially unbaptized children, and Walpurga was involved as well. Odin, and spaefolk, were known to speak with the dead—with their spirits, sometimes incorporated, sometimes not. Spirits sometimes showed up to their own funeral or to their kinfolk, to speak to them about the circumstances of their death, give instructions about the affairs they'd left behind, or accuse their murderers. One could go to the grave of a relative for help and advice: Svipdag received protective magical spells at the grave of his mother Groa in the *Grogaldr* of the Poetic Edda. Often the wights of the homestead, land, farm, etc, were considered to be the spirits of founders or past owners or workers of the land, embodied in different forms as *nisse, tomte, heimchen,* and many other folkloric beings. There are a great many published accounts and studies of these beliefs; I've included some of them in the Book-Hoard / bibliography.

So, let's take it as given that there were widespread beliefs about the survival of 'somethings' after death among all the Germanic peoples, as there were among all their neighboring pagan cultures. My belief, and the underlying assumption in the following discussions, is that some of our souls do survive Midgard death and continue into various states of disembodied spiritual existence.

Does Orlog Influence the Afterlife State?

Obviously, we cannot know for sure any of the answers to questions about what happens in the afterlife. Here, I use reasoning, speculation, examples from old Heathen lore, and results of my own spiritual work, to explore (not definitively answer!) these interesting and meaningful questions about orlog and the afterlife.

The first question we'll address here is: how does orlog laid during life influence our afterlife state? We go through a transition between life, the death process, and the afterlife of our souls. What influence does orlog have on this process and its outcomes?

This question, it seems to me, links us more with a Christian worldview than a Heathen one. In the Christian view one's behavior during life, and the Deity's judgement on that behavior, totally controls the afterlife fate of the soul. If we translated this view into Heathen terms, we'd say that the orlog we laid during life is judged by the Norns / Wyrd and / or the Deities after we die, and our afterlife circumstances are set by their judgement.

Quite honestly, I don't see much of that in the more Heathen-oriented lore, except for the way our luck and

Orlog at the Time of Death

hamingja are developed during our life and may be passed on, as I discussed in the previous chapter about "Hamingja as Legacy." In terms of 'judgement' in the afterlife: some souls go to Valhalla. They are chosen by the Valkyries on Odin's instructions, because Odin wants them in Valhalla due to their warrior skills. He's collecting his army for Ragnarök. This is not really 'orlog' and 'judgement.' It's related to those, because the warriors during life laid orlog in the sense of developing their warrior skills and strength, and the Valkyries / Odin 'judged' them worthy of Valhalla. But this isn't the same as the Christian situation; it is not a moral judgement on their souls, but a practical choice: Odin wants them for his own purposes.

In my humble opinion, a lot of the hype about Valhalla in the Old Norse poems was based on two purposes. One was the benefits that the poets gained by praising their patron and his warband, assuring them they'd go to Valhalla because of their courage and war skills. That's how poets made their living, whether the people they sang about actually made it to Valhalla or not. The other purpose, I think, was to energize the warrior spirit, encouraging youngsters to want to be warriors, and warriors to fight bravely. Martial music, songs, poetry, and hero-tales have always been used, in cultures around the world, to inspire people to do what in normal circumstances seems like a bizarre way to behave: subject themselves and others to brutality, maiming, and bloody slaughter, and feel good about doing so.

I am certainly not mocking courage, skill, endurance, self-sacrifice, and the determination to defend one's own, all of which I deeply respect. I'm thinking here more about the social / political role of the image of Valhalla. I think that

Orlog at the Time of Death

under Christian influence, as well as this socio-political influence, we lose sight of what Valhalla really is: not so much a Christian-like heavenly reward for warriors, *per se,* but something Odin has set up for his own purposes. Those purposes include shaping the circumstances of what comes after Ragnarök: a world free of the beings and influences that war against the Gods during Ragnarök...at least, temporarily free. Odin is laying his own orlog, and his own long-laid plans, by his choices and actions preparing for Ragnarök, and the Einherjar are a part of that.

Orlog does appear to influence the afterlife of warriors: they are chosen for Valhalla or for Freya's Folkvang because they were warriors during Midgard life—presumably as a result of their Midgard orlog. We must remember here that 'orlog' also means 'war, battle, strife.' But it has that meaning because of *what leads up to* that war or strife, not necessarily what comes *after.* Orlog comes from the past: it consists of the circumstances that lead to war or strife, in a collective, societal sense as well as the orlogs of each individual who's involved with it. As warriors, victims, others who are affected by war, their orlog leads them into that situation. But does their orlog follow them out of it—out of life and into death? I'm less sure about that. As I said, in the example of warriors' deaths in battle, orlog leads them into that situation, but after their death it is not the Norns or orlog that decide where they go; it is Odin or Freya, according to Norse myth.

Likewise with death under other circumstances. Many people's souls go to Hel; even that feisty old Norse brawler, Egil Skallagrimson, expected to head for Hel when he died. Here are the last lines of his poetic masterpiece, *Sonatorrek:*

Orlog at the Time of Death

I shall, even so, gladly
With good will
And without looking back,
Await / abide Hel.
(my translation)

skalk þó glaðr
góðum vilja
ok ó-hryggr
heljar bíða.
https://heimskringla.no/wiki/Sonatorrek (B1)

This relief sculpture shows Egil Skallagrimson carrying his drowned son. The sculpture is by Anne Marie Carl-Nielsen, and is located in Skallagríms-garður, a park in Iceland that holds the haug or grave mound of Egil's father Skallagrim and one of Egil's sons.

Hel was not considered a bad place to be, for most people. Take a look at the attitude of a famous Frisian war-leader here. (Ancient Frisia became today's Netherlands.) The engraving on the following page depicts a Frisian king or duke, a Heathen named Redbad or Radboud (d. 719 CE.) He fought against the Frankish efforts at Christianization, with wins and losses. At one point he considered baptism as a political expedient, but backed out at the last minute, as shown in the engraving. The story goes that as he was about to be baptized, he asked the bishop whether he would see his

Orlog at the Time of Death

departed kin when he went to the Christian heaven. Upon being told that 'no, his Heathen kin would not be in the Christian heaven,' Radboud stated that he would rather be in Hel with his Heathen kin, than go to heaven by himself. A typically Heathen sentiment! To me, this indicates that Radboud did not at all believe he would be facing punishment, misery and despair in Heathen Hel. Instead, he considered it a reasonable, and more homelike, alternative to Christian heaven as a place to spend his afterlife in company with his kin. His reaction also indicates a genuine and firm belief in the afterlife and in Heathen Hel. He would not have given up the clear political and strategic advantages of Christian baptism unless he truly believed in, and wanted, an afterlife existence with his Heathen kin.
(https://en.wikipedia.org/wiki/Redbad,_King_of_the_Frisians)

The ancestral connection in the afterlife was of the greatest importance for many Heathens. Looking at other traditional beliefs around the world, we can see that most of them include faring to the ancestors after death and becoming ancestral spirits in turn. In general, the afterlife destinations of souls in these old traditional beliefs, including Heathen ones, depend less on any kind of divine judgement, and more on the nature of the soul itself. For example, I argue in my book *Heathen Soul Lore Foundations* that the Hugr / Hyge /

Orlog at the Time of Death

Hugi soul is an ancestral one, who naturally continues after death as an ancestral spirit. The *saiwalo / sawol / sele* —the soul that gives us the word 'soul' in modern English—is naturally drawn to Hel and associated underworld domains like the green fields of Frau Holle. Other souls may go on to become guardians of the home or the land, familiar spirits from folklore in many cultures including Germanic ones. The Ghost soul, our Spirit, I believe is drawn to the God-Homes: not only Valhalla or Folkvang, but to the home of whichever Gods the person was closest to during Midgard life.

Does orlog play a role in these afterlife destinations and the details of their circumstances? One might argue in favor of that, in the sense that our actions and deeds during life prepare our various souls for their afterlife destinations and activities. I do not think, however, that the Norns have a strong hand in this process as it relates to the afterlife, though that is only my impression. I can't think of any really Heathen lore to point to, that would prove or disprove the idea that while the Norns shape our Midgard life, our afterlife is not up to them. My belief is that it is the *orlog we lay ourselves*—our own choices of deeds and actions, our own choices of mental and spiritual focus during life, and our personal relationships with the Deities—and not the orlog the Norns lay for us, which ultimately conditions the destinations and the states of our souls in the afterlife.

To put this simply: I believe that while the Norns shape and condition our Midgard lives, it is our own contributions and responses to our orlog during life, and our relationships with the Deities and other Worlds during life, that shape and condition the afterlives of our souls.

Orlog at the Time of Death

Let's look at an example of this, quoting the great Beowulf's last words. The *Beowulf* poet was Christian, and that shows in some of the passages in the poem. But he knew perfectly well that Beowulf himself was not Christian, and I think the poet did well in imagining how Beowulf himself, as a Heathen, would have approached the moment of his death. As Beowulf lay dying after killing the dragon, he spoke to his brave thane Wiglaf, saying:

" 'Wyrd has swept all my kinsmen toward *metod-sceaft*, those undaunted eorls. I shall go after them.' (He refers to the shaping of *metod,* similar to wyrd.) That was the old man's last word from his *breast-gehygd* (the Hyge or Hugr in his breast) before he chose the high battle-flames as, outgoing from his breast, his Sawol (soul) sought its soothfast doom." *(Beowulf* lines 2814-20, my translation, parentheses mine.)

Soothfast (*soðfæst*) means 'true, trustworthy, honest, just.' The last thing Beowulf speaks of is his brave, undaunted Heathen kinsmen gone before him; he intends his Sawol / soul to follow them to his soothfast doom, his honorable place in the afterlife. He is fully expecting this to happen naturally, for his Sawol to join his kin. He is not pleading with a Deity for a merciful judgment on his Sawol, but rather setting his own intention for his afterlife destination. Beowulf knows he has earned his honorable place in the afterlife by his worthy deeds, the orlog he himself has laid during his lifetime, and he makes a confident statement to that effect. For all the influence the Norns may have had over his life-events, it is *Beowulf's own responses* to the conditions the Norns laid for him which earn him the right to join his ancestors in their soothfast doom.

Orlog at the Time of Death

As I believe: the Norns may have a large influence in shaping the circumstances of our Midgard life and death, but *it is up to us and our Gods to shape the passages of our souls into their various afterlives.* This is what we spend our lives doing—choosing how we respond to the conditions that the Norns, Wyrd, orlog have laid. I suggest that it is greatly to our benefit if we pursue this in full awareness, knowing that our own choices and deeds in this life shape the conditions of our souls in the afterlife, just as the Norns and the orlog they lay shape the conditions of our life in Midgard.

Does Orlog Stop when Midgard Life Ends?

We've gone over some thoughts about the role of orlog and the Norns in the transition between life and death, and where our souls may head to in the afterlife. While it's impossible to be sure of what ancient Heathens thought about the role of orlog after death, here is my reasoning about their view of this question, "Does orlog *continue* to influence us in the afterlife, or does orlog stop when Midgard life ends?"

To begin our chain of reasoning: what do the Norns do? They 'choose life,' choose the event and the circumstances of our entry into Midgard life. They shape our Aldr, our lifespan and Time-Body with its processes of growth, maturation, and decline. They influence and gather up the significant deeds and events of our lives and lay them as orlog in the Well. They may predestine the time and circumstances of our death. All of this has to do with our *life in Midgard:* its beginning, its end, and what happens in between. This doesn't say anything about our afterlife situation.

Orlog at the Time of Death

I don't see evidence, myself, that old Heathens considered that our personal orlog continues to operate on our souls after our life in Midgard ends, though certainly the orlog that we've laid during our life continues to affect events in Midgard after we're gone. That's an important distinction: orlog we've laid *during life* becomes part of the Well, of What-Is, and continues to be active in Midgard. But what about after that life is over?

The word 'orlog' referred to death, in the majority of instances where it was used in ancient times, and often, so did the word 'wyrd.' To me, that implies an end: an end to our orlog along with the end of our life in Midgard. Our orlog-while, predestined for us, has now taken place, has been fulfilled. Its role is done. Our soul, or souls, no longer exist in the physical plane of Midgard after we die; they now exist elsewhere. We have left *Alda Vé* behind: the sacred space of Midgard itself which supports and gives life to *alda börnum,* children of Aldr, human beings given orlog by the Norns. Let's look at this phrase, *Alda Vé,* and what it implies about the Aldr soul and the circumstances under which it lives—and comes to an end.

Alda Vé

"The wise lack for little, for Oðrœrir has come up to the rim of **Alda Vé.**"
(*Hávamál* vs. 107 in Old Norse, 106 in translation, *Poetic Edda.*)

A *Vé* is a sanctuary, a temple or other sacred space; this verse is a reference to a mysterious 'sanctuary or sacred place of the Aldr.' This verse refers to Odin's theft of Oðrœrir, the mead of poetry and wisdom, when he drank it out of the

Jotun Suttung's vats, escaped, and flew back with it in eagle's form to Asgard. We're told in *Gylfaginning* that "Odin gave Suttung's mead to the Æsir and to those people who are skilled at composing poetry" (prose *Edda* p. 64, Faulke's translation). These skilled poets and wise folk are humans, *alda börnum,* 'children of Aldr' (this term is discussed in Chapter 5). Once Odin stole this mead from the underworld domain of the Giants and brought it up to Asgard, it also became available to humans living in Midgard, by Odin's grace or *heill.*

Alda Vé or *Vés* is a mysterious reference. I've seen the phrase translated as "sanctuaries of men," implying human temples to the Gods, but I don't buy in to precisely that understanding. "Vé," or in some texts "Vés," is in the singular form, not plural 'sanctuaries.' This phrase refers to the sanctuary of humans who each bear the Aldr soul shaped for them by the Norns. What is this 'sanctuary of humans?' What is the sacred place of the Aldr soul, where *alda börnum, eldi-barn*—time-children, mortal beings—live?

As I understand it, the 'sanctuary of humans' is Midgard itself: the place that Vé, son of Borr and Bestla, and his brothers Odin and Vili shaped out of Ymir's corpse as a sanctuary for human and earthly life in the midst of the cosmic chaos surrounding it. *(Gylfaginning* in the prose *Edda,* p. 11.) The God's name itself, Vé, is a clue to this understanding: he represents the power of making holy, of sanctifying; he is an embodiment of holiness. The only place in extant Old Norse lore that I'm aware of where Vé's name appears is in this context of shaping Midgard: the sanctuary of earthly life, protected from chaotic forces by encircling mountains and sea or rivers. His role in the shaping of Midgard was to give it the quality of holiness, of a sanctuary imbued with the power and blessing of the Gods: our earthly home of Alda Vé.

To me, this reference to Alda Vé is strong evidence that the Aldr's domain of life and action is seated in Midgard, not in any of the Worlds where other human souls or spirits may reside in the afterlife—souls such as the Ghost, Hugr, Mod, Ferah or Fjör, and Saiwalo / Sawol / Soul. *Alda börnum* in Old Norse, *eldi-barn* in Old Saxon: these terms for 'human being' imply that we are children of Time, mortal beings. Our Aldr life-span is time-limited; our Aldr life-soul is limited in space to the Midgard domain.

Orlog at the Time of Death

Recall what I wrote in Chapter 5 about 'what the Norns shape': our Aldr-soul itself, along with the lifespan it governs, the timing of significant personal events, and the flows of spiritual nourishment and life-force the Aldr feeds us, which fuel our body, souls and lifespan. Old Norse *aldr-lag* and Anglo-Saxon *ealdor-legu*, the laying-down of Aldr, mean 'death, destined death': here we see that the Aldr soul 'lays' or 'sets down' its life functions at the fated time, the end of our lifespan. There is a clear parallel between *ør-lög, or-læg, ur-lag*, on the one hand, and *aldr-lag, ealdor-legu*, on the other hand. Both are shaped by the Norns and given to us as humans. Both refer to one's death, the moment when orlog, 'what has been laid down by fate,' comes to pass, and the moment when one's *ealdor / aldr* life-force or life-soul is itself laid down, given up to death, and one's lifespan comes to an end.

I believe that the essence of the Aldr soul—the mortal Time-Body—which is shaped for us by the Norns is rooted in Midgard life, in the space that was shaped by the Gods for our human lifetimes to play out (and for the lives of other earthly beings as well). Aldr holds the vitality of our body and the Werold of our lifetime and life experience in Midgard. This makes it more likely, based on its nature, that it does not survive the end of physical Midgard life as an entity in itself. What would be its function as a soul, if it were no longer associated with a physical body that requires nourishment, growth, health, change through time, and with a Werold of life-experiences that require timing, shaping, and connection with Midgard orlog?

Aldr does have a function outside of Midgard: it feeds our deeds, as strands of orlog, back to the Norns for their action of weaving the ever-growing fabric of space and time. But Aldr performs this role specifically *while living in Midgard*. Midgard is Aldr's realm of action, the place where orlog and wyrd play out in human lives, interacting with all other life forms, physical and spiritual. Our Aldr souls are active agents of the Norns in Midgard, working with them to lay and fulfill orlog. Input, feedback, and throughput between the Norns and Midgard flow through the Aldr soul dwelling within each of us, together weaving the orlog of This-World: Alda Vé. Other beings besides humans, and natural processes, of course play major roles as well, but here we are primarily focused on the roles of human orlog.

Summary of Aldr's Roles

Now let's look at what happens with respect to orlog and Aldr as our body and our mortal lifespan reach their wyrded end. In Chapter 5 I discussed the roles of the Aldr during life, and I return to the subject in Chapter 19. In summary, during Midgard life our Aldr:

- governs our lifespan and the timing of significant events during our life (including physical changes as we grow, mature, and decline),

- functions as a form of life-force nourishing us both spiritually and physically during our Midgard life,

- shapes the experiences of our lifetime into a meaningful whole, our Werold or personal world, and

- connects us with orlog and the Norns, forming the linkage between our mortal body and personhood, the Norns and their work, and life in Midgard.

Orlog at the Time of Death

What happens with Aldr when this work is done?

What Happens to Aldr at Death?

Let's take a look at the fate of Aldr itself after physical death, based on my personal understanding. When our physical body's life, supported and shaped by our orlog and our Aldr soul, is 'laid down' here in Midgard, I believe that Aldr returns to the Norns and the Well. Recall that, according to *Gylfaginning*, Urð's Well lies in the same place where the Æsir's *rökstola*, their seats of judgement and truth-seeking, are placed (p. 17 in Faulkes' *Edda*). Aldr comes in spirit-form to this sacred place, carrying its Werold and its orlog with it, its weaving of all the experiences and deeds of our life. I believe that at this time Aldr is still accompanied by our other souls who survive physical death.

At this time, Aldr and its companion souls face the judgement of the Deities and the Norns, as a formal acknowledgement of the worth of our life and deeds. We experience this, I believe, not so much as a moral judgement or verdict, but more as a recognition—hopefully one of honor and blessing—of the deeds and events of our life, given by the Great Beings of our troth. They acknowledge the true worth of the orlog we have laid by our deeds, the Werold we have woven and its cost to us—all the struggles and triumphs, losses and gains, giving and learning, that went into its weaving—and they acknowledge its value. They bear witness as the Norns speak our life's orlog and lay it in the Well.

After this godly acknowledgement of the orlog we have shaped during our life in Midgard, our souls separate, each to its appropriate destination. The Aldr itself returns to the Well and is dissolved therein, along with its Werold, and becomes part of the Worlds' orlog, of All-That-Is, that lies in the Well and influences all that comes into being.

This, now, is not the afterlife of a personal being, a soul. Rather, Aldr has dissolved itself as an individual being, along with its individual orlog; they have been laid as a layer in the Well and become part of the natural process that feeds into the World's orlog as a whole.

When the Norns draw up a new Aldr-soul to give to a child in the womb, this new Aldr is shaped by orlog from the Well, including orlog laid by previous Aldr souls and their Werolds. But this is not the same thing as the rebirth of an individual personality—that fate of personal rebirth is left to others of our souls, in my view.

Synopsis and Some Unanswered Questions

The question of whether, and how, orlog operates in the environments our souls inhabit in the afterlife is a complex and fascinating one, but it's beyond the scope of this book. From my perspective it's a question that is closely meshed with Heathen soul lore as I understand it and needs to be explored in that context, which would take us far afield from our present course.

Thus, I'll close this chapter with a synopsis of my reasoning about orlog at the time of death, and some unanswered questions about orlog in the afterlife. I do this in the spirit of a quotation from the French political philosopher Baron de Montesquieu (1689-1755): "One should never so exhaust a subject that nothing is left for readers to do. The point is not to make them read, but to make them think." This applies to myself, as well…there's still a lot more for me to think about here!

Orlog at the Time of Death

I. How Orlog Functions in Midgard

When we are alive in Midgard orlog acts upon us in several ways, as we've covered in previous chapters. To summarize:

> 1. Orlog is laid through the workings of choices and deeds, which result in causes and effects:
> (a) on the individual level and
> (b) on the collective level.

Our choices and deeds affect us individually and are likely to have effects on others as well. The deeds of other individuals, and the actions and orlog of various collectives and the society we're embedded in, may influence our orlog as well as theirs.

> 2. Orlog is shaped and spoken by the Norns; this can involve:
> (a) their actions resulting in causes and effects,
> (b) fateful, wyrded interventions chosen by them, coming from outside the workings of cause and effect.

Again, these actions of the Norns can impact us both on the individual level and through their effects on the collectives that we are a part of.

> 3. Deities act in Midgard as well, and their actions also influence individual and group orlog—ours, and their own.

These conclusions leave many questions unanswered relating to orlog after death. Here are some of the ones I ponder.

II. Rebirth into Midgard

There is a fair amount of evidence for a belief in 'rebirth' in Norse lore—at least for some people, under certain circumstances. The fact that it is noteworthy to mention such rebirths in the sagas and poems seems to hint that it doesn't necessarily happen to everyone—at least as it was understood in the past.

> 1. This is a complicated topic to pursue, because it involves a number of sub-questions:
> (a) Who gets reborn, and why?
> (b) What is it that gets reborn? Personality? Soul? Luck? Orlog? Hugr? Ghost?
> (c) What is the mechanism or process whereby rebirth happens? That is, what triggers rebirth for some people? Does it have to do with their orlog in their previous life?

A good number of books about old Heathen beliefs offer overviews of their concepts of rebirth, including Hilda Ellis's (Davidson's) seminal *Road to Hel.* My own studies on Heathen soul lore indicate that the Hugr soul is likely to be reborn, while the Hamingja-spirit is not reborn, precisely, but rather it remains in disembodied form Midgard when the person dies, and is then passed on or inherited by another living person, as I discussed in the previous chapter about "Hamingja as Legacy." Of course, it's quite possible that the Hamingja rejoins the same person after that person is reborn into Midgard, giving something of a reincarnation effect. There are a great many questions that remain on this topic, including this one:

2. Assuming that rebirth into Midgard is a possibility, to what extent does the orlog we laid during our past Midgard life influence the conditions of our new, reborn life in Midgard? If the Hamingja rejoins its previous self when that self is reborn into Midgard, presumably it would bring whatever orlog it bears with it for the newly-born person. But that seems not always to be the case, and it isn't clear how much of the orlog or the personhood is carried by Hamingja, which is not an actual soul, in my understanding, but rather a spirit-being that is attached to us during Midgard life.

III. The Operation of Orlog in the Afterlife

And finally, questions concerning the function of orlog, if any, as it relates to our souls in the afterlife domains:

1. Does orlog influence human souls while they reside in the afterlife domains, either permanently or temporarily while awaiting rebirth? Does causality itself operate in the same way in other Worlds as it does in Midgard and the physical universe as we know it?

2. If orlog and causality in some form do operate in the afterlife worlds, to what extent is the orlog we lay *during our afterlife* influential in the conditions of our reborn life in Midgard?

3. For souls who stay in the afterlife and are not reborn, how does orlog work, or does it not affect them? My sense is that the orlogs of whichever God or Goddess we reside with would have some influence over our souls too, but I don't know how much. For example, Odin's

Einherjar share in his and the Worlds' orlog of facing the Ragnarok battle. The Einherjars' orlog *during life in Midgard* resulted in them being chosen for Valhalla. Odin's and the Æsir's orlog of Ragnarök influences their fates in the afterlife. But do they also accrue personal orlog while in Valhalla, the way we do during life in Midgard?

4. Do the Norns relate to us in the afterlife the same way they do in Midgard? My own vague sense is that they do not, at least not in the same ways as in Midgard. The more I think about this, the more it seems to me that human orlog—emphasis on 'human'—as we know it, is really a Midgard phenomenon. Though orlog does affect the Deities, and affects our souls in a collective way through our association with those Deities in our afterlives, I have the feeling that the Norns have less direct influence over us in the afterlife, while the Gods and Goddesses and the workings and patterns of the afterlife Worlds have more weighty influence on our souls in the afterlife.

These are all deep and intriguing questions I like to ponder, but they'd require a full book (or books) to explore them in more depth. Now that our minds are attuned to weird ideas about orlog, however, let's move on to some more weird ideas in the next part of this book.

Part IV: Orlog Metaphysics

or

Some Weird Ideas about Orlog

A spiral-shaped depiction of geological ages of the Earth, apparently spiraling out from the Big Bang, or out of Ginnungagap! We can see a parallel between the geological ages and formations of the Earth, and the orlog laid by us and all beings associated with the Earth.

17. The Evolving Nature of Orlog

"The process of occurrence of events and the continual accumulation of more and more of them into the pattern of the past present a system of growth that is never finished. As the Norns daily bring their nurture to the tree (Yggdrasil, the World-Tree), they express the power of this sequence or pattern of the past up and out into and upon the world of men; as these 'past' events sustain and feed the tree, they bring into being the events of the here and now; as 'present-day' events occur, they fall from the tree (as 'dew') back into the well (Urð's Well) and join themselves into the ever increasing complexities of the past, restructuring it, reinterpreting it, continually expressing more and more about the interrelations of all actions." (Bauschatz p. 20-21, parentheses mine.)

Process versus Substance

Here is something of a conceptual challenge that I think is important to understand as we strive to grasp ancient concepts of orlog but evolve them into something relevant for Heathens today. Just as I wrote earlier that there's a

The Evolving Nature of Orlog

difference between the details of any specific cause-and-effect event, versus the process of causality as a phenomenon, there's also a difference between the *substance* of orlog and the *process* of orlog. I think it would be easier if there were two different words for these things, but there are not, as currently recognized, though 'orlog' versus 'wyrd' might eventually be worked into such definitions. I won't do so here, though, because when I've tried to work out such definitions for myself it seems to create more confusion, not less! Process and substance of orlog are not separate things, they are part of an integrated whole, but for the purposes of the following discussion it's useful to look at them individually.

The Process of Orlog

The *process* of laying orlog continues the same over time, and in both modern and ancient Heathen understanding, we use metaphors of layers laid in the Well or plastered onto the Tree to describe this process. In Bauschatz' beautiful imagery, the Tree sucks water from the Well, and after the water-sap runs through all the life and beings upon the Tree, drops the water down as dew, representing deeds and events. Significant deeds fall within the Well and are recycled back to nourish the Tree and all life upon it; insignificant deeds fall outside the Well as ordinary dew and have no influence. (See Bauschatz chapter IV: "Action, Space, and Time.")

We've discussed in earlier chapters how this process is envisioned as 'shaping,' 'scoring (runes),' 'laying layers,' and 'speaking.' This process is captured by *verbs,* the words of action that describe what the Norns do as they lay the layers. The process of orlog, however it is envisioned

208

metaphorically, is presumed to be unchanging. The Norns / Wyrd lay layers, they shape what is coming into being, they speak orlog: this is how it happens, it always has happened this way, and always must happen.

A freshly-cut tree showing its growth rings and the changes growth brought about, such as the atypical patterns on the right of the image. The Norns tend the Tree, keeping it alive and growing, able to change and adapt as this tree did.

The Substance of Orlog

The *substance* of orlog is a different matter: this consists of the *layers which have already been laid*. The substance is not captured by verbs, words of action, but by nouns: 'what is.' These layers have been laid already and lie outside the direct influence of the Norns or others in present or continuous-present time.

These already-laid layers are not the same today as they were when the Eddas and other ancient poems were composed. The layers lying at the 'surface' of orlog, so to

The Evolving Nature of Orlog

speak, those that are most influential in our daily lives today, are not the same now as they were then. Many years have passed since then, many layers of dew-drops have been added to the Well, centuries of rings have grown upon the Tree.

Orlog itself has accreted many more layers since that time: that is what it does. It grows and develops based on the layers continually being laid down, and those layers subtly influence the ones that accumulate above them and below them. The World Tree, nourished daily by the Norns, has grown, and the Norns have spoken daily, over the past thousand years, whether people are aware of this or not!

This photo shows the weathered growth rings of a tree that was felled around 1111 CE. The tree was therefore alive and growing during the time that the Old Norse poetry contained in the Eddas was being composed. This is a mesmerizing image of a central 'well' around which rings of orlog have been laid. It shows the fissures and changes that can occur in those layers of orlog as time progresses and the

substance of orlog evolves. But in one way it is not a good image of orlog and the Tree: this trunk is long dead. It shows the substance *of orlog laid down and fixed in the past. It's an image of substance and past processes, but not an image of current life and growth.*

Process Creates Substance

Once these layers have been laid, they take on a character and process of their own. Here's an analogy involving rocks and soil that illustrates how this works. Rocks are laid down on the Earth's surface by either volcanic or sedimentary action, but they don't stay the same over time. Both types of rock can be changed by the pressure and heat of tectonic forces into metamorphic rock, having different features.

Even patterns laid in stone may change, subject to the forces of the living earth. Here layers that were originally flat underwent some upheaval and humped up over the cave or fissure below.

The Evolving Nature of Orlog

All types of rocks on the surface are subject to erosion and deposition as sand, silt, and clay, and further geologic changes after that, including changes into sedimentary rock. Tectonic movement and other geological processes can result in layers being reoriented—horizontal layers becoming more vertical, and even inversion of lower layers on top of higher ones.

Soils that develop over different kinds of rocks have different properties even when the surface soil constituents are similar, coming from decomposing plant and animal materials. Soils are categorized by types and subtypes, as plants and animals are by species, and soils can and do evolve into different types with different characteristics over time, influenced by what lies below them, what is deposited on top of them, and by the water that flows through it all, just like the water of the Well of Wyrd.

Soils *evolve* under the influence of their climate, surroundings, and inputs, almost like living things; they don't just sit there. Plants, animals, people, microorganisms, waste products, weather, depositions and erosions by wind and water—all of the activities and materials on and below the surface—influence the metamorphosis and evolution of soils.

And not only that: churning and mixing of soil layers occurs constantly. Earthworms, burrowing animals, grubs, and other organisms mix soil around from layer to layer. Freezing and thawing cause upheavals in the soil and move rocks up to the surface. Water dissolves chemicals from the surface and carries them down to lower layers, which then are changed by this input, while rising groundwater brings up dissolved minerals from below. Soils, whose very nature is defined by layers, are not static, and neither is orlog itself, an equally dynamic, layered phenomenon involving many complex processes.

This photo shows different layers that have evolved within this soil profile, each layer having features which can be differentiated by soil analysis even when they are visually similar. Soils illustrate both process and substance. Soil changes itself, evolves according to its own physical, chemical and microbiological processes. Midgard life comes from the soil and returns to it. Soil is the source and sink of earthly life, and its supportive foundation, as orlog supports the metaphysical ordering functions of Time.

We can liken the *processes of rock and soil formation* to orlog as a process. We can liken the *substances*, the specific composition of individual rocks and soils themselves, to the substance of orlog. These substances are always changing, always subject to processes of alteration and transformation, albeit very slowly and imperceptibly from a human perspective.

The Evolving Nature of Orlog

I suggest that orlog is the same: what is laid down in the past is there, it supports and shapes what is layered above it, but it, too, is subject to slow changes and transformation into something subtly different. That changed substance, in turn, affects what grows above it, the new layers laid down by the ongoing processes of orlog.

Orlog Evolves as Process Creates Substance

I've argued here that orlog is subject to evolution in the sense that, through its natural processes and the work of the Norns, it undergoes changes in its substance through time. The layers of orlog that are most influential in today's world—the 'top' layers, so to speak—are not the same as the most influential or 'top' layers that existed centuries ago when information about Heathenry was being recorded in the writings we have today. A lot of orlog has been laid between then and now!

And not only that: the 'soil' of orlog has been stirred as old information becomes available and important to us today, as we are positioned at the 'surface' of the substance of orlog. The old writings, archaeological evidence, folklore, and other evidence of ancient Heathen beliefs and practices, burrowed into and dug up from ancient layers of orlog and brought into awareness in today's world, are now creating new layers of orlog in modern Heathen consciousness and action. These older layers influence us today as Heathens, but so do all the layers of orlog that have been laid between then and now: layers laid by centuries of history and cultural change, changes in religion and philosophy, discoveries of science, and many other influences.

The Evolving Nature of Orlog

These layers of clay deposited in a floodplain are intersected by a natural vertical channel cutting through the layers. In the same way, we may seek to penetrate through layers of orlog in search of knowledge from the past.

I suggest that it is a valid exercise to approach an understanding of the *substance* of orlog through modern ideas and thought processes. In elder times, orlog meant primarily 'time and circumstances of death', and this was, in general, not heavily influenced by the individual but set by the Norns or Wyrd. Nowadays, influenced by modern scholarship and Heathen thought, and modern ways of thinking generally, we tend to think of orlog as something we mostly create ourselves (whether knowingly or not) through our choices and deeds during our lives.

If we understand that orlog-substance slowly and subtly reshapes itself through time, then it's valid to believe that *both* understandings of orlog are genuine: both the ancient, more deterministic or fatalistic understanding of orlog, and the modern one that incorporates a greater role for personal choices and our responsibility for them. Over centuries of

The Evolving Nature of Orlog

time, orlog-substance has shaped human thought and deeds, *and been shaped by them in turn.* As soils physically, chemically, and microbiologically reshape themselves over time, so does the substance of orlog. The greater degree of fatalism, as seen in old Heathen and other old Pagan attitudes, has been modified by layers of science, philosophy, history, culture, changes in outlook. As a result, we may conclude that orlog is something which we *can and do* influence by our choices and actions today, more than was the case in the more fatalistic past.

Orlog and the Norns / Wyrd still determine the conditions that influence our choices and actions; they are conditioning forces as I discussed in previous chapters. But many modern Heathens believe that our own Will plays a strong role as well. My understanding is that *the Norns themselves shaped this change in the substance of orlog.* I think they shaped this change while Heathenry was mostly 'underground,' below the level of everyday consciousness, during the centuries after conversion took hold and before the re-emergence of modern Heathenry. They, and we—generations of humans—brought about this evolution in the substance of orlog. Through this development they are helping us to mature spiritually—mature through the passage of generations and all the learning and experience that we accumulate and build on, year by year, including the rediscovery of Heathenry and the wisdom it brings as we grow it forward.

Bauschatz gives a powerful description of the living, growing nature of the Well—the symbol of Time—and the Tree: the symbol of Space. The Tree is the shape of three-dimensional Space, of the concrete, 'real' world as we know it—our World of Midgard, and all the other Worlds as well,

The Evolving Nature of Orlog

material within their own contexts of space. As do natural trees, this great Tree of Space expands and grows as the abstract becomes concrete and what exists in potential form becomes actualized through the deeds and actions of living beings. The Well, as he discusses, is not a static container of still water, but a powerfully active, upwelling wellspring.

"Within the well, the power of all events past still surges, writhes, twists, whelms, and weaves the whole of this greater reality 'out'"...out into the domain of the Tree, nourishing its growth and change. (Bauschatz p. 125. I love this description!).

The Norns and orlog and the Well are not static, have never been static and never will be. Their work is to nourish the World-Tree—the ever-evolving shape of all the Worlds— and help it grow. Growth means change, and our souls need to expand to encompass such changes, while still and always remaining rooted in *skǫp Norna,* the shapings of the Norns.

*Embodiment of the Aldr soul into a newborn,
under the auspices of the Norns.*

18. The Body as Orlog

Orlog as Nourishment

The nourishing, growth-promoting power of orlog and the Norns is not focused only on the great metaphysical entities of the Well and the Tree. I mentioned 'nourishment' as one metaphor for orlog earlier, in the context of the Aldr lifespan and life-soul or life-force (Chapter 5). Both nourishment and orlog consist of *accumulations.* Nourishment consists of layers of food, drink, and what we breathe, which we lay down by consuming and metabolizing them day by day; this continuously forms and re-forms our physical body and fuels it for the full span of our life. Unfortunately, anti-nourishment in the form of unhealthy and toxic substances are also accumulated day by day in our bodies as well, and these too affect our orlog in terms of our health and functioning during our lifetime.

Both nourishment and anti-nourishment serve as physical forms of orlog, laying layers within our bodies that affect our abilities, our health, and how we experience our lives, and thus affect the quality of our deeds which are laid as layers of orlog in the Well. Our own body is part of our orlog, laid down in the layers accumulated day by day from all the substances we take in and metabolize, along with our habits, our thoughts and emotions.

Genetics and Epigenetics

Going even deeper, we see that our genetic makeup and the action of epigenetics lay foundational layers of orlog within our bodies, their capacities, abilities and actions. Genes carry the orlog of our physical inheritance from our ancestors. Epigenetics describes the effects that our daily exposures, actions, and physiological responses have on modifying the actions of our genes, switching them on or off, altering their expressions in our body and its life-sustaining activities. These genetic and epigenetic activities have strong shaping effects on our body and its activities.

The Conditioning Effects of Orlog

There's another way that understanding our body as orlog helps us understand orlog itself, as a phenomenon. Just as with orlog, there are things about our body that we can change, and other things we cannot. The changes we can make usually require effort—often very strenuous effort, like improving our fitness, managing our weight, or managing chronic conditions to maintain the greatest wellbeing we can under those circumstances. We may be able to postpone the effects of aging through diligent actions, but eventually aging will occur if we live that long.

It's the same with orlog: some of the orlog-conditions in our lives are things that we can change with a lot of dedicated effort. Some conditions of orlog we can't change; we must simply figure out how to deal with them the best way we can.

Process and Substance

Each day we lay layers of orlog in our body and in our life-circumstances, interweaving them with layers of genetic and epigenetic activities. Those layers shape our actions and reactions, which in turn shape the next layers of orlog that we lay. This *process* of laying layers of cause and effect—through genetic and epigenetic action, nourishment and anti-nourishment, behavior, habits, thoughts, emotions, actions and deeds—creates a *substance:* our body and all its reactions, abilities, and structure. That substance—our body and our self—in turn conditions and influences what we do with it today, tomorrow and the next day, which in turn lays more orlog-layers with their subtle conditioning effects on our present state of being and our actions. The condition of our body, its underlying structures and its many subtle reactions, are the *substance* of orlog that has been laid during each day of our past. This substance or substrate affects our present actions, the ongoing *process* of laying more layers of orlog day by day through our choices, behaviors, words and deeds, all of it creating who we are in this life.

The Body as Orlog

Body and Time-Body.

19. Time and the Time-Body

"These maids shape / make people's **aldrs** (skapa monnum aldr); we call them Norns." (Gylfaginning in the prose Edda)

"In one day was my **aldr** shaped, and all my life laid down" (Skirnismal vs. 13, Poetic Edda).

(My translations.)

Bodies in Space and Time

It is not only our physical body which contains layers of orlog that influence and are influenced by how we live our lives. I believe we have another, metaphysical 'body' that is even more subject to the shaping of the Norns. Here, I'm following on from discussions in Chapter 5: "What Do the Norns Shape?" I envision that we have something I call a Time-Body that is analogous to our physical body, but exists in time rather than in three-dimensional space. I suggest, further, that this Time-Body is the same thing as our Aldr life-force or life-soul that I discussed in Chapter 5, but for now I'm referring to it as the Time-Body. Let's start by

Time and the Time-Body

looking at features of our physical body, then extend that analogously to this Time-Body idea.

Our physical body occupies a certain physical space and has given dimensions: height, depth, width. We fill these dimensions with our body's shape or form. The space our body occupies is unique: no other physical object can occupy the space that our body occupies unless we ingest or absorb it into the inner spaces of our body like our stomach or lungs. We can move around in space, carrying our own body-occupied space with us, and we interact with all that is around us on physical and other levels.

The shape our body occupies in space defines us each as a unique individual with a multitude of characteristics—characteristics that our body has developed through many different processes: through genetics and epigenetics; through work, exercise and activities; illnesses, injuries and disabilities; body care, nutrition, and non-nutritive substances; training, habits, and customs; the effects of maturation and aging; and many more. In subtle and not so subtle ways, our physical body records and reflects much about the story of our life in the layers of physical substance that it lays down to shape itself.

So, our physical body is three-dimensionally defined by its shape or form that occupies a unique place in space. I suggest that we have another, different kind of body as well: a body in Time rather than Space. What is the defining characteristic of this Time-Body, that makes it analogous to our body-shape in space? What gives our Time-Body its 'shape'? I see this as *continuity:* our continuity in time for the duration of our life, our life-span. Our physical body holds its place in space by its three-dimensional shape or form—that's how we claim the space we occupy. Our Time-

Time and the Time-Body

Body occupies its place in time through the process of continuity: the continuity of who we are, our life-span, our Werold, our experiences, our sense of self, our life-story, our body itself, all maintained throughout our life. The continuity of who we are holds and shapes our place in time, as our physical body shapes our place in space. The characteristics of our Time-Body change over time and so does our physical body. They both—physical and time bodies—are affected by all our experiences in life as well as by our processes of growth, maturation and aging.

In time-lapse photography and animations, you can see the stretched-out shape of a body that occupies consecutive spaces in rapid succession, like the photograph of a flower unfolding from a bud, a person running, a stream of light from a star moving through the sky or a car's headlights as it drives. This is the best illustration I can think of to help us envision what the Time-Body might 'look like,' with its stretched-through-space feature mimicking continuity in time.

However, I think that 'what the Time-Body looks like' is a misleading way to go about understanding the Time-Body. Our physical senses are designed to operate in physical space and tell us things about that space, so when we describe something we use concepts like 'it looks like this, sounds like this, acts like this, etc.' Within Time, the abilities analogous to the physical senses are 'experience' and 'memory,' and the way those two work together. These are what we use to detect, process, and understand aspects of time, as we use our physical senses to detect, process, and understand aspects of space in Midgard. When we communicate along the lines of: 'yesterday I experienced this, and here is my memory of it,' we are operating from our

Time and the Time-Body

Time-Body, working through our physical body to physically communicate something.

Of course, experience and memory depend on what happens in space as well as in time. Space and time are interwoven, and our physical and time bodies interact with each other during every moment of our lives. But it's useful in our philosophical pursuit of orlog here to understand something about their distinctions as well as their interactions. To understand the Time-Body a little better, let's start with the obvious question: what is Time?

Time as Change

In conventional physics, 'time' is defined as 'change;' time is measured as the interval during which some kind of change occurs. Atomic clocks measure the frequencies of the vibrations that occur when electrons jump back and forth between higher and lower levels of energy: these are very tiny and very rapid changes suitable for extremely accurate scientific observations. At the level of everyday human experience, easily observable changes happen constantly: we move around to different positions in space, engage in different activities, interact with different people, speak words in changing sequences, breathe in and out at different speeds, eat and digest our food, observe children and adults as they change and grow, experience changes in day and night and the seasons; even the thoughts we think are constantly changing.

This is how we perceive time: through different experiences, and our observations and memories of them. Time, for us subjectively, is the flow of changing circumstances throughout our lives along with the physical traces they leave, and the memory with which we keep track of them. We sense time through experience and memory, as we sense our physical surroundings, the space we are in, through our physical senses. In both cases, we depend upon our powers of observation and thought to make sense of all this.

There is an additional way we learn to sense time as we mature: through an understanding of cause and effect—the understanding that under normal circumstances events or effects are caused by 'something,' and that 'something' occurred before the event that it caused. The cause happens first, followed by its effect, which may in turn be the cause of some new effect, and so on. Whole complex networks of interweaving causes and effects are common in human experience as well as in nature, and link us back to the complexities of orlog and the Norns. It's often very difficult to fully understand all the causes of some complex event, but we can still operate on the assumption that things are caused by other things, and whatever caused that thing to happen occurred *before* the event, not after it. Cause comes first, effect follows.

These are ordered sequences of changes through time, and they shape our human perception of what time is. They are also how our Time-Body understands and makes sense of the world it lives in, the world of Time: it understands Time through sequences of changing events, through continuity of awareness and experience, and the memory that ties these things together. Just as our physical bodies can become injured or ill and malfunction as a result, so can our Time-Body when we experience problems with memory and awareness, which in turn affects our experience of our life and the shape of our Werold.

Causality and the Time-Body

In Chapter 9 I suggested that one of the vital roles the Norns fulfill as great Powers is by ordering the processes of causality. Our Time-Bodies sense this work of the Norns and strive to understand how we humans fit into that process, which leads to our efforts to understand matters of free will, determinism, and predestination. Causality, determinism, and predestination are matters of importance to our Time-Body because they fundamentally have to do with our relationship to Time.

Causality is based upon sequences of changing events through time and how those events relate to each other.

Determinism, on a personal level, presents us with the question: "how did I get to this point in time, what will I do now that I am here, and why will I do it? To what extent is my next step, 'the future,' already determined by the past, and to what extent am I free to make a choice, to deviate from the influences of the past?"

Predestination implies that there is a force or a being which has the power to control my Time-Body's trajectory through time so that I arrive at a predetermined 'destination' per schedule. This destination is set for me long before I ever get there, maybe before I even conceive of it being in my future.

Causality, determinism, and predestination are all phenomena that lie beyond the sphere of full human control. Free will is human; it is within our own individual reach to decide and act upon. How these phenomena—causality, determinism, predestination, and free will—interact with each other in our individual lives involves our relationships with the Norns and orlog, with the Deities, and with all the complexities of Midgard life.

Time as Relationship

'Time as change' is not the only way that Time may be perceived. Winterbourne, and scholars whom he draws upon including Bauschatz, see the old Germanic idea of time as, in fact, not a temporal concept at all, but a relational one:

"…in place of any abstract chronology, Norse mythology presents us with *time as genealogy.* This is an idea that assists us in understanding how it is possible that in Germanic mythology the past becomes more powerful through the flow of time; it does not recede in significance, because the past is, paradoxically, fullest *now,* in the present." (Winterbourne, p. 49).

This is a feature, I would say, of a great many pre-literate societies as well as the Norse and Germanic. Their histories are contained in memorized lists of genealogies; time periods are designated by the reigns of kings, by battles and other significant events that happened during them rather than by numbering the years. Winterbourne notes that time in the *Völuspá,* for example, is not presented as an ordered series of events related to each other in time, but rather time is designated by names indicating what happened during them, such as an 'axe age,' or 'the first war in the world.' What relates those different periods of time to each other is not a regular, organized time-sequence, but rather how the significance of events that occurred then relates to the significance of other events in the tale. Significance and interrelationship, rather than linear sequence, are the important factors, as I discussed also in Chapter 6, "Time, Tense, and the Norns."

Bauschatz contrasts the realm of the Tree, the representative of actualized, three-dimensional physical reality, with that of the Well as the container of what is abstract, conceptual, and not fully known.

"Within the well, the interrelations among actions rather than actions themselves are of paramount importance; here within the realm of the well, are the motives and reasons for and the final causes of the acts that occur within the realm of the tree" (Bauschatz p. 125).

Time as a Container of Meaning

This leads us to Bauschatz's very extensive examination of old Germanic ideas of time and space, discussed especially in his Chapter IV on "Action, Space, and Time." He describes time as a 'container for events,' symbolized by Urð's Well. All events of significance that occur in the Worlds fall into this Well and constitute the past. I'll repeat here this passage from Bauschatz that I quoted in Chapter 6:

"The past, as collector of events, is clearly the most dominant, controlling portion of all time. Man's world stands at the juncture of this past and the non-past, that is, at that point, the present, in which events are in the process of becoming 'past.' The past is experienced, known, laid down, accomplished, sure, realized. The present, to the contrary, is in flux and confusion, mixed with irrelevant and significant details. What we nowadays call 'the future' is, within the structure of this Germanic system, just more of the nonpast, more flux, more confusion." (pp. 138-9)

Time, in this view, is not related directly to cause and effect, or to the orderly passage of days and years, or to change. Instead, time is the 'space,' or the container wherein humans, Deities, other beings, and their deeds of significance form interrelationships. This is time as 'duration,' and as 'what endures.' Spaces and places—especially sacred or otherwise significant spaces such as a temple or a battlefield—provide context and depth of meaning to the actions that take place in them. So, also, does time, especially sacred or significant times: holy tides, festivals, commemorative days or events.

Within the containers of time and space, the interrelationships of beings and their actions take place which shape the course of events in all the Worlds and give them meaning. Time itself is given meaning because it provides the 'container' within which those relationships are formed and fixed in place. In the form of orlog they are collected and kept in Time, maintaining their existence and influence. As Bauschatz discusses in depth, the World-Tree provides the structure of space, which is constantly growing and expanding because it is nourished by time and orlog from the Well. Together they encompass the cosmos.

Time, contained within the Well, provides the opportunity for significant events and relationships to build and grow, accumulate, play out, be experienced and remembered, and to influence what is now coming into being. The more 'past' that flows into the Well, the more there is for us to work with, on personal, cultural, historical, and spiritual levels. This provides the context for our Time-

Body's experiences and memories. As our physical body engages in actions and relationships in Space, our Time-Body experiences and remembers them in Time.

Time-Body / Aldr Soul and Werold

Here we've looked at several quite different concepts of time, all of them valid and relevant to our pursuit of understanding orlog: time as change, time as the context for causality, time as genealogical relationships, time as a container or a field within which actions and events occur and interact with one another in complex ways. Time as a container 'stores' those actions and events that are of true significance, and these contents of the 'container of the past' in turn feed into the significance and power of new actions and events taking place in the 'non-past'—the state of flux that constitutes the 'present' and 'future.'

This is the context within which our Time-Body or Aldr soul has its being and creates its Werold or personal world, our own personal container of time that encompasses the span of our life. Within our Werold we weave our networks of relationship and significance, we lay down layers of orlog as our life-span progresses. Our Aldr soul gives us the capacity to sense Time itself, to understand and work with it, at least on a practical and everyday level. It enables us to view our own life-time as a whole: as a weaving that extends through time, where we can look backwards, and to some extent make projections forward in time, in our quest to understand and shape our Werold.

Our physical body and our Werold can both be seen as expressions of orlog-substance, shaped from layers of substances and experiences we have consumed and metabolized within the space-time container of Midgard.

Time and the Time-Body

We ourselves are woven into the larger constructs of the Well and the Tree by the Norns, first when we are born and placed into our initial life-contexts, and then by the direct and indirect influences of the Norns, other Deities and beings including humans, our own deeds, and the influence of all that goes on around us during our lifetime.

In a way, we can think of our Aldr soul as an agent for the Norns in Midgard, with respect to our own personal life and life-span. Our Aldr life-force nourishes and strengthens our living being and extends it through time, just as the Norns nourish and strengthen the World-Tree with the sacred white mud of the Well, supporting its life in time. Aldr takes the meaningful experiences of our lives and weaves our Werold out of them, just as the Norns gather the significant events of the Worlds and lay them into the container of the Well to shape the orlog there. Our Werold is the shape of our personal orlog: the orlog that comes to us from outside sources, past and present, and the orlog that we lay for ourselves. The quotations I gave at the beginning of this chapter talk about the Norns shaping people's Aldrs, as our Aldr shapes our Werold out of the totality of our life-experience and governs the length of our life on behalf of the Norns. I see the Aldr or Time-Body as a soul closely associated with the Norns and orlog: shaped by them, connected to them, and working with them during our life in Midgard.

Time and the Time-Body

"The Quantum Leap" sculpture.

This image looks a little like the Time-Body would look, leaping through Time, with the segments representing the body moving through time rather than space.

20. The Quantum Nature of the Norns' Work

Formal philosophy may sometimes look at phenomena in a rather fixed way, as 'either / or;' 'if it's this, it can't be that.' Determinism versus Free Will. Causality or Chaos. True or False. There are other, more ambiguous perspectives that can be taken, however, including insights gained from quantum theory in physics. I am not necessarily suggesting—or denying—that the Norns are somehow 'quantum beings' or operating on the quantum level as physics currently understands it. Rather, in this chapter I'm using a few aspects of quantum theory as analogies to deepen our understanding of how the Norns shape orlog. (Note that there are a good many, quite different ways that quantum physics interprets and explains the phenomena that are observed in that field of study. My discussion in this chapter is based, metaphorically, on only one set among a number of possible interpretations. I include one website that briefly summarizes different interpretations in the Book Hoard under 'Quantum Theory'.)

Needless to say, if you find quantum physics to be an uninteresting or baffling subject, you are welcome to skip this chapter! I like to approach a subject from as many different angles as I can think of, to get a more solid sense of it, but it's understandable if you consider some of my approaches to be a bit too far out.

I'm beginning with an image, a vignette, a brief tale, of the Norns and especially the one named Verðandi in Old Norse, whom I call the Gatekeeper or the Midwife of the Quantum Realm. Following that, I'll turn to three basic aspects of quantum theory and relate them to the three Norns and their functions in shaping orlog.

Fractal

Gatekeeper of the Quantum Realm

Verðandi rules the domain of Becoming: the very instant of time when a being or a deed ripens from the layers Wyrd has laid and springs forth to lay new layers and respond to Skuld's tuggings, faint or strong, upon its thread of life. Her name means 'Becoming / coming into being.' Hers is the

The Quantum Nature of the Norns' Work

point of the needle, the edge of the knife, the imperceptible moment when something moves from 'not-being' into 'becoming.'

As 'becoming' moves into 'become,' Skuld attaches strands of shild / debt / obligation to that which has become. This is a metaphor for the action of causality, of cause and effect. Skuld's name comes from a form of the word 'should,' and implies that 'given this thing / event / action / being / situation which has now come into being, this is what 'should or must' result from it.'

Then the deed or event or being rolls over into Urðr's domain of 'what-is,' what has happened, what has been accomplished and completed, entered into Being. It is tethered lightly or strongly to Skuld's domain of 'what should be,' depending on many complex factors, and those tugs from Skuld's tethering threads create the function of causality. In the meantime, the next instant of Becoming arises and moves on, into the same pattern. That very moment of Becoming is Verðandi's domain.

I like to picture Verðandi both as a midwife into Being, and as the gatekeeper of the quantum realm. A *potentiality* arises in the quantum realm and is 'called to' or 'attracted to' Verðandi. This potentiality could manifest as a deed, a person, a situation, an object, a thing, event, or phenomenon of any kind. She then midwifes its birth into the domain of Time and Being as we know them. It's as though the potentiality of a deed, a situation, a being, a moment of Time itself, is the 'soul' of that thing, and she calls this soul into its 'body,' which is its reality in this Space-Time where it is enacted into being. It is then given a wyrd—that is, it takes on its role in causality—and is embedded into the solidity of 'what-is,' Urðr's domain. Verðandi remains at the gateway of the quantum realm, midwifing the next births into being.

Verðandi's foundation is in the present moment: never past, never future, never 'perfected' in the sense of completed and finished, always budding into the perpetual Now. Thus, she stands as the sacred gatekeeper of the quantum realm, at the imperceptible edge where Might-Be becomes What-Is.

Norns and Three Phenomena of Quantum Physics

Here I want to discuss three basic aspects of quantum physics that I relate to the Norns, and that could have some bearing on some of the contradictions or quandaries that inevitably arise when striving to understand these mysterious beings and their even more mysterious work of laying orlog. Here are the three quantum phenomena I'm discussing, which I state briefly below and then go on to apply them to each Norn in more detail.

1) *Wave function collapse.* "*Wave function collapse* means that a measurement has forced or converted a quantum (probabilistic or potential) state into a definite measured value. In various interpretations of quantum mechanics, wave function collapse…occurs when a wave function—initially in a superposition of several eigenstates—reduces to a single eigenstate due to interaction with the external world. This interaction is called an *observation* and is the essence of a measurement in quantum mechanics, which connects the wave function with classical observables such as position and momentum. Collapse is one of the two processes by which quantum systems evolve in time…
https://en.wikipedia.org/wiki/Wave_function_collapse

The Quantum Nature of the Norns' Work

Various interpretations of quantum mechanics explain this phenomenon differently. In the metaphorical context of the Norns' work I interpret it this way: Verðandi's sacred act of observation, taking place at the very instant of Becoming, turns a potential or a probability into an observable or experienceable phenomenon, a 'reality' in this space-time that we occupy. I relate this *wave function collapse* phenomenon, which moves something from a potential to an actual state or single *eigenstate,* to **Verðandi's domain** of the perpetual Now.

2) *Quantum entanglement.* "In quantum physics, a group of particles can interact or be created together in such a way that the quantum state of each particle of the group cannot be described independently of the state of the others, including when the particles are separated by a large distance. This is known as quantum entanglement."
https://en.wikipedia.org/wiki/Introduction_to_quantum_mechanics

I consider that quantum entanglement is analogous to the inescapable interconnections among our deeds, actions, our relationships with others, and the resulting ethical implications, as these relate to **Skuld's domain** of debt, obligation, and consequences.

3) *Wave-particle duality.* "Wave-particle duality is the concept in quantum mechanics that fundamental entities of the universe, like photons and electrons, exhibit particle or wave properties according to the experimental circumstances. It expresses the inability of the classical concepts such as particle or wave to fully describe the behavior of quantum objects. During the 19th and early 20th

centuries, light was found to behave as a wave then later was discovered to have a particle-like behavior, whereas electrons behaved like particles in early experiments then were later discovered to have wave-like behavior. The concept of duality arose to name these seeming contradictions."
https://en.wikipedia.org/wiki/Wave%E2%80%93particle_duality

I relate this wave-particle duality, this ambiguous nature of 'What-Is,' to **Urð's domain** of wyrd / orlog laid in the Well, which can take on different objective and subjective meanings, connotations, and implications depending on our angle of view.

Verðandi's Domain: Collapsing into an Eigenstate

Starting with Verðandi as the initiator of a new being, deed, or event: I've called her the Gatekeeper or the Midwife of the Quantum Realm. As I see it, the quantum realm is a feature of Ginnungagap, the gap of sacred and magical potential that is perpetually spun out between the two poles of Fire / energy and Ice / entropy. All-That-Is arises from this Gap, and undergoes shaping by Powers, Deities, and cosmogonic processes.

I envision Verðandi rather literally as an observing entity standing at the gateway between that which exists only in potential form, and that which exists at the macro level in the world we know: objects, phenomena, events, deeds, decisions, choices. She 'midwifes' the passage of these phenomena from potential to actual, and her presence as an observer on the edge of Ginnungagap, the cusp between 'what might be' and 'what is,' is what catalyzes or enables that passage to happen. As 'what might be' transitions from the quantum realm into 'what-is,' the realm of Midgard, it collapses from a probabilistic state into an observable one.

When that observable phenomenon enters our space-time with its own 'shape' and properties, in quantum mechanics this is called an *eigenstate,* from German *eigen* meaning 'one's own, belonging to oneself.' In quantum mechanics terms:

"Because of the uncertainty principle, statements about both the position and momentum of particles can assign only a probability that the position or momentum has some numerical value. Therefore, it is necessary to formulate clearly the difference between the state of something indeterminate, such as an electron in a probability cloud, and the state of something having a definite value. When an object can definitely be "pinned-down" in some respect, it is said to possess an eigenstate."
https://en.wikipedia.org/wiki/Introduction_to_quantum_mechanics

In terms relevant to this book, Verðandi's shaping creates the *eigenstate* for each being, event, phenomenon, that moves from potential into actual form. When it moves from the potential to the actual state it takes on its own individuality, its own characteristics, direction, momentum: its *eigenstate*.

Verðandi is the one who collapses Schrödinger's cat into aliveness or deadness by her function of observation or midwifing between the realms of 'potentiality' and 'actuality.' She is the catalyst that causes the 'potential' to become the 'actual' and to take its own shape, its *eigenstate,* as it does so.

Skuld's Domain: Quantum Entanglement

Moving on to Skuld: quantum entanglement deals with particles whose attributes have been entrained together, such as their direction of spin. No matter how far these particles are later separated from each other, changing the attributes of one results in a like change in the others. At the level where Skuld works, here is how I see this entanglement operating. We enact a deed or make a choice, and that has consequences down the line in our life and most likely in the lives of others as well. The more closely 'entangled' we are with others, the more our deeds and choices affect them as well as us. This is not something we can escape from or opt out of: it is inextricably entangled with our reality.

"Any measurement of a particle's properties results in an apparent and irreversible wave function collapse of that particle and changes the original quantum state. With entangled particles, such measurements *affect the entangled system as a whole.*" (my italics)
https://en.wikipedia.org/wiki/Quantum_entanglement

We can apply this understanding metaphorically in this way: the 'measurement of a particle's properties' is equivalent to solidly fixing something in physical space or in mental or emotional space. When something is measured scientifically it is fixed, recorded, solidified, as shown in the following description:

"Before a photon [a quantum particle] actually "shows up" on a detection screen it can be described only with a set of probabilities for where it might show up. When it does

appear, for instance in the CCD of an electronic camera, the time and space where it interacted with the device are known within very tight limits. However, the photon has disappeared in the process of being captured (measured), and its quantum wave function has disappeared with it. In its place, some macroscopic physical change in the detection screen has appeared, e.g., an exposed spot in a sheet of photographic film, or a change in electric potential in some cell of a CCD."
https://en.wikipedia.org/wiki/Introduction_to_quantum_mechanics

The location / existence of the quantum particle has been fixed in place through measurement / observation, but that process has caused a great change, a wave-function collapse, to happen to the particle, which then affects all the other particles it is entangled with. In subjective human terms, once a 'potential'—an impulse, a thought, an intention, a creation of our imagination—has been fixed in place by being spoken of, acted upon, or expressed in other ways, it has follow-on effects on everything / everyone that is 'entangled' with the speaker or actor. It has 'collapsed,' like a particle's probabilistic wave-function, from an unexpressed potential into a deed enacted in space and time. Because we are all, in many and varied ways, entangled with many other beings, phenomena, and events, what we say and do has effects upon them—perhaps tiny, meaningless effects, or perhaps larger, significant effects. And their words and deeds have effects upon us.

These effects are, to use another metaphor, equivalent to what I see as threads, strands, strings, ropes, cables, that Skuld attaches to the tapestry of our lives: our words and deeds, our choices and decisions. Bauschatz notes that:

The Quantum Nature of the Norns' Work

"Skuld seems to make reference to actions felt as somehow obliged or known to occur; that is, the necessity of their 'becoming' is so strongly felt or clearly known that they present themselves as available to be incorporated into the realms of Verthandi and Urth" (p. 14). "All occurrences (of *skulu* -> *Skuld)* express constraint, obligation, necessary continual action" (p. 13).

Using the analogy of weaving a complex tapestry, we can envision that a thin thread of shild / debt / obligation / consequence, attached to a particular orlog-thread in our tapestry of life, equates to some very minor pull on our wyrd-threads in that direction, one which we can overcome or change if we choose. A strong rope or cable, a powerful attachment of shild to our orlog, will be difficult or impossible to overcome: it approaches the force of 'necessity.' It will pull us strongly in the direction that Skuld has designated in response to the complexity of orlog that we have laid and that has been laid for us. In my view, shild / debt / obligation can range from being simply a slight tug in the direction of our orlog, to stronger influences pulling us in a specific direction, to the strongest of influences: necessity.

We can see the effects of our deeds on others and the world around us as 'entanglement in Space,' but I suggest that entanglement in Time is just as potent, and connects with our own orlog. We can view our past self and the deeds and choices of that past self as one particle, and our present self as the other particle with which it is entangled. What our past self did is affecting the state of our present self, and the same can be said about the deeds of our present self affecting the state of our future self.

The Quantum Nature of the Norns' Work

These 'Selves in Time' can be considered entangled particles, and it's an interesting philosophical question as to whether the effects of the quantum entanglement can work backwards in Time as well as forwards, when it comes to orlog. That's what we try to do with wergild or restitution, as one example: somehow mitigate, rebalance, repay by our present deeds for what happened to the other entangled particles—other persons in the past, or our own past self—as a consequence of our choices or deeds in the past. And we can try to work forward in time: making good choices, undertaking worthy deeds now, to lay desirable layers in the Well for our future self and for other persons and events that we affect by our actions.

The entanglements resulting from our actions, deeds, decisions—and our efforts to understand, acknowledge, and affect their impacts—lie within Skuld's domain. All of this complexity is based upon 'entanglement' as the *operational requirement* for the work of Skuld. If there were no entanglement, no necessary connection, between ourselves, our actions, and all the other beings and their actions upon the Tree, no shild / debt / obligation would arise from our actions. The concept of skuld / shild / debt / consequences rests upon and depends upon entanglement or inescapable interactions among beings and their deeds. Entanglement is not optional; it is a fact of life, and Skuld oversees the playing-out of this phenomenon.

Urð's Domain: Wave-Particle Duality

"The concept of wave–particle duality says that neither the classical concept of 'particle' nor of 'wave' can fully describe the behavior of quantum-scale objects, either photons or matter."

The Quantum Nature of the Norns' Work

Now we come to Urðr, who rules the domain of What-Is, what has been completed, established, put into place; what lies within the Well. We might think of this as unchanging: what happened, happened—there is no changing it. This is true, of course. Yet there's another factor at play when it comes to 'the Past' and human perceptions of and reactions to that Past. As individuals, families, cultures, nations, we base some of our self-image, our understanding of the context of our lives, and our reactions to other people, on the past experiences of ourselves and of the groups we belong to. Our interpretations and our subjective sense of what happened in the past may have a large impact on our current decisions, actions, and attitudes.

Literature, films, historical analysis, psychoanalysis—many explorations have been made along the lines of: "what if this is not really what happened? Was there another side to this historical account that we're not told about? What if this influential person in history was actually different than what has been told about them? What if the story told in history is incomplete or even false? What if these events in my family history were greatly misinterpreted? What if I experienced a trauma that I don't remember, or 'remember' a trauma that never happened the way I thought it did?" And so forth. Exploring and answering such questions, at the personal or the cultural or societal level, can bring about many reactions and changes in understanding and attitudes. And with those changes, the personal or cultural orlog may shift direction, making subtle changes in its structure.

What Wyrd or Urðr has already laid down does not cease to exist. Yet what is laid down on top of those layers, the next layers that come, may reflect changed circumstances that Verðandi and Skuld have brought about,

The Quantum Nature of the Norns' Work

which in turn can affect our perception of and experience of 'the past' that we have access to. For humans, the Past that is real to us, subjectively, has as much power as the objective Past that lies within Urðr's domain. Skuld may make us aware of a debt, obligation, consequences arising from the past that we were previously unaware of, and that changes things for us even though 'the past' was not changed. Verðandi may sensitize us to a fuller awareness of what is now coming into being, which may open our eyes to a wider view in Time and Space. Our *perception* of the past has been changed, and that affects us in many of the same ways that orlog, the objective past, does. Our view changes, our perception and attitudes change, and with it our actions and reactions.

Here's an example: some terrible experience that many people lived through, like a war. The objective event was what it was: fighting, destruction, many actions by many people, much suffering. Yet, the impacts on each person, and what they did with the rest of their lives after the war, may differ considerably. Some might recover and make the best of their circumstances, others might not. Winners and losers will have different attitudes and interpretations of what happened. History is famously written by the winners, but the viewpoints, experiences and events relating to the losers might later resurface and change many people's interpretations of what happened and why it happened.

Thus, we lay new layers of orlog—these new, varying interpretations of the past—on top of the older layers. The resulting orlog then incorporates the effects of our changed attitudes and actions. This in effect changes the past, in the sense that the new layers we've laid are the result of, and influence our understanding of, the older layers. This is

The Quantum Nature of the Norns' Work

difficult to explain and picture! It involves shifting perceptions, subjectively shifting foundations, which are in turn part of the objective layers that Urðr lays down. This is why I liken it to the quantum theory of wave-particle duality.

Objective past, actual events, laid down by Urðr into the layers of orlog, can be thought of as 'particles' in this analogy. Subjective past as events experienced and interpreted by humans can be thought of as 'waves.' Depending on the 'experimental design, or method of observation,' on the ways we try to observe, perceive and understand the past, we may see something more like 'particles' or more like 'waves' as we plumb the mysteries of What-Is. Both objective and subjective perceptions are real to us, both have meaning, and shape our understanding and our actions.

I'm suggesting that at least from a human perspective, the Past / What-Is / Urð's domain can take on the ambiguous 'both / and' shape of quantum phenomena like light as both a wave and a particle. We think of the Past as fixed, but again from a human perspective and experience, reinterpretation of past events, new knowledge about past events, learning about past events from other people's perspectives, and so forth, really can change our present state of awareness and affect the actions we might take based on that new awareness. These reinterpretations themselves become new layers of orlog laid in the Well, and they affect future actions. Likewise, different people who all experienced the same event in their past may shape very different trajectories leading from that past event to their present—and different—states of being. Subjectively, 'the past' was a different thing to each of them, even when factually they experienced the same concrete event.

The Quantum Nature of the Norns' Work

This seems to me to resonate with the ambiguous nature of quantum reality as we currently understand it. Both objective 'particles' and subjective 'waves' of history and the past are contained within Urðr's domain. Based on a quantum physics analogy, our approach to understanding the past—our 'experimental design' or method of observation—affects whether we perceive 'waves' or 'particles.' Archaeology and paleontology lean more toward the objective, for example, but are still influenced by interpretive theories. Examining the personal letters and diaries of people who experienced a significant historical event, like a revolution, from different sides and perspectives offers a more subjective viewpoint that nevertheless sheds light on important aspects of history which can be obtained no other way. Even more subjective, though deeply meaningful, are methods like meditation and spaeworking or trance-working to understand aspects of our personal past, transpersonal past, ancestral past, or Heathen religious mysteries which are 'lost' to objective methods of study. There are many different 'experimental designs' or methods of observation that we might use to explore the past and the workings of orlog: both the mundane past and the more spiritual and esoteric aspects of it; and both objective and subjective aspects of all these layers of orlog.

In the reality of human experience and in the pursuit of wisdom rather than physics, I would say this: we perceive *both*—subjective and objective layers of orlog—laid together inextricably in the Well, however we approach our examination. For humans, at least, this 'wave-particle duality' of subjectivity plus objectivity inevitably shapes the layers that are laid there by our human actions, and shapes our understanding of the resulting orlog. We can never be

The Quantum Nature of the Norns' Work

100% objective and factual in our attempts to understand the past; there are too many unknowns, and our own cultural and personal contexts inevitably introduce subjective interpretations. And *therein lies its meaning, its significance, for us.*

We can't force orlog to appear to us as purely objective 'particles,' not waves, or vice versa. For us as humans, we are always dealing with 'both / and' views of the past: both objective and subjective views influencing each other. Personally, I think this is a good thing, because both viewpoints, subjective and objective, are essential for developing an understanding of orlog that leads to true wisdom. Wisdom incorporates not only factual, objective truth, but the deep meaningfulness that arises from subjective experience as well.

This exposition of objective / subjective experience of the past as particle / wave duality is only one example of how paradoxical understandings lie within the Well. There are many other ways we can apply the analogy of dual-manifestation to understand the domain of the Norns. As one contributor to this book, Svartheiðrinn, suggests, Wyrd herself is like the quantum phenomenon of light being both a wave and a particle. In Chapter 8, contrasting orlog and Wyrd, I noted the ambiguity of the ancient references: Wyrd sometimes appears as a personal being, other times as an impersonal phenomenon or process. Wyrd herself, in Svartheidrinn's and my perception, seems to have no issue with sometimes appearing as a person, other times as an impersonal phenomenon: both a particle and a wave. It seems as though she is presenting us with an existential riddle, like a koan, challenging us to plunge more deeply in our efforts to understand who and what she / it is.

The Quantum Nature of the Norns' Work

As for how Wyrd, the Norns, and the Deities themselves understand orlog: this is a mystery for us to pursue in our relations with them and by learning from them. Perhaps they stand outside the wave-particle dualities of subjectivity / objectivity and of personal being-ness / impersonal phenomena. They may have a completely different view of how things work, something other than what we understand as 'objective / subjective,' 'personal / non-personal.' I find this an intriguing idea to pursue with them!

The Quantum Nature of the Norns' Work

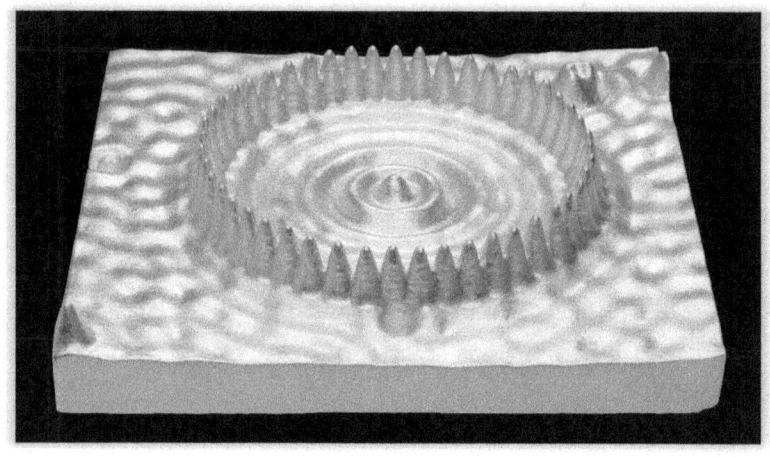

"The Well (Quantum Corral)"

A reproduction in gilded wood illustrating a physics phenomenon called a 'quantum corral.' The original image, published in Europhysics News, is described as a "scanning tunnelling microscope image of a circular 'quantum corral' made from 48 Fe (iron) atoms arranged in a 14.26 nm in diameter ring on a Cu (copper) surface." The sculpture artist renamed the image as "The Well."

Meditation on this image in the context of orlog and the Well provides some fascinating insights, in my experience, especially with respect to Bauschatz's descriptions of how the Well and the Tree work, with dew-drops falling from the Tree into the Well. The cone-shapes making up the ring each look like a miniature evergreen tree surrounding the Well and the water dropping into it...another interesting symbol to consider in meditation.

21. The Work of the Three Wells

> *"There are...three wells at the base of Yggdrasil: Urth's Well, which is most obviously the well of the 'past'; Mimir's Well, which is the well of wisdom, and Hvergelmir, the well that is 'serpent-infested' and that 'seethes.' All three wells suggest fluidity, accumulation, and containment.... What their juncture uniquely signals...is a meaningful joining of 'wisdom' with a 'past'...that still 'writhes' like a serpent and 'seethes.'"* (Bauschatz p. xix.)

While we're on the subject of 'weird ideas,' I'd like to share some of my thoughts about the three great Wells described in Norse mythology and how each of them relates to orlog, in my understanding. Each Well is located under one of the roots of Yggdrasil, as Snorri recounts in the prose Edda (p. 17). Beside one root are found both Urð's Well and the doomstead or assembly-place of the Æsir where they gather each day to discuss matters of the Worlds, make decisions and judgements. This positioning of the Norns' Well in the same place where the Æsir meet implies a close connection between the decisions of the Æsir and the orlog that the Norns lay in their Well. The implication is that the speaking of the Norns and the decisions of the Gods interact with each other, together arising from orlog in the Well, and at the same time laying new layers of orlog therein.

Mimir's Well

Mimir's Well is considered the Well of wisdom, memory and inspiration, and lies under the root which stretches out toward the realm of the Jotnar. Clues and hints in Norse poetry tell or imply that this well contains Oðrœrir, the Mead of Inspiration; that Odin drank from it to gain the wisdom of the great fimbul-galdors; that Odin's eye and Heimdall's hearing lie within the Well; that Mimir drinks mead from it daily, and Odin consults him for wisdom. Snorri tells us that this Well "has wisdom and intelligence contained in it and the master of this well is called Mimir. He is full of learning because he drinks of the well" *(Gylfaginning* in the prose *Edda,* p. 17). Though not entirely clear, Mimir's name is generally regarded as meaning "the rememberer, the wise one, and is etymologically related to Latin *memor"* (Simek p. 216), and also to modern English 'memory.'

Here is a photo of our shrine to honor Mimir's Head and Well. The head was carved by my husband; it is placed over a small pond on our homestead, overshadowed by a huge Yew bush, reflected in the pond here.

Mimir's Well is a place not only of wisdom, but also of the power of memory upon which wisdom rests. I envision

The Work of the Three Wells

Mimir's Well as functioning in a similar way to Urð's Well: as a container of memories—individual memories, ancestral memory, folk-memory, the collective unconscious—which are laid in layers within the Well as all of us go about living our lives, generation after generation. As 'significant' deeds fall into Urð's Well and are laid there as orlog, so also 'meaningful' memories are laid in Mimir's Well and ferment together into wisdom under the influence of Oðrœrir, the wode-stirrer, the fermenter of inspiration. When Mimir drinks from it daily, memories and wisdom are distilled together within his great being. My thought is that Odin's raven Muninn originated from this Well at the time that Odin was given a drink from it, after he came down from the Tree.

So, if we take this view, we can see that Urð's Well and Mimir's Well work in parallel ways, laying layers of orlog and of memory. The knowledge of these things leads to wisdom and to inspiration. History, poetry, tales, philosophy, culture, science and technology: all of them draw from memories, orlog, knowledge that was laid in the past. All of these aspects of culture and wisdom are woven out of that knowledge, those memories, which are fermented into wisdom and give rise to inspiration. Inspiration, expressed in a multitude of ways and actions, gives rise to new things: ideas, art, discoveries and inventions, insights, enlightenment. Thus, I believe, these two Wells of orlog / wyrd and of memory and inspiration work together as major drivers of human culture and history, wisdom and evolution, at the individual and the collective levels.

The Work of the Three Wells

Relationship between Mimir's and Norns' Wells

Here's an off-the-wall idea that strengthens the parallels between the work of Urð's Well and Mimir's Well. I find this speculation intriguing, though it is not well-attested in the lore. The Swedish scholar Viktor Rydberg has a lot of ideas that other scholars may not agree with from a research point of view, but which I find are enlightening and inspiring from a mythological point of view. One of those ideas goes like this, building from known myths to pure speculation:

(1) The 'boy and girl' that are generated under the arm of the proto-Giant Ymir are not named, but Rydberg suggests that they are really Mimir and Bestla. *(Vafðrudnir's Sayings, Poetic Edda,* v. 33)

(2) We are told in *Gylfaginning* that Bestla is the mother of Odin-Vili-Ve, while their father is Borr (prose *Edda,* p. 11).

(3) Rydberg suggests, through a very convoluted argument, that the Norns are *niptur,* or kinswomen, of Mimir (Ch. 85, vol. 2). The word *nipt* could mean either sister, daughter, or daughter of one's sister. In this view, the Norns could be daughters or nieces of Mimir, though unlikely to be sisters if the generation of Mimir and Bestla, alone, from Ymir is accepted.

If we add to this the idea that Bestla is Mimir's sister, and that there are instances of brother-sister matings in old Germanic and other mythologies, we could conclude that the Norns could be both daughters and nieces of Mimir through his sister Bestla.

The Work of the Three Wells

This is wildly speculative from a scholarly viewpoint, but from a mythological and cosmogonic perspective I find it attractive and meaningful. It provides a nice mythological structure: three brothers—Odin, Vili and Ve—shape the Space of Midgard by sacrificing and reshaping Ymir, while three sisters, the Norns, shape events in Time through their work with orlog. Together, they are shapers of Time and Space. They also all give gifts that shape our human-ness. *Önd, oðr, lö/la, læti, litr* are given to Ask and Embla by Odin and his brothers / comrades, turning the trees or logs into humans, while the shaping of orlog, of our fate of human-ness and all that fate implies, comes from the Norns. *(Völuspá* vs. 17-21 in the *Poetic Edda.)*

These sets of three beings are, in this view, half-siblings, with powers different than, but equal to, each other. Bestla is the mother of all of them; Mimir is the father of the Norns and the maternal uncle of Odin, Vili and Ve. There are additional clues in the lore, besides these speculations, indicating that Mimir and Odin are likely uncle and nephew through their relationships with Bestla, but I must emphasize that their relationships to the Norns are highly speculative.

This mythological viewpoint can further strengthen an understanding of the connections between the Wells of Mimir and the Norns. The work of the Well of orlog and wyrd is based upon—engendered by—the work of the Well of memory and inspiration, from father to daughters, in this view. I find this idea very meaningful, myself, and choose to include it in my understanding of Heathen mythology even though it is not well supported in the lore.

The Work of the Three Wells

There's Quantum here too...

If you've made it through the previous chapter about the quantum nature of the Norns' work, you may notice some aspects of the quantum analogy operating in Mimir's Well, too. Individual memories are particles, and they conglomerate together as *quantum entanglement*. We can't separate memories into individual bits, unconnected with their larger contexts in time and space. They come as packages of entangled particles. If our understanding of one memory, or piece of a memory, changes, this will affect the memory-bits that are entangled with that piece. If we suddenly bring into conscious awareness a memory that was previously unconscious, that changes the impact of many other memories we have.

The phenomenon of PTSD is one example of this entanglement: a cue or trigger occurs either in the outside world or in the memory, and it sets off a cascade of other highly debilitating memories that are associated with it. PTSD is very difficult to treat because of this memory-entanglement where so many cues cause the PTSD reaction instead of being seen in a different, harmless context.

Many forms of psychotherapy, and some forms of spiritual work too, focus on both remembering and reinterpreting one's memories so this memory-entanglement phenomenon can work positively and supportively rather than causing suffering and disability. We can see this as laying new layers of orlog to help address the effects of previous events.

This kind of work can apply to memories from one's current life, and to past lives and collective memories as well. This brings in something that I view as analogous to a *wave-particle* phenomenon. Our individual memories and current

The Work of the Three Wells

lifetime can be seen as particles. These particles are embedded within waves of larger contexts and events and are moved around and shaped by these turbulent waves: collective events of history and culture, of our families going back in time as well as larger collectives and the collective unconscious. When we make a choice or decision, take an action, interpret things in a certain way, shape our memories: how much of that comes from our own individuality—our own 'particle'—versus all the influences that work on this particle from the complex 'waves' of culture, society, history around us? It's not always easy to discern what is a 'particle' and what is a 'wave' within the Wells of Mimir and the Norns!

So, we can see analogies to quantum entanglement and wave-particle behavior in the contents of Mimir's Well. What about the *Eigenstate?* Recall that 'Eigenstate' refers to what happens when something collapses out of a cloud of probabilities / possibilities into a phenomenon with its own observable characteristics—an actualized rather than a probabilistic state. This is exactly what happens during inspiration! We sort of swim through a cloud of possibilities as we brainstorm—possibilities like the form a piece of art or a poem or song might take, or seeking a discovery of some kind, or the solution to a problem that's bugging us—and as we brainstorm, inspiration happens. Out of these clouds of vague possibilities, inspiration causes an Eigenstate to coalesce into being—the thing we're looking for: art, song, solution, discovery, new idea, whatever, that our inspiration has shaped and our actions solidify for us.

This inspiration is an expression of wode or óðr, which is inspired by Oðrœrir, the wode-stirring mead that resides in Mimir's Well and is Odin's gift to poets, scholars and wise-folk. Snorri says that those who drink of Oðrœrir become skalds (poets), or become *frœðamaðr:* wise, scholarly, knowledgeable persons *(Skaldskarpamal* p. 62 in the prose *Edda).* In this quantum analogy I would call the Eigenstate a manifestation of wode / oðr working upon a cloud of memories and possibilities lying within Mimir's Well, catalyzing the formation of a new idea that is then manifested into observable reality through us as living beings.

Hvergelmir and the World-Mill

Here are my thoughts about the nature of Hvergelmir and its role in the operation of the cosmos and of orlog. These ideas are based on old lore about the beginning of the Worlds, but move on from there into ideas influenced by modern understandings.

The cosmic polarities of Fire and Ice, energy and entropy, spin out between them a force-field which is mythically represented as Ginnungagap, the space where manifestation arises. In the center of that gap, the push-pull activity of Fire and Ice creates a maelstrom of energy called Hvergelmir, the Roaring Cauldron of cosmogenesis. Out of this cosmic Well flow the Elivagar, rivers of turbulent energy that eddy and curl around areas of empty space to create fields of potential where the Worlds can come into being as Eigenstates, manifesting out of potentiality into actuality through the shapings of the Great Powers.

The Work of the Three Wells

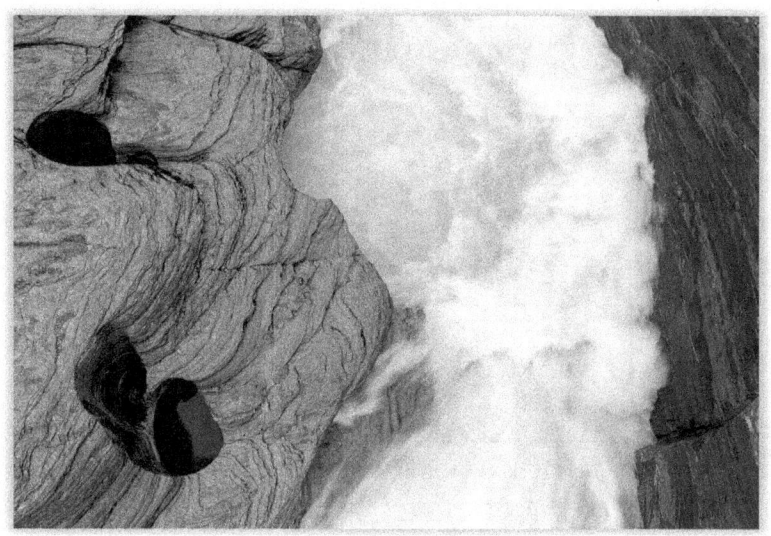

An image of Hvergelmir, the Roaring Cauldron, enclosed by layered rock formations symbolizing layers of orlog.

Another image that is widespread in Indo-European and other mythologies is the World-Mill, an image that captures the turning wheel of the heavens and the changing seasons from the perspective of Earth. (See deSantillana's *Hamlet's Mill: An Essay on Myth and the Frame of Time.)* The sea is called 'Hamlet's Mill' (Amlode's mill) in a passage from *Skaldskarpamal* (prose Edda, p. 92), and maelstroms / huge whirlpools in the ocean are attributed to the presence of a giant mill on the bottom of the sea. A legend about Amlode / Hamlet tells that he pretended to be insane and called sandbanks "meal (flour) from the mill of the storms," perhaps a reference, again, to the sea as 'Hamlet's Mill.' *(Saxo Grammaticus, Book Three.)*

Here the imagery reflects the ocean's churning, grinding power. As this giant mill under the sea turns, it creates the tides and the movements of the heavenly bodies around the earth. It also grinds up stone into sand and clay.

A drawing by Olaus Magnus, Swedish cartographer (1490 – 1557). "On the Maelstrom and the Tides of the Ocean."

Viktor Rydberg in his *Teutonic Mythology,* chapter 80 (vol. 2) discusses this grinding action of the World-Mill, in particular as it relates to Ymir and other giants. The idea is that when giants (who are rock-beings) die, they are placed in the World-Mill and ground up into sand and clay, then cast up onto the shores of Midgard to form the soil of earth. Hence the kenning for sand as the 'meal from the mill of storms.' The famous line from the fairy-tale 'Jack the Giant-Killer' echoes this myth, where the giant threatens to 'grind Jack's bones to make his bread.'

A more recent branch of Heathenry, Urglaawe, is based on Deitsch ('Pennsylvania Dutch') traditions and folklore. The Mill plays an important role for them in the form of Holle's Mill, the mill of the Goddess Frau Holle, which 'processes' people's souls for rebirth, as Hamlet's Mill 'processes' giants for recycling. (Schreiwer p. 46.)

When we put all this imagery together—Hvergelmir, the World-Mill, Hamlet's Mill, Holle's Mill, the mill at the bottom of the sea churning out sand and storms—we have a consolidated image of a cosmic process out of which new things arise (cosmogenesis), but which also breaks down and processes what is old and worn out into different forms for recycling. The roaring turbulence of Hvergelmir lies at the root of this process, powered by Fire and Ice, churning out a perpetual process of cosmogenesis. In its upper layers we can envision the World-Mill, powered by Hvergelmir's energy, which turns the Worlds and recycles the materials of those worlds.

Entropic Inversion and Orlog

In different terms, I envision this as a process of entropic inversion. The second law of thermodynamics describes entropy as an inevitable or necessary process where ordered systems gradually become disordered, losing the energy needed to maintain their ordered structure, and eventually break down altogether. When I describe this as a 'necessary' process I'm linking up with Skuld's domain here. But for her, I believe, this 'necessity' works both ways.

It seems clear to me that the shapings of all three Norns together are directed toward an underlying order, and an increase of complexity, that supports biological life and social systems, even when individual events may be disruptive. While we are gestating in the womb, the physical and spiritual elements that make up our being are gathered together and intricately ordered and coordinated. This is 'uphill' work from a physics point of view, requiring large inputs of energy on both physical and spiritual levels. As I see it, our Aldr soul plays an important role in this process as one who nourishes us with life-force to support this ordering process. As we age and decline, our energy diminishes and eventually at death all the life-energy is gone and the body decomposes. The time of *aldr-lag,* of *ealdor-legu,* arrives, when our Aldr is laid down in death. This is entropy at work, and the same process occurs within ecosystems and social systems.

The Norns are in charge of both ends of this process of weaving energy into functioning systems, and the necessary breakdown of those systems caused by entropy—the 'orlog-while' of each system or being. They choose life for us, and set the terms of our death. They, along with the wisdom and memory of Mimir's Well, shape the rise and fall of societies and cultures through layers of orlog. The waves of energy and entropy ebb and flow, and along with them, all the phenomena of life in Midgard. Underlying this process are the actions of Hvergelmir and the World-Mill, the genesis and the breaking down of that which was generated, in a perpetual ebb and flow.

When I use the term 'entropic inversion,' what I mean is this ebb and flow, this building up and breaking down, but then the reversal of that flow into building up again—flowing out in an ongoing process of renewal. When anything comes into being, energy at some level is required to create and maintain it. When that energy is dispersed it breaks down and loses its ordered nature. In physics, that's the end of the story. In myth and on the spiritual levels, it's not. While Ice, as entropy, imposes stillness, stability, stagnation, Fire perpetually generates more energy—energy that is uncontrolled, unshaped, unstable. Where they meet in the middle in Hvergelmir, this roaring cauldron contains both potentials—energy and entropy, force and form, flux and stability, creation and destruction: all mixed together in potential form.

The Work of the Three Wells

How does this apply to orlog and its manifestation in the Worlds? I think this link comes through the 'necessity' of the Norns and Wyrd, and it works in a circular way. First, there is a necessary movement toward life and order, followed by the necessity of disorder and dissolution, but then there is again the movement toward genesis and renewal. These flows shape the Worlds of life, then move toward Ragnarök and their breakdown. And after the breakdown and a time of quiescence, the Earth arises again, green and fertile, out of the waters of the sea....and out of the World-Mill and Hvergelmir underlying those waters.

The seeds of decline and dissolution are laid at the beginning of anything that is coming into being. But the cosmic processes of generation and regeneration lie even deeper than that, inverting the action of entropy and dissolution. All that becomes, dissolves, but also forms the raw material for new beginnings.

We can make conscious use of this process, on an individual spiritual level, when we wish to transform harmful layers of orlog in our lives into more life-supporting layers, and lay new threads on the loom of wyrd that is our life. This work is energized by love for self and others, by trust and faith in Heathen works and ways, and by work with the Holy Ones. It uses as its raw material the wisdom and inspiration from Mimir's Well and the orlog that lies in Urð's Well. But it also depends profoundly on work with Hvergelmir and the World-Mill: being willing to let go, to accept loss and sacrifice, to repay our shild, to pay whatever price must be paid, to allow to die that which must die: the full acceptance of necessity. All is cast into that great, churning cauldron of inversion and transformation, with no way of knowing what may then be cast up again by the

The Work of the Three Wells

World-Mill onto the shores of our inner being, to be gathered up and laid as new layers of orlog in our life.

I have created a ritual that is based on this work of the three Wells, which you can use to structure such a process of transformation if you wish. It's presented in Chapter 31: "Wyrd and Shild: A Ninefold Rite of Life-Renewal." This chapter on The Work of the Three Wells provides the theoretical basis for that ritual.

An ancient, sacred well in England enclosed in a stone hut.

Part V. Heathen Perspectives on Orlog Today

Masses of molten rock seethe below the surface of the Earth, then erupt to become layers laid at the surface. They wear away by erosion, are deposited in layers again, and slowly become covered by new layers. Then these layers of solid rock laid down in ancient times slowly writhe up again to the surface of the Earth, re-orienting and even changing into different minerals under geologic pressures. They are still layers laid by Earth and Time; they have not disappeared, but they have shifted and altered.

The molten, churning depths of the Earth itself, far below the surface, echo the seething layers of evolving orlog, and of Hvergelmir, the Roaring Cauldron of cosmogenesis, breakdown, and renewal.

22. Orlog and Wyrd: Some Modern Perspectives

Orlog and wyrd are not simply strange ideas from the past...well, they are not anything 'simple,' in any case! Many modern people—Heathens, Wiccans, Pagans, Animists, esotericists, mages, and others—understand and work with wyrd, in many different ways and contexts. One reason we've focused on orlog here, more than on wyrd itself, is because the term 'wyrd' is used in so many different ways and contexts today. Orlog is a less familiar term, especially outside of Heathenry, which makes it easier to focus on its older meanings and contexts aside from modern ideas about it. Throughout this book, of course, our reasoning and discussions are obviously modern people's thoughts and conclusions about orlog and wyrd, even though we try to tie our thoughts to ancient understandings. In this chapter I'll mention just a small sample of the many modern Heathen perspectives on these topics.

Orlog and Wyrd: Some Modern Perspectives

A Modern Summary

Here is a summary of some modern Heathen perspectives on the difference between orlog and wyrd, as discussed by Ben Waggoner in *Our Troth vol. 3: Heathen Life.*

"The usual interpretation today is that *ørlǫg* is the sum of all the deeds and choices of a person's ancestors. *Ørlǫg* is the basal layer of wyrd, which determines the shape of life from beginning to end, and it determines how much main and luck a person will receive. ... Wyrd, on the other hand, is used to refer to the way that individuals' choices and deeds shape and constrain the outcomes of their lives. You can't do much about your *ørlǫg*—but you shape your wyrd every day, and ultimately those shapings influence the *ørlǫg* of everyone who comes after you." (pp 70-71).

In this perspective, orlog is the past, wyrd is the present which also shapes what is coming into being in the future. Wyrd shaped in the present ultimately lays or becomes the orlog of our pasts and shapes what is coming into being in the next generations. This perspective is focused on 'living Heathen' in daily life, living life with and through a Heathen understanding of how life, orlog and wyrd work.

A Nature-Psyche Approach

Matthew Ash McKernan is a psychotherapist focused on helping people to heal through the context of their relationships with Nature and with Wyrd. In his beautiful book *Wyrdcraft: Healing Self & Nature through the Mysteries of the Fates,* he describes the Web of Wyrd in this way.

Orlog and Wyrd: Some Modern Perspectives

"Our life-threads weave together, along with the life-threads of countless other beings and things, near and far. Each thread is composed of countless finer threads, each with its own constellation of elements, raw materials, patterns, and stories, as well as its own purposes playing out within the greater weave and web of life into which we are all woven... called the Web of Wyrd. Within it, everything is connected to everything else: all plants, all animals, all ecosystems, all matter, all phenomena, all purposes, all meanings, all processes, all possibilities—all interwoven. (pp. 1-2)

He explains further: "Wyrd, too, is a feeling. In fact, wyrd is an experiential phenomenon. Wyrd is first and foremost sensed... Wyrd is not an abstraction of some bigger-picture being or force that remains forever out of reach; it is a lived experience in the here-and-now. Yes, wyrd can be understood intellectually, but it can only be *known* somatically, emotionally, and relationally—within and through your tender mortal body." (McKernan p. 17)

This is an embodied ecological and psychological approach to understanding wyrd as oneself embedded within a greater whole, where attunement with that whole promotes health for the individual and the whole, together. The focus here is less on Time and divisions of time, more on our interactions in Space, within the Web, shaping and nourishing the World-Tree.

A View from Heathen Magic

Cat Heath is a Heathen who has developed an approach to magic based solidly on her many years of research into and experimentation with old Heathen practices and Heathen-

Orlog and Wyrd: Some Modern Perspectives

oriented folklore. She lays out this approach in her book *Elves, Witches, and Gods: Spinning Old Heathen Magic in the Modern Day*. Cat offers this insight on how orlog and magic intersect.

"When we enter this world we have *ørlög*, or "primal-law." This is what the Norns give us. And as time goes on, our actions, the relationships we build, and the choices we make all set down new layers of action. Over time, if we make the same kinds of choices, and continue to act in a certain way, we may find that our life seems to have recurring themes that crop up again and again. On a magical level, I've found it useful to view magical workings in a similar way." (p. 105)

(Following this, Cat offers examples of magical workings drawn from historical sources, which lead her to this conclusion) "…if we wish to create permanent magical change, that change must be worked repeatedly and over a period of time. In other words, we must set down enough layers of magical action for the desired result to become one of those recurring themes in life." (p. 106)

Here we see the practice of magic tapping into the process of orlog, so as to actively / magically lay desired layers in orlog. This practice can also apply to other ways of making changes in one's orlog, such as changing bad habits into good ones.

A Devotional Perspective

Here is the response of a modern Heathen, Zachary Kolb, during a discussion in a Norns devotional group about the question 'Can we have a personal relationship with the Norns?'

"When it comes to the Three Keepers, Shapers, and Weavers that are the Norns we commonly think of, to me their presence is so great and diffused that we know them without realizing it. In everything Wyrd touches, we know them, we feel them, and they feel us, they *know* us. But our minds cannot fully comprehend them, so it makes knowing them in the form of a more personal relationship untenable. That said, the personal nornr that works as part of our Disir *can* form a more personal relationship with us. As can the Gods who act in direct accord with them. So, in a roundabout way, I'm saying yes and no and a secret third thing."

A Tale-Teller's Insights

Here is one more perspective I'd like to share. One of the many factors that make JRR Tolkien's writings so appealing is his sense of the old Germanic cultures and mindsets. That includes the sense of orlog—not the term itself, but the sense of it—that permeates his tales of Middle Earth. I like this description of his approach:

"No reader of the *Lord of the Rings* (1954-5) can fail to notice how the past grows ever more present in its unfolding story. …landscapes increasingly bear witness to the events of thousands of years before that have continued to resonate down through the centuries… (People, places, artifacts)…all tying the fate of the present to a destiny laid down in Middle Earth's deepest history." (Day, p. 8.)

There is much in this that resonates for me: the idea of the landscape itself being involved, just as much as people and other beings are involved, with the unfolding of fate. We are a part of the landscape, and it is part of us. All of us are interwoven: heroes, *einherjar*-type champions, may stand out from the crowd, but they depend on the 'smaller' players just as much as those players depend on the champions. We are all part of an interactive whole, and this insight sheds light on another vital perspective for us here: the need to consider group and collective orlog as well as individual orlog. The next three chapters, on collective orlog and orlog that arises from people's long-term interaction with the land, delve more deeply into these vital interconnectivities of orlog.

23. Collective and Group Orlog

An Overview of Collective Orlog

Legacies do not come to us only from individuals; we all partake in legacies and influences that come to us from the orlogs of groups and collectives that we are embedded in, from the family on up to humanity itself. In the modern Western world there is a great deal of emphasis on individuality, more so than in other cultures in other places and times, including ancient Heathen cultures. In older, more traditional cultures, Heathen included, the collective nature of orlog and fate were more in the forefront of their minds. We are all integral parts of groups and collectives, whether we deliberately choose to be, or not, and of the orlogs that these collectives create. Both individuality and the more interconnected group-consciousness have their strengths and weaknesses, and in truth both forms of awareness are essential, I believe, for the full development of human experience, spirituality, and for the full maturation of ourselves as ethical beings.

Individuality promotes the ethical stance of personal responsibility: "I am responsible for my deeds, responsible for and to myself, and responsible for developing my full

Collective and Group Orlog

being in all dimensions: my abilities, talents, wisdom, the powers of my body, mind, heart, and souls, in my own unique ways. I am called to be true to myself, and be the best that I can be." This stance is a strong and good one. But none of us exist in a vacuum; we are part of collectivities that reach much farther in space and time than our own individual lives. Our responsibilities—as individuals and as members of multiple overlapping collectivities in space and time—extend beyond the scope of our individual lives. An understanding of orlog on group levels as well as on the personal level hugely enhances the breadth and depth of our grasp of orlog as a whole.

Orlog is entangled with our genetic heritage, with culture and history, with political, social and economic structures, with the development of languages and dialects, knowledge, technology, with the movements and actions, conflicts and cooperations of small and large groups of people. All of what we are, individually and collectively, consists of layers laid throughout history, and what we make of, and build upon, those layers. As individuals we are embedded within these larger layers of group and collective orlog, whether we recognize and acknowledge that, or not.

A difficult ethical question lies in the concept of group shild—moral debt or obligation—that results from the actions of any group or collective that we are a part of, that we participate in and benefit from. We are inescapably a part of groups and collectives that extend beyond ourselves in time and in space: for example, our economic system and the actions of our government, and our culture, society, and kinship relationships that extend into the past. To what extent is each individual responsible for the shild, the debt or moral obligation, that is / was accrued by groups and collectives that the individual is a part of, or an inheritor of? These are painful and difficult issues fraught with disagreements; there are no quick and easy answers to these questions.

One of the ethical points that belongs in these considerations is the difference between 'guilt' and 'responsibility.' We may have little or no personal *guilt* or blame for decisions and actions that we were not personally involved with and could not have prevented. But our membership within the larger group involved in those actions, and the benefits we gain from that membership, may indicate that we have some *responsibility* to participate in acknowledging and mitigating whatever harm was done by that group. It's important to keep this understanding of the difference between 'guilt' and 'responsibility' in mind as we ponder these aspects of orlog. I discuss this further in Chapter 31, "Wyrd and Shild: A Ninefold Rite of Life Renewal."

In many cultures and places around the world, people believed in the past, and believe now, that there is such a thing as 'the fates of nations, people, tribes, cultures.' Orlog is in operation at this level, too, though the true orlog may be quite different, and less appealing, than the 'great destiny' that groups of people may imagine for themselves. Too often, the 'great destiny' of one group may take no account of the 'destinies' that other groups may have, which can bring about conflict between them.

Recall that in the old non-Norse Germanic languages 'orlog' also had the meaning of 'battle, conflict, adversity, strife.' Group orlogs may often lead to conflict, and result from conflict, in layers laid over time between competing groups of people. We can easily see, by looking around the

Collective and Group Orlog

world today, how layers of history lead to ongoing conflict among groups: culture wars, social and political conflict, economic and class conflicts, struggles over identity, rights and freedoms, religious and ideological conflicts, conflicts over land and resources, warfare, exploitation, oppression, and rebellion. Conflicting interpretations of the orlog / history underlying each group that participates in the conflict play a major role. The longer and more deeply orlog has been laid by the history underlying each conflict, the more intractable and embedded in orlog the conflicts become. This is a bitter and frustrating legacy of the human condition, and needs to be countered by the gradual and deliberate laying of layers of frith to counteract the 'strife' aspect of orlog.

Group / collective orlog and the shild that is included within it is a huge subject; it reaches deeply into the roots of being for us as individuals and for all groups and collectives. Orlog is laid by deeds and actions, and groups engage in these just as much as individuals do. The older and more cohesive a group or collective is, the more impact their orlog has on them, and perhaps on others as well—for good and for ill. Identity, culture, sense of belonging, customs, language, belief systems: all of these are part of who we are, and all of them are rooted in the orlogs of collectives we are embedded in, from the family on up to humanity itself. All of them strongly influence us as individuals: they are the social, cultural, and spiritual environment or ecosystem within which we individuals—and our orlog—are embedded.

The topic of collective orlog is a much greater one than we can delve into in this book, but we do have other chapters that pick up on various strands of the topic. Sara has a short essay, following this one, that gives an everyday personal example of what individual orlog embedded within group orlog looks like. Sara's Chapter 24 on "Orlog of our Relationship with Land" explores the topic in more depth, and I address it again in Chapter 25, "Beyond Individual Orlog." In Chapter 26 about "Oathing in Symbel" and Chapter 27 on "The Symbel Mysterium" I consider aspects of group orlog in the context of this Heathen ritual. We encourage you, as you think through and work through the material we offer in "Part VI: Orlog Awareness in Practice," to consider how group and collective orlogs as well as personal orlog play out in your own life and your own spiritual journey.

Sara: Personal Orlog Embedded in Group Orlog

By Sara Axtell

What can it mean to consider our orlog not just as individual humans, but as families, as communities, as whole cultures? I have come to believe that these layers are often intertwined, and that the patterns of action that are most resilient (or intractable depending on perspective) involve threads of orlog from multiple levels. Let's look at a hypothetical example and try to identify the different levels of orlog at play.

A woman (let's call her Laura) and her partner (let's call him Brian) are experiencing conflict. She finds herself taking on the bulk of the chores in their shared household. Rather than discussing her feelings with her partner, she holds her emotions in, and her annoyance comes out in other ways, leading to arguments and ill feeling. Her partner is aware

Collective and Group Orlog

that something is wrong, that his partner is in distress, but does not understand why and does not ask.

What layers and levels of orlog might be shaping this situation? First there is the orlog that shapes the work that each partner does to support the household. Each of the partners have patterns of action that were laid in earlier romantic relationships. Perhaps in Brian's past relationship, there was a pattern of his female partner doing the inside-the-house chores while he performed the outside chores. While in Laura's prior relationship, she and her partner talked each week to plan who would do which chores.

Those personal orlog patterns interweave with family patterns in the orlog. Perhaps they each grew up seeing their mothers engaging in the same household work. Brian has continued this pattern in the orlog while Laura has tried to shift it. These patterns exist in the context of larger cultural patterns, where many generations laid patterns of sharing household work in a way that fell along gendered lines. (Of course, there are also different ways of dividing household work that are also in the Well, albeit not as strongly, and Laura is trying to reweave her own thread into these alternate patterns.)

There is also orlog that shapes the way the two are communicating. Again we may start by looking at individual layers of orlog. Perhaps in an earlier relationship, Laura's partner berated her each time she attempted to express her feelings. In response to this, she learned to keep her feelings to herself. Perhaps when Brian was a teenager, family members often asked him to share his feelings in a way that felt intrusive. In response he began laying a pattern of not sharing his own feelings, and not asking about others' feelings, in order to respect their privacy.

Collective and Group Orlog

These personal orlogs are not laid in a vacuum. There is also broader orlog at work. Gender shapes how we learn to express our feelings and talk about our needs, or how we don't talk about our feelings and needs. People of our gender, over generations, have laid patterns around emotional expression and communicating needs (perhaps embedded in societal patterns and power structures). We inherit these patterns and may either take them on or reject them, push against them, and work to shift them. There may also be cultural patterns at work. If Laura and Brian are of Scandinavian-American origin, for example, they may have inherited a pattern of stoicism, of not sharing feelings, or of communicating them through silences and things left unsaid.

We can quickly see how any situation in our lives may be connected to multiple threads of orlog on multiple levels. When we want to try to change a situation, or heal the weave of orlogs, we may attempt to do healing on any of these levels, or all of them at once. I think that is why healing orlog is often aided by a collective process in which we are talking together about the patterns that are in play and how we might change them together.

Collective and Group Orlog

Note: This discussion mirrors a theory in social science called the social ecological model, that posits we are all nested within concentric circles of influences, for example, family, community, and societal influences. Look here for an overview:

https://www.ebsco.com/research-starters/environmental-sciences/social-ecological-model.

24. *Sara:* Orlog of Our Relationship with Land

By Sara Axtell

Weaving Patterns

The weaving metaphor for orlog gives us tools for understanding how the patterns we are currently living have evolved, and ways we can begin to transform or heal patterns that are damaging. To work with this metaphor, it helps to understand some fundamentals of weaving. In the photo on the next page, you see a weaving project on my rigid heddle loom. There are warp threads (the vertical threads in this photo) and weft threads (the horizontal threads). At the outset of a weaving project, the warp threads are strung onto the loom. They are stable; they provide a structure. They don't change during the course of the weaving. The weft threads are threaded back and forth through the warp. They are more dynamic, more changeable.

Orlog of our Relationship with Land

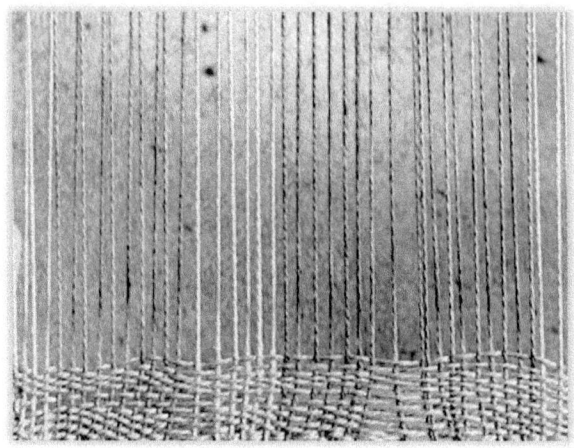

Karen Bek-Pedersen (2009), in her work on weaving as a metaphor for fate in medieval Scandinavia, sees the warp threads as orlog–set but not revealed until the weft of our actions shows the pattern. We can understand the warp threads as fundamental truths that create our reality. Our actions are woven into these fundamental truths. Different weft threads can change how these fundamental truths look as they unfold.

Primstav

I am a part of a learning community that is studying the orlog of our relationship with land. The group is called "Primstav: Land, Time, and Unsettling Ourselves." The *primstav* is an old Norwegian 'perpetual calendar' that describes human-land relations in different seasons. Symbols carved on this wooden primstav mark the times that certain work should be done on the farm, when land ceremonies should be performed, and the actions of plants and animals who share the landscape. A primstav is about the size and shape of a yard stick (or *lefse* turner!) and has two sides—one for summer and one for winter. Here is an example of a primstav, also called a runic calendar, from the Norwegian Museum of Cultural History. (Unfortunately, my own primstav does not show up well in a black and white photograph!)

Figure 1. Summer side

Figure 2. Winter side

What I share in this essay represents some of my own learnings from our primstav study, from my personal perspective as a Norwegian descendant who is racialized as white and living in what is now considered the midwestern

Orlog of our Relationship with Land

United States. But I believe that any of us could use a similar approach to understanding the orlog of any feature of shared culture and the ways that our personal and family orlog intertwine with that feature. We can trace back the layers of orlog to understand what shapes our current realities and potentially look for earlier threads of orlog to reweave into our everyday lives.

Relating to the Land

In terms of my current example, many would say that in this historical moment, there are severe ruptures in our relationships to land (e.g., Hjarnø Rasmussen, 2021; Wyn, 2023). We can see the impacts of these disruptions in our sense of kinship with Nature playing out in the climate chaos we are all experiencing. But also in a sense of uprootedness, and a yearning for connectedness.

How did this disconnection happen? And what could be a pathway back to a deeper sense of connection? In this essay, I will offer some ideas for how we can use weaving as a metaphor to understand our relationships with the landforms, plants, animals, and other-than-humans we live among as an example of how we can examine this cultural or group level of orlog.

What comprises the warp threads of this orlog, the fundamental truths that structure the realities of these relationships? I think we could argue that our dependence on landforms and on other species—the *feorh-cynn* or *feorh-kin,* an Anglo-Saxon word for the 'kindred of living beings'—is one of these fundamental truths. Plant-and animal-kin provide us with the food we eat and the air we breathe. How we act within these relationships is the weft. We have examples in the lore of practices that allowed earlier generations to be generatively engaged with the web of relationships in which they were a part. What events and circumstances led to such dramatic changes in these relationships?

There are so many layers and complexities, it is difficult to grasp the enormity of it. But here are some of the weft threads that we have studied in our Primstav learning community. These by no means represent the only important layers in the orlog, but I offer them to spark our thinking. I encourage you to reflect on your own personal, family, and cultural histories and the threads of orlog that contribute to your own relationship to land. (Note: for an examination of how these histories have unfolded in Canada, see Wyn's excellent series, *How the Northern European Forest Commons Can Inform Modern Heathen Practice in Canada.*)

Gift for a Gift

Norse and Germanic cultures (as with many traditional cultures across the globe) centered reciprocity with the *landvættir*—the land-wights or land-spirits, plant-kin, animal-kin and landforms in their kinship circles. These acts formed the rhythm of the seasons: offering a loaf of bread to the field at the beginning of summer, leaving the last stalks of grain at the harvest, preparing porridge for the nisse—the house-wight or farm-wight, and special foods for the birds and cattle during Jul / Yule (Hjarnø Rasmussen, 2021).

In the following illustration of my orlog-weaving, we "read" the orlog from the bottom up. The ur-layer of my (not very expert) weaving is an interweaving of browns and greens representing the circle of feorh-kin into which we are weaving our own presence. The next layer is handspun linen weft representing these practices of gift for a gift.

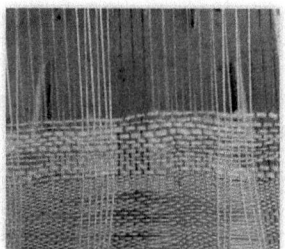

Odal land

Odalsrett, meaning 'the rights associated with ancestral land' in Norwegian, describes an ancestral relationship with land in which generations of a family, including both living and dead members, had a relationship with a farm. Caring for ancestors through practices like offerings at grave mounds was part of the obligations in this odal relationship (Zachrisson, 1994). Within the concept of odal land was a sense of belonging to the land: "The man possessed the farm, but at the same time the farm possessed him" (Gurevich, 1985, p. 48 as cited in Zachrisson, 1994). In 1814, *odalsrett* was enshrined in the new Norwegian constitution at a time when other Scandinavian countries were dismantling their parallel legal frameworks for ancestral land. One argument that was made in favor of maintaining *odalsrett* was that land was not a commodity and the nature of humans' relationship to land should be maintained (Dackling, 2021). This relationship with land both expresses and builds upon the gift for a gift relationship and strengthens the layer of kinship in the weave.

In the photo on the next page, above the lower layers of brown and green, I have woven in a layer of tan colored hand-spun wool yarn to represent this extension/expansion of gift-for-a-gift practices.

Land Consolidation in Norway

In the 1800's and early 1900's, there was a series of transitions in the patterns of settlement and land use in Scandinavia, overviewed by Lundberg (2008). Prior to 1870, the farm buildings of multiple families were arranged in a cluster, called a *tun*. Each farm complex used an open field strip system in which different areas of the farm were divided into strips, or *teiglag*. This word for a strip of land incorporates the word 'lag' or layers, here laid horizontally next to each other rather than vertically the way we usually envision orlog. The process of dividing and apportioning these strips was based upon the complex orlog of ownership, relationships, and rights extending over centuries.

Each family had rights to multiple strips of each section of the farm, so that there was a kind of patchwork of these strips, with different families' holdings interspersed with other families' holdings. Grazing lands were held in common, as were some of the areas used for peat harvest. This organization of farms dates back at least as far as the early medieval Gulating law code, replacing an earlier system of common ownership called *jordfellesskapet*, meaning 'the shared earth-cupboard.'

From 1870 to 1910 land was consolidated and reallotted, so that rather than multiple strips, each family had fewer, larger holdings. This led to breaking up the cluster of farm homes, and a disruption of the associated social structure. It also allowed for and was facilitated by changes in farming technology. A spade was a tool well suited for working multiple strips or fragments of land, but consolidated holdings were better suited for horses and plows. Similar to enclosure in Britain, these land consolidations created a system which emphasized individual holdings and a shift away from collaborative farm work.

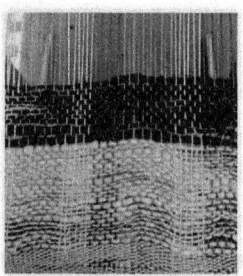

These changes are represented here by a layer of dark blue wool. It is a stark contrast, a departure from the structures that had supported the earlier relationships in which people had been embedded.

Emigration and Becoming Settlers

The early and mid-1800s saw other dramatic social and economic change in Norway as well. Changes in the textile industry and growth of the iron and metal industries were early contributors to industrialization (Danesi & Øvrebø, 2022). Changes in transportation facilitated greater internal mobility within Norway. An economy based on money was replacing earlier economic relations. And in the midst of these changes a depression emerged in 1879 that damaged both industry and agriculture (Semmingsen,1960). Along with a sharp population increase—between 1815 and 1865, the population of Norway doubled—these changes led to a mass emigration from Scandinavia in the mid-1800s.

Many who emigrated came to the upper midwest region in what was becoming the United States of America. Bergland (2020) described the role that Norwegian settlers played in the larger project of settler colonialism in the United States. Through war and broken treaties, Indigenous Nations were forcibly removed from their territories, and the fiction of 'empty' land for European settlement was created. Norwegian emigrant Ole Rynning's 1938 publication *A True Account of America* reinforced this fiction when he advised potential emigrants that, "Indians have now been transported away" (Bergland, 2020, p. 20).

In our primstav study group, many feel that this violence became interwoven with our relationship to land. "For descendants of settlers, reconnecting to our European roots requires us to face these histories, a task that often collapses into guilt, overwhelm, and immobilization. We need communal rituals and structures to support such an intense reckoning" (Axtell et al., 2024, p.29-30).

Development of the U.S. Food System

Settler colonialism re-shaped the landscapes and ecologies of what is now the United States, for example, through damming waterways (Harper, 2022) and clear-cutting forests

Orlog of our Relationship with Land

for the timber industry *(The Decolonial Atlas,* 2014). Policies like the Homestead Act (National Park Service, n.d.) and the Dawes Act (National Archives, 2022) imposed individual ownership and European style agriculture onto the landscape. Economic and infrastructure developments like commodity markets, the railroad system, and food processing companies helped to shape our current food system (Champion, n.d.) which requires extensive irrigation, pesticides, and herbicides and has led to erosion and depletion of groundwater (Center for Sustainable Systems, 2024.). It also leaves many of us who reside in the U.S. distant, both geographically and spiritually, from the sources of our food. The system is both a cause and a reflection of our relationship with land in this moment.

In the next layer of weaving here, I have represented these layers as pink and purple, which to me look unnatural and removed from the greens and browns further down in the weave.

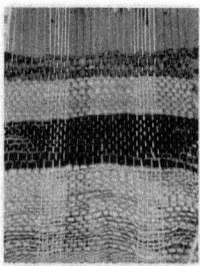

Joining new weft to our orlog

Reworking the Pattern

The weight of this orlog can be overwhelming. It can be hard to see around it or imagine anything different. But understanding a pattern can help to loosen its hold. It can

Orlog of our Relationship with Land

help us to step outside of the pattern to try something different. It can help us to find a pathway to something healthier by identifying threads within the weave that we can reconnect with and re-work into the orlog. Many of us are working to re-engage our reciprocal relationships with the land through offerings and ceremonies, or by helping to care for the soil and the waters. We can respect Indigenous sovereignty and participate in solidarity actions. We can re-invigorate the idea of the commons, through things like community gardens, tool and toy libraries, and other elements of a sharing economy. We can localize our food systems through community-supported agriculture or farmer's markets. We can't unweave the patterns that have been laid, but we can weave again the patterns that helped us to stay connected to the circles of kinship that support us.

References and Resources for this Chapter

Axtell, S., Brown, C., Brune, J., Lovett, K., Lovett, M., Springer, M., & Vangsness, A. (2024). "Healing roots and unsettling legacies." In Bremer, S. and Wardekker, A., *Changing Seasonality: How Communities are Revising their Seasons.* De Gruyter.
https://doi.org/10.1515/9783111245591

Bek-Pedersen, K. (2009). "Fate and weaving: justification of a metaphor." *Viking and Medieval Scandinavia,* 5, 23-39.

Bergland, B. A. (2020). "Norwegian migration and displaced indigenous peoples: Toward an understanding of Nordic whiteness in the land-taking." In *Nordic Whiteness and Migration to the USA* (pp. 17-34). Routledge.

Center for Sustainable Systems, University of Michigan. 2024. "U.S. Food System Factsheet." Pub. No. CSS01-06.
https://css.umich.edu/publications/factsheets/food/us-food-system-factsheet

Champion, B. (n.d.) "Historical Development of U.S. Food System."
https://www.k-state.edu/mog/resources/Historical%20Development%20of%20 U.S.%20Food%20System.pdf

Danesi, R., & Øvrebø, P. (2022). *Manufacturing in historical national accounts: when was Norway industrialised? Identifying the time of the Norwegian industrialization using empirical evidence on business cycles and growth* theory based on new historical GDP figures (1816-1939). Master's thesis, Norwegian School of Economics.

Dackling, M. (2021) "Traditional or modern peasants? odelsrett and bördsrätt in parliamentary debates, 1810 – 1860," *Scandinavian Journal of History,* 46:1, 63-83, DOI:10.1080/03468755.2020.1778519

Gurevich, A. J., & Campbell, G. L. (1985). *Categories of medieval culture.* Routledge.

Harper, L. (2022). *Leech Lake Band of Ojibwe: TRUTH Project report.*
https://sites.google.com/view/truthproject

Hjarnø Rasmussen, R. (2021). The Nordic Animist Year. Nordic Animism.
https://nordicanimism.com/nayear-book

Lundberg, Anders. (2008). "Changes in the land and the regional identity of western Norway. The case of Sandhåland, Karmøy." In *Nordic landscapes. Landscape, Region and Belonging on the Northern Edge of Europe*, 344-371, Editors Michael Jones and Kenneth R. Olwig. University of Minnesota Press.

National Archives. (2022, February 8). Dawes Act (1887). https://www.archives.gov/milestone-documents/dawes-act.

National Park Service. (n.d.) "About the Homestead Act." https://www.nps.gov/home/learn/historyculture/abouthomesteadactlaw.htm.

"Primstav: Land, Time, and Unsettling Ourselves." https://www.facebook.com/groups/2354134371472956

Semmingsen, I. (1960) "Norwegian emigration in the nineteenth century." *Scandinavian Economic History Review,* 8:2, 150-160, DOI: 10.1080/03585522.1960.10411427

The Decolonial Atlas. (2014, November 3). The Deforestation and Colonization of the United States. https://decolonialatlas.wordpress.com/2014/11/03/the-deforestation-and-colonization-of-the-united-states/

Wyn, M. (2023, April 4). *An Introduction to the Forest Commons of Northern Europe.* Hearthside. https://hearthsidecommunity.blogspot.com/2023/04/an-introduction-to-forest-commons-of.html

Zachrisson, T. (1994). "The Odal and its Manifestation in Landscape." *Current Swedish Archaeology,* 2(1), 219-238.

25. Beyond Individual Orlog: Deep Suffering and the Role of Frith

Some people, far too many, experience terrible situations that seemingly have no way out, and may offer little opportunity for any change of external circumstances that they can choose for themselves. I won't go through a list of examples; people of all kinds, around the world and in all times, certainly including the present, find themselves in such situations. Nor can we, from the outside, define whether a person is actually in such a situation: sometimes the bonds are not visible or even definable to the outside eye. Sometimes the person experiencing it is the only one who knows it is happening.

All religions and philosophies have examples that they can point to, to show their followers how to interpret and deal with such seemingly hopeless situations of suffering. Sometimes it is the founder of the religion, such as the Buddha or Jesus, who models a path. 'Stoic' philosophy practiced by Greeks and Romans is enjoying a return to popularity in modern times with its useful precepts. The Roman Platonist philosopher Boethius wrote a book in 523

Beyond Individual Orlog

CE while he was in prison awaiting his unjust execution, called *The Consolation of Philosophy*. His book was compatible with both philosophy and religion, and was influential throughout European history. Often examples are found among the saints, sages, wise ones, philosophers, heroes, who follow the paths of their beliefs and serve as inspirations to others who are struggling and suffering under impossible conditions. Very often, these spiritual heroes started out as ordinary people thrown into extraordinary situations who somehow found their way through and out the other side, in a spiritual / philosophical sense, even when their external circumstances did not improve.

Heathenry also has guidance to offer when facing great ordeals, as we discuss in this book, and of course there are other sources of Heathen rede and support, as well. Here, I want to speak specifically to the question *'what is the role of orlog in bringing about the very worst of situations, apparently un-earned and perhaps inescapable, in someone's life?'*

Do we Blame the "Wretched Norns"?

Snorri Sturlason, in his *Gylfaginning* in the prose Edda, offers an unsatisfactory answer to this question. The character Gangleri is in the hall of High, Just-as-High, and Third, asking questions to which these three beings (perhaps Odin and his brothers, or a tri-partite Odin) give answers based on Heathen mythology and belief. Gangleri says:

" 'If norns determine the fates of men, they allot terribly unfairly, when some have a good and prosperous life, and some have little success or glory, some a long life, some short.' High said 'Good norns, ones of noble parentage, shape good lives, but as for those that become the victims of misfortune, it is evil norns that are responsible.' " (Faulkes' translation, p. 18.)

Immediately prior to this question, High had noted that the norns come from different parentage, some from the Æsir, some from elves, some the daughters of Dvalin (dwarves). Presumably he is referring here to the 'lesser norns,' personal fate-beings who oversee individuals, rather than to the three great Norns. This was quoted from an older Heathen poem, but Snorri's interpretation above, given through "High," gives a very superficial and class-based answer to the perpetual question as to why some have good fortune, some have bad. Elder Heathens did sometimes blame Norns, greater or lesser, for misfortune. The miserable dwarf Andvari, sometime-keeper of the cursed treasure-hoard of the Nibelungs, complained that "A wretched norn *(aumlig norn)* shaped us (me) in ancient days." *(Reginsmal* / Lay of Regin v. 2, Poetic Edda.)

I find this attribution of ill-fate to evil norns and good fate to good norns to be pretty superficial, quite honestly. It offers nothing of substance upon which to hang any deeper spiritual or philosophical understanding, nor any guidance for ethical action. Whether the few clues we have represent true, deep-thinking Heathen views, or represent only the scoffing misunderstandings of Christians describing Heathen views, is difficult to say. It does seem that ancient views, among Heathens and other European pagan cultures such as Greek and Roman, were quite fatalistic and did not give much agency to humans when it came to 'fate.' This is one of the areas of Heathen thought that needs to be brought into the present cultural environment of our Heathen renaissance through deep discussions among modern Heathens, and not remain stuck in the ambiguous clues we have from the past.

Comparing Orlog and Karma

In pursuit of that aim, then, I return to the question: 'what is the role of orlog in the very worst of situations, apparently un-earned and perhaps inescapable, in someone's life?' And I will add: 'how can an understanding of this question help one to deal with such orlog, such an ordeal?' One answer to these questions comes from a modern Western understanding of the idea of 'karma,' a topic I discussed in a different context in Chapter 15. 'Karma' would say that a person's misfortunes in this life come as consequences of past misdeeds, if not in this life then in previous ones. Very severe misfortune results from truly evil deeds, likely committed in past lives. The ethical response here is to face the misfortune with that understanding, accept that in facing it one is 'paying one's shild,' and that good will come from responding in this way, in future lives if not in the present one.

There is certainly much to be said for that understanding. It is ultimately 'fair,' it offers an ethical way to respond to one's circumstances, and it offers hope for some future good to come of it. The downside of this perspective is that it can result in blaming the victims of misfortune, and being indifferent to social and material conditions that result in people (and animals) living lives of misery. The idea is that 'they earned it; let them live it out, it's good for them.' Cultures where this concept of karma is firmly entrenched may exhibit this attitude collectively as a society, even though individuals may show a more actively compassionate nature.

Overall, there does seem to be much similarity between karma and orlog. Both see that actions and deeds laid in the past result in today's circumstances; both acknowledge, in their own terms, the value of 'paying shild' so as to turn the situation around if that's needed. And yet...deep thought along Heathen lines always leads me to question how far that apparent similarity extends. Traditional belief in karma indicates that there is no alternative to simply living through whatever circumstances karma has brought about; it is essentially a passive experience that must be endured, and virtue lies in that endurance. Heathen culture (and Western culture generally) tends to take a more active attitude—fighting against it in some way—which sometimes works out well and sometimes makes things worse, especially when there is not a full understanding of the circumstances, including the orlog involved.

The Role of Heathen Frith

One thought I have is that both karma and modern understanding of orlog focus on the individual and their deeds, in past and present lives. Modern Westerners tend to take a very individualistic view, and that view has definite strengths in terms of ethical values and a sense of individual responsibility. On the opposite side are schools of thought that attribute all individual circumstances to 'society,' 'education,' 'the system,' to collectives of one form or another, and see the individual as the helpless dupe of circumstances beyond their control. In the past, Heathens who were caught up in wars and other grim collective fates were more likely, I think, to see themselves as pawns in a collective orlog or in the overarching orlog of their king or leader, than to interpret their fates in a solely individual way. The use of the word 'orlog' to indicate 'war,' as well as an individual's fate, certainly points in that direction.

Collective orlog at many levels is real and is influential—I believe that ancient Heathens would agree with this assessment. An individual's suffering in the present moment could reflect strands of different orlogs interacting: past and present life-orlogs of the individual, as well as past and present collective orlogs that have inescapably caught many individuals up in their nets.

Looking at this situation as a Heathen philosopher, I find the idea of 'karma' in the sense of total individual responsibility for one's situation to be too limiting for a comprehensive spiritual understanding. What it leaves out is the whole aspect of human interconnectivity, of quantum entanglement, of Heathen frith itself. It leaves out the question of why it was, and is, so important to pursue and maintain the social relationships of frith at all levels.

Frith in its deepest sense refers to the behaviors, attitudes, and commitments that support a closely-knit and well-functioning community. When frith is broken, or is never established within the circle of the family in present and past generations, everyone suffers, ill orlog is laid for all. When frith is broken or never well established at the level of a society, strife, war, rebellion break out and consume that society. When frith is broken, or is not well established between humans and their Deities, great misfortunes ensue, as well as good things that might have happened being missed out on. This, too, is a strong traditional belief that underlies all pagan religions.

Beyond Individual Orlog

The breaking of frith, or the failure to establish and maintain it, plays a strong role in the development of harmful orlog at both individual and collective levels, among humans and among other beings as well. There are a number of tales in our mythology that show how Deities and other non-human beings brought harmful orlog on themselves due to breaking frith in various ways.

The sociologist James Russell wrote a book that has much to offer the Heathen philosopher and historian, called *The Germanization of Early Medieval Christianity: A Sociohistorical Approach to Religious Transformation.* He cogently argues that Germanic Heathen customs and beliefs *(forn siðr* and *sköp Norna,* in our terms) were so different from those of Christianity that medieval Christianity had to undergo some fairly radical transformations in order to persuade—or confuse the Germanic peoples into converting. The Christianity that emerged at the end of this process had become as much Germanized, as the Germanic peoples had become Christianized, according to this fascinating analysis. Among the strongest reasons Germanic peoples were more resistant to conversion than those of the Roman Empire was their foundations of frith that depended on Heathen customs and beliefs.

"The decline in familial and national solidarity in the Roman Empire may be contrasted with the high sense of familial, communal, and tribal solidarity among the Germanic peoples. These kinship ties originated in fundamental interlocking sociobiological relationships, and were supplemented by the more elective *comitatus* relationship… …a closely knit social system with strong bonds of kinship and vassalage…" (Russell p. 128.)

Beyond Individual Orlog

The *comitatus* refers to the oathed war-band, a deeply-rooted tradition from Proto-Indo-European times, and vassalage refers to the frith-relationships within social hierarchies where each level had important and well-defined responsibilities toward the other levels of the relationship.

Russell continues, writing about "the high group solidarity of Germanic society and the anomic social environment of early Christianity. ...these disparate social environments contributed significantly to the development of disparate world-views, value systems, and religious attitudes." (p. 131.) The term 'anomic' refers to 'a state of social disintegration, rootlessness, or disorientation caused by a breakdown of established social norms and values.'

This Heathen world-view of closely-knit social bonds that structure both mundane and spiritual relationships underlies, I suggest, an ancient Heathen understanding that orlog encompasses both the individual and the collectives of which the individual is a part. The fate of a person is influenced by the fate of the groups they belong to, and influences them in turn. This is the foundation for the idea that the deeds of a great hero, such as Beowulf, could influence the orlog of his people just as much as influencing his own orlog.

Here, also, was rooted the belief that it was wrong for an oathed warrior to survive the death of his leader in battle: their orlogs were intermeshed and the wyrded death of the warrior needed to occur in tandem with his leader's. One who survived a battle, an attack, or other deadly circumstance when they 'should not' have survived was *fæg* or *fey,* doomed to a death that had simply not caught up with them yet, and this put them into a very weird frame of mind where they would behave abnormally and undertake risks with no thought of consequences.

The Orlog of Signy the Volsung

The same close interweaving of orlog often occurred among kin or married couples. An example of this which is very hard for the modern mind to understand is the death of Signy the Volsung in the *Völsungasaga.* She was married unwillingly to her husband who turned out to be a treacherous foe to her kin, killing her father and most of her brothers. Signy engaged in a long, subversive, and cruel scheme to bring about her revenge and her husband's death by the hands of her twin brother Sigmund and their incestuous son Sinfjotli. And yet, when her husband's hall was in flames, Signy refused her brother's invitation to come away with him and start a new life. Instead, she turned and walked back into the burning hall to die with the husband she had spent years and the lives of her other sons plotting against.

According to the medieval text of this old oral tradition, Signy's rationale was that "I have worked so hard to bring about vengeance that I am by no means fit to live. Willingly I shall now die with King Siggeir though I married him reluctantly." (Byock's translation, p. 47.) I am not sure that an ancient, traditional Heathen mindset would agree that bringing about a terrible vengeance proved that someone was not fit to live; they tended to be rather in favor of terrible vengeances (let me emphasize that I am not!). My own idea of Signy's motivation is her recognition that her orlog, willy-nilly, was tied to her husband Siggeir's through their marriage and all of the eventful, if hateful, actions of their lives together. Her life was focused on her vengeance against him; she brought about the deaths of her sons with Siggeir, and tricked her brother into siring an incestuous son with her, whom she raised to be brutal himself, all to bring about her vengeance. This vengeful focus on her husband over the course of many years created tight bonds of orlog between them, which she acknowledged and acted upon in her choice to die along with him. As she saw it, her orlog-while, her time of death, had come simultaneously with the completion of her vengeance: that was how her life had been shaped. It was not she alone who had shaped it; her kinship bonds, both familial and marital, played major roles as well.

In his introduction to *The Saga of the Volsungs*, Byock makes the following observation. "An overriding theme of tension between marriage and blood bonds runs through the saga. For generation after generation, strife with kin by marriage brings a series of misfortunes on the Volsungs. Marriage creates new kinship alliances, which are vital for societies like the one pictured in the saga… Even though pledges were exchanged between lord and retainer, the most trustworthy defense lay in the family." (p. 10.)

Orlog is Context

There are themes running through this example from the *Völsungasaga* that relate to both individual and familial / group orlog, and also to hamingja as it is passed down as a family legacy. These are topics that demand a fuller exploration than we can offer here, but I want to make these points. I believe that a Heathen view of orlog is not entirely an individual matter, unrelated to any larger social context. I believe it's true that the more terrible and unjustifiable an individual's situation might be, the more likely it is that collective orlog is playing a significant role, as well as possibly past-life orlog. I don't believe that 'evil Norns' simply assign horrible fates to people randomly. I also don't believe that we stand alone, in evil fortune or in good.

We exist in context with others, past and present, human and non-human, and within collective systems. Earlier, I suggested that both determinism and free will play important roles in our choices and deeds. In the same way, orlog is both individual and collective—not just one or the other. Just as we are often subject to conditions that are determined beyond our control, but must use our own Will to choose how we will face those conditions, so also it is important to acknowledge that the orlog we each face and work with, day by day, is woven of both personal and collective strands. We have to live with collective orlog as well as personal, and figure out how to deal with them both. Sara's writings in this book, as well as mine, point out that the best way to heal harmful orlog comes about when we do what we can to heal collective orlog as well as our own personal orlog.

And in the final analysis, we can turn to our Holy Ones, working in frith with them, to help us deal with suffering and adversity. We and they relate together as individuals and as groups, where frith is the essential foundation of those relationships. Whether or not we can find immediate relief in the physical world through them, they can always guide us toward developing a philosophical and spiritual stance that strengthens our stamina, enhances our might and main, grows our wisdom, and keeps our focus on laying new and better orlog in all ways that we can. When those new layers of orlog encompass strands from the Gods and Goddesses as well as our own personal strands, that orlog takes on amazing qualities that are worth the work that goes into them! In the next chapter I'll discuss one of the powerful ways we can undertake such a project.

Note: The following articles of mine offer more in-depth discussion of Heathen frith, if you are interested. They are on my website, HeathenSoulLore.net.

Heathen Frith and Modern Ideals
https://heathensoullore.net/heathen-frith-and-modern-ideals/

Frith, Friendship, and Freedom
https://heathensoullore.net/frith-friendship-and-freedom/

26. Oathing in Symbel

Note: Chapter 4, "The Ancient Role of Symbel," provides important background information for this chapter.

"Speech is the means by which the fact of any action is made explicit and the way in which its continuing present is assured" (Bauschatz p. 109).

The Modern Heathen Symbel or Sumble

We've described orlog as the 'laying of patterns' in numerous contexts in this book. The Heathen ceremony of symbel or sumble is a powerful way to lay patterns in orlog, and to begin the reworking of existing patterns when needed. As background to this chapter, you may want to review Chapter 4 "The Ancient Role of Symbel," and keep those points in mind as you read through this chapter. Chapter 23 on "Collective and Group Orlog" is also relevant here.

Symbel is one of the two standard ceremonies among modern Heathens, along with the Blót, and is usually included in abbreviated form within the Blót. In its simplest group form it proceeds like this: a designated person raises a horn or other drinking vessel and opens the ceremony by hailing the Heathen Deities—all of them together, or sometimes one in particular if the symbel or Blót is dedicated to that Deity. Participants follow around the circle in turn, each hailing one or more Holy Ones. During the second round, ancestors, heroes, admired persons are hailed. For the third round, some groups will hail the Landwights, others consider it an open round to speak their hearts in whatever way they wish. Some groups may do this more formally and include the Braga-Full—hailing the group who hosts the symbel, its members, and other such acknowledgements. Sometimes the symbel is performed very formally, with carefully structured steps and customs meaningful to the group performing it. Other times it may be informal—springing up around a campfire spontaneously, for example, or held among a relaxed group of Heathen friends. For many groups, the level of formality falls between those two styles.

Oathing in Symbel

There is one symbel event that does require a degree of formality, however: swearing oaths. These should never be done lightly, whether it involves the swearing-in of group officers or others in authority, relationship oaths such as betrothal or blood-siblinghood, or oaths to accomplish a certain deed. Oaths are a powerful means of both influencing and fulfilling our orlog; they need to be carefully thought-through and faithfully carried out or we risk serious damage to our orlog.

For this reason, some Heathen groups appoint a Thyle or Thul for the symbel, an experienced and mature Heathen who serves as a reality-check during the process of oathing. The Thyle may challenge a person's ability to perform the oath, as was done during Beowulf's symbel in Hrothgar's hall

Oathing in Symbel

in the *Beowulf* poem (see Chapter 4). The purpose for this is to make sure that the oathing person has thought through all the ramifications and requirements of the oath. If it becomes clear during the challenge that the person has not done this, then the Thyle might either suggest some modification of the oath to make it more achievable, or suggest that the oath-taker wait and prepare more thoroughly before making the oath in a future symbel.

In acknowledgement of the power of Skuld, some groups require that a person swearing a formal oath in symbel should also state the shild or penalty that they will pay if they fail in their oath, even if the failure is due to circumstances beyond their control. The purpose here is to make clear, and to accept, that failed oaths inevitably affect one's orlog and involve the accumulation of shild, of metaphysical debt. The shild-penalty that the oath-taker offers as part of the oath-swearing is an acknowledgement of the seriousness of the oath and its consequences. We can see how serious the offered shild could be, in the example of Beowulf oathing to slay Grendel or die in the attempt: if victory is not achieved then death will be the shild that he agrees to pay (see Chapter 4).

In a modern setting, the shild might take the form of a deed of service for one's Heathen or non-Heathen community, a substantial donation to a worthy cause, helping to clean up a natural area, planting a tree and caring for it, memorizing a long passage of significant Heathen lore and reciting it in symbel, or any other deed that seems appropriate. The cost or difficulty of the shild should match the significance and difficulty of the oath. For a great, challenging, perhaps life-changing oath, the shild should also be costly and difficult—a 'heavy' oath requires a 'heavy'

Oathing in Symbel

shild to compensate for its potential failure, though it needs to be something one can realistically do. For a more minor oath, the shild can be relatively light. Matching the 'weight' of the shild to the 'weight' of the oath is something else a Thyle and / or the other symbel participants can help the oath-taker establish.

If the oath is fulfilled, the oath-taker gains much might and main, spiritual power, increase of luck and hamingja, an honorable reputation among Heathens and the Holy Ones, and lays an influential and beneficial layer of orlog in the Well. If the oath is not accomplished, a commensurately negative layer of orlog is laid, that may bring about harm in complex and unforeseen ways. One's reputation or *gefrain* will of course suffer, as well. Paying shild for a failed oath may partially—not completely—mitigate some of that harm. If one fails in keeping the oath, and then also fails to pay the promised shild, of course the orlog-harm and reputation-harm are multiplied exponentially.

It is in hopes of preventing such failure that a Thyle or other person may challenge one's oath in symbel and require one to prove the seriousness of intent regarding both the oath and the promised shild. Part of this challenge could involve the oath-taker giving examples of previous oaths or serious commitments they've undertaken that have been successfully accomplished. This action was part of the ancient symbel formalities described in the *Beowulf* poem and analyzed by Bauschatz in his Chapter III, "Beowulf and the Nature of Events."

One's *gefrain* is an important factor here: Heathens who have built a reputation for serious commitment, truthfulness, strength of will, previous successful oathing, and keeping their word are unlikely to be challenged during

Oathing in Symbel

oath-taking. Someone whose reputation is unknown, who has not yet built such a reputation, or whose reputation is a bit spotty or doubtful might well be challenged—and this is to their ultimate benefit. They can thus learn to use appropriate oathing practices as a way to grow into the stature of an honorable *gefrain.*

Once an oath has been achieved, or has failed but one has paid the required shild, this should be reported in a subsequent symbel as the completion, the final act, of that oath-taking. Verðandi stands witness at the moment when we take our oath, then hands that promise over to Urð to lay in the Well as an accomplished fact: 'the oath has been sworn; this is now laid in orlog.' Then Verðandi watches again as the actions of the oath are accomplished. Once the oathed action is completed, by formally boasting it in symbel it is handed over to Urð's domain to be laid in the Well as another layer of our orlog: a strong, shining layer that brightens our entire wyrd by the honor it achieves.

As Bauschatz describes this process of boasting an accomplished oath: "Speech is the means by which the fact of any action is made explicit and the way in which its continuing present is assured" (Bauschatz p. 109). Once the oath, now achieved, has been laid in the Well, it continues to influence what is coming into being: it is not 'over and done with.' This is why failure to achieve an oath, without paying shild for that, is so harmful: *the influence of that failure continues to affect the course of events through orlog.*

Skuld is not left out: the oath is a form of 'what-must-be,' and so is the shild that's stated along with the oath. When we have sworn an oath, Skuld emphasizes that sense of 'what-must-be, what needs to happen' in our life, urging us to the accomplishment of the oath and creating unease and difficulties if we are slack in that pursuit. Keep in mind that Skuld is a Valkyrie as well as a Norn—one who hovers over the battlefield or the field of struggle and striving in our daily life. This imagery of Skuld as a Valkyrie, spear in hand, hovering over our daily actions can certainly strengthen our motivation to fulfill our oath in a timely manner! If we fail in the oath (whether that is our fault, or not—the reason does not matter), shild is owed to her and she makes sure it is paid, whether by our own honorable payment of our promised shild, or by disruptions and harms occurring in our daily life.

If we fail our oath but offer no excuses and simply pay our promised shild, this also should be reported during symbel, so that 'our accounts are settled,' so to speak, in the eyes of the Norns and the Gods as well as the eyes of our fellow Heathens. Paying shild is an honorable deed, too, and is thus laid in the Well and helps to establish our reputation as someone who honors our given word, without excuses.

Taking an oath and achieving it or paying the price are part of what we do to build our reputation among our fellow Heathens as well as all the Holy Ones. Marking these steps in symbel is how that reputation becomes laid in orlog, and also how it becomes fully known to these all-important companions of our lives.

A Modern Heathen Concern

Some modern Heathens believe that the failure to accomplish an oath boasted in symbel damages not only the luck and orlog of the one who oaths, but also the luck and orlog of all who witness that oath in symbel—the 'luck of the hall.' This is an additional reason for the work of the Thyle to weed out untrustworthy oaths before they are finalized, and it's also a reason to be very cautious about allowing oathing in symbel at all—especially if it is a large group with many members whose reputations are unknown to each other.

If one believes that the orlogs of all witnesses are damaged by a failed oath, this caution is understandable. It results in an unfortunate situation, however, when personal Heathen oathing in symbel is strongly discouraged or not allowed at all (except for the swearing-in of group officers, whose reputations may be better known). As I and many Heathens believe, oathing in general and especially in symbel is a very powerful way to grow our Heathen might and main, to improve our lives and strength of character, and to nurture bright and shining reputations as the Heathen forebears valued. (The name 'Robert,' by the way, comes from Anglo-Saxon *Hreþ-beorht,* meaning 'fame-bright.') If fear of consequences results in no opportunities to oath in symbel except in solitary practice, that chokes off a very important avenue for Heathen spiritual development, as I and others believe.

In the rest of this chapter I offer some perspectives to take into consideration as you and any Heathen group(s) you practice with explore the deeper meanings of Heathen symbel and decide how you will handle oathing during symbel. I also suggest some further resources about practicing Heathen oathing at the end of this chapter. I want to note that you and other Heathens might disagree with any of the perspectives I offer; I don't pretend to know 'the one and only right way' to do anything in Heathen practice! I have thoughts about these matters and I share them here, but your views, beliefs and practices, and those of any

Oathing in Symbel

Heathen group(s) you're a member of, are up to you to decide.

Risking Luck versus Risking Orlog

I mentioned earlier that some Heathens believe that a failed symbel-oath impacts the wyrd or orlog of everyone present who witnessed that oath. Because of this severe risk, some are reluctant to allow any oathing in symbel, or attend any symbel where oathing might take place. Of course, people have a right to this belief, but I have a partial—not complete—counter-argument here: that witnessing a failed oath in symbel may affect our luck, but not our orlog, under most circumstances. This argument is based on the difference between luck and orlog, which I discuss in Chapter 14; it might be helpful to review that chapter in the context of this discussion. Here are the salient points of my argument.

(1) **Luck and orlog are not the same thing,** though they are related and have some effect on each other. While Heathens in the past saw orlog as being certain and fixed, luck is complex, variable; the outcome of the luck or unluck is not 100% certain in any given circumstance. Orlog is under the governance of the Norns / Wyrd and is stored in Urð's Well, with all the metaphysical 'weight' that this storage implies. Hamingja-luck is managed by lesser luck-bearing spirits; it is stored in objects we possess and use, in our surroundings, and—significantly—it is 'stored' or inherent in our relationships with others, both human and non-human. Both luck and orlog manifest in the events of our lives, but they do so in different ways though they may overlap at times.

Oathing in Symbel

(2) **Luck is something that can be relatively easily (compared to orlog) gained or lost.** Many folklore practices, 'superstitions,' and magical practices, in the past and in the present too, are focused on gaining good luck or warding off bad luck. Changes in one's orlog are not so easily achieved, requiring hard work, focused intent, and the recognition that changes in orlog depend mostly on our personal work with the Norns / Wyrd, rather than on the influence of 'luck,' other people, and our surroundings.

(3) **Luck is 'contagious;' orlog is not,** and I think this is an important point when considering the impacts of oathing in symbel. This is especially true of hamingja-type luck. People in the past (and present!) wanted to associate with someone with a lot of luck—a king, chieftain, leader, someone who demonstrated luck and success in their life, with the understanding that this hamingja or good luck could 'rub off' on them. By the same token, they didn't want to be associated with unlucky persons or enterprises because of the belief bad luck is contagious as well. People around the world believed and believe in things like good-luck tokens whose luck is considered 'contagious' in the sense that the luck contained in the token can spread to themselves and their activities and events of their lives.

In contrast to luck, I think orlog in elder times was viewed in a different way. Most often, they considered that orlog meant 'the time and circumstances of death,' and the events leading up to that—with the implication that the Norns / Wyrd have shaped one's lifespan and life circumstances to lead to that death. Just because one person's lifespan ends and death comes about in a specific way doesn't mean that

Oathing in Symbel

their 'orlog-while' is contagious for other people around them. Yes, of course the event leading to that death may affect others as well: a battle, a plague, a famine, a disaster will cause large numbers of people to die together. But it wasn't one person's orlog that affected those around them and caused their death; it was each person's orlog affecting that person individually, as well as the overarching, impersonal effects of group orlog and world-orlog.

What I suggest is this: we do not substantially risk our own orlog because of what others say in symbel, and what they do or fail to do afterwards (with exceptions that I'll discuss in the next section). There may, on the other hand, be some effect on our luck and the 'luck of the hall' when unlucky, disastrous oaths are sworn, or when sworn oaths or shilds fail to materialize. Whether this is an acceptable risk for you and your group is something you will have to decide.

One thought that is meaningful to me is this: the risk of bad luck for everyone is a motivating factor both for the person oathing and for all in attendance. It creates a more weighty seriousness of intent for the oathing person to achieve their oath if they realize that their fellow-Heathens will be impacted by their failure. It can motivate friends and fellow-Heathens present at the symbel to support the oath-taker in the achievement of their oath: offering encouragement and advice, following up in a friendly way to make sure they're on track, helping in practical ways if that seems appropriate. It causes the oath-taker and all present to take seriously the acts of oathing and of community support for each member of the group in symbel; it builds community and commitment.

The idea that we are all subject to a certain degree of risk—loss of luck—if one of us fails is very supportive of group solidarity, especially with a closely-knit group. It also has the potential, if it is not handled appropriately, to create hard feelings in the group when failures happen. This approach or understanding of symbel dynamics has its pro's and con's, certainly, and it's up to individuals and Heathen groups to decide whether the shared-luck benefits of oathing in symbel that I've outlined here are worthwhile for them, or not.

But I want to make this point again: I believe that it is luck—individual and group luck—rather than individuals' orlogs, that is at play in this *group* dynamic of oathing in symbel. The *oathing individual's* orlog is obviously involved, and so is the orlog of any oath-helpers the oathing person might have, who stand with the oather, vouch for them, and commit to helping with the oath. But the individual orlogs of each of the witnesses are not substantially impacted, in my understanding, except under the circumstances I describe next.

Oathed Bonds and Group Orlog

Luck is contagious; orlog is not. There is, however, a similar effect at work with the orlogs of people who are closely related to or oathed to each other: not contagiousness precisely, but linked or interconnected orlogs. Such links are created through specific bonds, formed by oaths, kinship, or lives that are linked together in other significant, long-term ways. For example, the marriage-bond: two people swear specific oaths to each other during the wedding, and those oaths do create an orlog-bond, a linkage between their orlogs. What comes to one spouse through their orlog is likely to affect the orlog of the other spouse as well. That connection plays out during their married life and affects

Oathing in Symbel

any children they might have. It's likely to reach out farther, to grandchildren and perhaps extended families as well.

Orlog plays an important role in kinship through family dynamics. For example harmful layers laid in orlog, such as patterns of spouse or child abuse or neglect, tend to get passed down through generations, affecting their descendants' choices of spouse and their child-raising practices. Helpful layers of orlog, such as a family culture of facing and overcoming hardship together in wise, dynamic and practical ways, also spread their beneficial influences through the generations.

Some Heathen groups require an oath in order to join them. This is usually a simple oath taken by each individual to the group as a whole, rather than to any specific person such as the group leader. A few Heathen groups require more complex hold-oaths or oaths of fealty, where there is a hierarchical structure similar to ancient Heathen social structures. Each member functions within a network of oaths of loyalty and obligation to those 'above' and 'below' them in the hierarchy, with the leader of the group holding all the oaths together. This structure of hold-oaths, when they are properly fulfilled, is intended to generate luck as well as solidarity, might and main for the entire group. It also creates stronger interconnections of orlog than is the case for groups who are not bound by oaths to each other.

For Heathens who are bound to one another by close kinship or by oaths—whether through marriage, blood-siblinghood, membership oaths, or hold-oaths of fealty—I believe it is true that their orlogs are more closely linked than among Heathens who are not formally oathed or closely related to each other. In such cases, failing to fulfill an oath in symbel may significantly affect the orlog of the group as a whole, as well as their individual and group luck. Usually these groups are aware of this risk and structure their oathing procedures with great care, including substantial support for the oath-taker by the others to whom they are oathed, to ensure a successful achievement of the oath.

Individual Oaths and Group Orlog

What about group orlog in groups where the members are not oathed to one another? Here is my thought about this. Orlog is a pattern, not just a one-off, especially when it comes to group orlog. If one person takes an oath in symbel and fails in the oath, I think the group orlog is slightly but not significantly impacted. But if there is a pattern of multiple failed oaths within the group, that is significant and may come about not only through the individual actions of each failed oath-taker, but even more because of how the group practices oathing.

A pattern of failed oaths is significant to group orlog and indicates that, as a group, they are not doing a good enough job managing the process of oathing. They may need to educate their members better in how to prepare for and take oaths, and how to proceed from there. They may need to make better use of a Thul or Thyle, and train such a person to guide their members in making achievable oaths. They may need to support their oath-takers better and follow up with them. They may need to improve the overall ethical culture or ethos of the group, placing greater emphasis on the importance of keeping their word, growing their honor and reputations.

In other words, the effect of oathing by an individual on the orlog of the group is interactive. Individuals are more likely to succeed with their oaths when their group has established good oathing procedures and offers support for the oath-taker. This success, when multiplied by many instances of successful oathing, does lay layers of good orlog for the group as a whole. Likewise, a succession of failed oaths shows not only the effect of such failures on the group's orlog, but may also be an indicator that the group's orlog is not supportive of successful oathing. The group's negative orlog in this respect will then negatively affect the likelihood of success for each individual oath-taker.

The obvious lesson is that as with all groups, what each member does affects the group, but what the group does affects each member, too. As Heathens with a deep understanding of orlog, we can work with these insights to enhance our experience of symbel, improve the success of Heathen oathing, and lay layers of orlog, luck, might and main, and shining reputations within the Well and within the circle of our lives and deeds in Midgard.

Further Reading:
See my articles "Oaths: What they Mean and Why They Matter," and "The Practice of Heathen Oathing" on my website: HeathenSoulLore.net. They are also included in my book Oaths, Shild, Frith, Luck & Wyrd.

https://heathensoullore.net/oaths-what-they-mean-and-why-they-matter/

https://heathensoullore.net/the-practice-of-heathen-oathing/

The Symbel Mysterium

⋖ O ⋗

27. The Symbel Mysterium

Modern Heathen symbel is a sacred rite that has deep roots. Underlying this mystery that is enacted by us here in Midgard is something deeper that I call a 'mysterium.' A mysterium, as I define it, is the sacred, shaping mystery underlying and giving meaning to any religious rite. It is the story we tell about the meaning of the rite, the mythology that underlies it, and the essence of meaning and significance that we enter into as we enact the rite.

In this chapter I'm offering a view of two different 'mysteria' concerning the ritual of symbel. One is the familiar mysterium of 'speaking at the Well of Wyrd,' the one that a great many—perhaps all—modern Heathens ascribe to. The other is an alternate mysterium based not on Urð's Well, but on Mimir's. As background to the following discussion you might like to review Chapter 21, "The Work of the Three Wells." The previous chapter on "Oathing in Symbel," as well as Chapter 23 on "Collective and Group Orlog" are also relevant here.

The Symbel Mysterium

Gathering at the Well of Wyrd

Queen Wealhþeow welcomes Beowulf to Heorot Hall and offers him the symbel-drink. By George T. Tobin.

In the following passage Bauschatz outlines the essential elements of symbel and its connection with the Well and the Norns. He is following the analysis he laid out, previously, of the symbel or *symle* in the *Beowulf* poem where Beowulf is welcomed to Heorot by queen Wealhþeow bearing the drinking horn to him, beginning at *Beowulf* line 612. When she hands him the horn, speaking 'wise words' to him, Beowulf drinks and swears his oath to slay Grendel that night.

"The elements of this typical *symbel* bear a close relationship not only to those already described by Tacitus but also to those isolated in the myth of Urth's Well. The cup…is an enclosure, in many ways like the *brunnr* (the well-spring). It collects and holds the intoxicating drink, one that is clearly beyond the ordinary. ... The act of drinking takes place in the presence of the act of speech...in such activity, the power of all other actions is brought to bear upon the ritual moment and fixes it within the ever-evolving interrelation of all present actions with the past. This combination of words, their denoted actions, and the semantic elements of the drink and the cup repeat the whole act of the continual speaking of the *ørlǫg* and the nurturing of the tree Yggdrasil, the central activities of the Norns. ... here also the ritual words spoken become part of this past. They disappear into the drink; as it is drunk, the speaker of the speech, his actions, and the drink become one, assuring that all now have become part of the strata laid within the well." (Bauschatz pp. 77-78.)

Bauschatz' work in analyzing and describing what I call the 'mysterium' underlying Heathen symbel has been highly influential in shaping the modern Heathen practice of symbel or sumble, giving this ritual a profound depth of meaning, significance, and beauty. But this action of laying orlog in the Well as a consequence of speaking in symbel has also given rise to concerns that the orlog laid by one person's words, especially oaths, could impact the orlog not only of the speaker but also of the other participants in that symbel, as I discuss at length in the previous chapter. In that chapter, I offer some thoughts that might mitigate some of this concern. In this chapter, I also offer an option for mitigating this concern, but it comes from a completely different direction. And this idea is worthwhile, I believe, not only in order to mitigate concerns about impacts of symbel on group orlog, but also as a worthy idea of its own, an alternate take on the symbel mysterium.

The Symbel Mysterium

Meeting at Mimir's Well

The association of Heathen symbel with the Well of Wyrd is a very beautiful and powerful one. But there is another Well to consider, too: Mimir's Well of Wisdom, Memory and Inspiration. To my mind, Mimir's Well is just as suitable for association with symbel as is Urð's Well, if not even more so—depending on the purpose of speech at that symbel. Mimir's Well is the repository of collective memory, the source of inspiration for words and deeds, and the source of inspired wisdom, including that contained within the Runes.

Laying our words, boasts, oaths, memories, thanks, and prayers into the Well of Memory, and then reaching in there to receive wisdom, inspiration and deep memories from ancestral and collective sources, is another inspiring image to help us structure the mysterium of symbel. The Well of Memory can store our oaths and boasts, memories and prayers, and keep them safely for future reference by ourselves and by others.

The difference is that there is not the explicit connection with orlog here, as there is with the Norns' Well. Of course, orlog is laid anywhere, any time that significant deeds and events occur—significant in the eyes of the Norns, whether we see it that way or not. But at Mimir's Well we are not deliberately trying to lay orlog, with all the implications of such an action. Instead, our focus is on memory, wisdom, and inspiration.

Think about what is spoken of most of the time, in most modern symbels. We offer prayers and petitions to the Holy Ones. We drink to the memories of loved and admired people. We share meaningful memories and wisdom we've learned from life experience. We may recite poetry or sing a song. We honor the deeds and achievements of friends, loved ones, people who've contributed to the growth of modern Heathenry, leaders and teachers. We boast our own deeds to set a good example, inspire others to do the same, and to lay them in Heathen folk-memory.

All of these actions are highly suitable for Mimir's Well of memory, wisdom, and inspiration, it seems to me. Mimir's Well holds as much mystery and meaning as does Urð's Well, and not only memory, wisdom, and inspiration. Mimir's Well and the mead it holds served as an initiatory medium for Odin when he came down from the Tree. It holds Odin's eye, which—lying in the Well—can see what it could not see if it were in Odin's head: memories, wisdom, inspiration that lie hidden in this Well. The same for Heimdall's hearing: he can hear the whispers hidden in this Well in addition to hearing all else that goes on in Midgard and other realms. Mimir's head itself...as I see it, Mimir's Well and his head are sort of fractal dimensions of each other, both reflecting what I call World-Mind.

Orlog, wyrd, and the mysteries of the Norns are of utmost importance and meaning, but so are the contents of Mimir's Well. Mimir's waters can flow into our own inspired words at symbel, speaking wisdom and the deepest truths of our hearts, celebrating our lives, our ancestors and heroes, our hopes and dreams and memories in company with one another. Many symbels do not even involve oath-taking, but all symbels involve actions relevant to Mimir's Well.

Actions of the Two Wells

There's an important question to consider when musing on whether Mimir's Well could or should offer an alternative or an additional mysterium for Heathen symbel. That is:

what are the actual *actions,* the dynamics, of each of the Wells? Each of them might look still and serene if we imagined standing there, viewing them at the surface, but there's a lot going on underneath the surface! It might be thought that Urð's Well is the more active one, with all of the activities and processes of the Well and its tenders, the Norns, that we've discussed throughout this book. We might be tempted to think of Mimir's Well of memory as simply a passive place to store things. Not so!

Here's a review of what I wrote in Chapter 21, "The Work of the Three Wells," about the relationships and similarities between Urð's and Mimir's Wells:

I envision Mimir's Well as functioning in a similar way to Urð's Well: as a container of memories—individual memories, folk-memory, the collective unconscious—which are laid in layers within the Well as all of us go about living our lives, generation after generation. As 'significant' deeds fall into Urð's Well and are laid there as orlog, so also 'meaningful' memories are laid in Mimir's Well and ferment together into wisdom under the influence of Oðrœrir, the wode-stirrer, the giver of inspiration.

The active word here is 'ferment.' The mead of wisdom and inspiration, Oðrœrir, is considered to be contained within this Well. Oðrœrir means 'wode-stirrer, inspiration-stirrer,' and it is brewed through the process of fermentation. It is a sacred drink with an extensive mysterium of its own, and a long history of sacred use in Indo-European myth and history. Mimir's Well is not simply sitting there holding memories and wisdom. It is actively fermenting memories, i.e. knowledge, experience, and meaning, into wisdom and then into inspiration.

Just as, working with the Norns and their Well, we can participate deliberately in the complex processes of orlog and wyrd, so we can work with Mimir's Well to ferment our memories, knowledge, and experience into wisdom and inspiration. And when we do this in symbel with others, we do it together as a group. We blend the memories and experiences of us as individuals into group memories and experience, then ferment them into institutional memory, group customs and shared history, that weave our individual threads into a meaningful group whole. This activity is as meaningful as is working with the Well of Wyrd.

Our Choice in Symbel

I'd like to point out that we, as Heathens with spiritual might and awareness, can choose where to direct our attention, intention, prayers, boasts, ceremonies. We can choose, at the beginning of symbel, whether to dip the symbel-horn into the Well of Memory and Inspiration, or into the Well of Wyrd. Our deeds in symbel and resulting from symbel are indeed likely to filter into the Well of Wyrd. There is no escaping that Well, and we must be mindful of that in symbel as well as in our lives generally. But as the basis of a convivial group ceremony, where most of the words spoken are likely to relate to ancestors and heroes, to memories, wisdom and inspiration in our Heathen lives, and where we want to speak our truths in deeply-inspired words: Mimir's Well has a great deal to offer as the shape of our symbel mysterium.

Even if a symbel is directed by ritual toward the mysterium of Mimir's Well rather than Urð's Well, anyone wishing to oath, or boast a deed completed, or announce the payment of shild at the Well of Wyrd can simply say so at the beginning of their speech: "I stand at the Well of the Norns / Wyrd and offer these words from my heart...." It's important to note the "I" here, rather than "we", though an oath-helper may choose to stand with the oath-taker at the Well, accepting the shared orlog of the oath in full knowledge.

The rest of those present can stand as witnesses, as guards of honor, warding the sacred space of the person facing Urð's Well, but not all deliberately linking their orlogs together. We can choose to risk some of our luck to help our companion by our presence at symbol, but keep our orlog out of range of the oath, so to speak. The rest of us are still over at Mimir's Well, sheltered under its root, while the oath-taker stands tall at Urð's Edge and accepts the orlog he or she is weaving with the oath.

Which Well Fits Well?

So, I offer this proposition: It might be worthwhile to think about the pros and cons of which Well we seek to connect with during any given symbol, and how each option might affect our conduct of symbol, the outcomes of our oaths and boasts, and the luck and orlog of the group holding the symbol as well as of the individuals present. Here are some questions to ask for this purpose.

Do we, as a group, want or need to shape and share a group orlog in this symbol? Is there a well-directed purpose for this? The symbol might be specifically *intended* to weave together and strengthen group orlog, and in such a case the Well of Wyrd is most appropriate. This would particularly be the case for a small, close-knit group who have history together, know and trust one another well, who may even have oaths of loyalty to one another. For them, each symbel may be a deliberate strengthening of group orlog as well as other purposes of symbel.

Another example is a wedding-symbel, ideally including the blood-kin as well as the close Heathen kin of the bride and groom; likewise an adoption or blood-siblinghood ceremony. Oaths and boasts in these contexts are specifically intended to link the orlogs of people together, and strengthen existing links. Group orlog-weaving in symbel at the Well of Wyrd fits well for these circumstances. The Well of Wyrd is also the appropriate setting for making an oath, or reporting on an oath achieved or shild paid for a failed oath.

Or is our aim to share a convivial ceremony with one another, perhaps in a larger group where not all participants are well-known to one another? The ceremony might even include guests who are not Heathen. Here, our purpose is to share the meaningfulness of our lives, our thoughts, our memories, our history and aspirations. We weave these together in symbel, and lay them, together, within the depths of World-Mind: Mimir's Well. There, they will ferment into a heady brew of group-memory, group-culture, and group-inspiration for future symbels to draw upon. But the fateful linkage of group orlog will not be as set, as powerful, as it would be at the Well of Wyrd.

As we develop the customs of our group, and as we prepare for each symbel, let us give thought to this: shall we knowingly weave group-orlog in this symbel, aware of what is involved with this? Or shall we convivially lay down a hearty brew of memory and inspiration, ready to froth up into our symbels yet to come? Both Wells are accessed by our thoughts and deeds, and influence us throughout our lives. But by deliberately placing ourselves in the vicinity of one or the other during a sacred ceremony, we emphasize and tap into the power of one more than the other.

Oath-ring made from an antique lightning rod, attached to our iron and steel Thor's Hammer. Made by my blacksmith husband, Rosten Dean Rose. This oath-ring holds our wedding oaths, among others, and has held them strong for more than a quarter century. The Hammer and the Ring have also blessed many Blóts and symbels over decades of our Heathen lives, as we've laid treasured memories and orlog into the Wells and drawn inspiration from them.

Part VI. Orlog Awareness in Practice

*"The Norns Urðr, Verðandi, Skuld, under the World-Tree,"
by Ludwig Burger.*

The Norns look very thoughtful in this drawing; they are sandwiched between a lot of stuff going on in the World-Tree above and below them! It behooves us to be thoughtful, too, as we pursue the deeper meaning of orlog in our own lives, and ponder how to work with it in all its complexity.

28. Ordeal: Dealing with Orlog Today

The root of the word 'ordeal' is Proto-Germanic *uzdailiją *meaning "that which is dealt out."*

What I want to talk about here is the connection between 'orlog', 'ordeal', and 'dealing' with ordeals and challenges in our life. 'To deal' means to distribute or apportion out, which is what the Norns do by choosing life, carving runes, shaping Aldr, laying layers, speaking orlog. But 'to deal' also means 'to deal with something, to handle it, take care of it, resolve a situation.' An 'Or-deal' is something that Or-log deals out to us, a life-challenge that we ourselves must deal with.

An 'or-deal' in a Heathen philosophical sense means *'the primal roots of a given ordeal-circumstance: the orlog, the weaving of wyrd, which has been dealt out for us to face here and now, in this place, in this time.'* An 'ordeal' has the connotation of a struggle, a challenge, a personal testing, and it is that, but it is more. It is fateful, it is a weaving of wyrd, a drawing-together of the strands of our life into a nexus-point of deep significance. Much of our past has gone into reaching this nexus-point of the ordeal, and much will lead forth from its outcome that will shape our time to come.

The ordeal of life is a challenge and a struggle, indeed, but more than that, it shapes the whole pattern of our Being, and shapes the meaning that our life holds. Our purpose in life is not to avoid or escape orlog and the ordeals that arise from it, but to rise to the challenge they offer: the challenge not only to meet the ordeal successfully, but to forge a pathway to emerge from the ordeal with greater wisdom, soul-qualities, and strength than we had when we went into it.

Orlog is Personal

"What we see so often in Norse literature is something that is perhaps unique in European paganism: an attempt to escape fate by living up to it—the near-opposite of hubris. In other words, the acknowledgement of fate provides the necessary presupposition for facing the challenges of life, which...are precisely made meaningful by it. It is a hugely impressive humanistic vision." (Winterbourne, p. 17).

Winterbourne is here implying something that appears often in ancient literature: our orlog is personal. When it unfolds into difficulties and challenges in our life it is our 'worthy opponent' against which we measure ourselves: our courage and determination, our vision, our ethical strength, our might and main. And perhaps most of all our wisdom, rooted in a Heathen understanding of the nature of orlog.

An ordeal, in my view, is defined as a serious challenge or difficulty that has developed in our life through the workings of orlog. In some cases it may be caused by our own mistakes, neglect of our responsibilities, or wrongdoing that we have committed and that we must work our way through, not seek to escape or excuse. Other times our ordeal may result from mistakes, neglect, or wrongdoing committed by others, which affect us and which we must deal with in our own life. Sometimes our own ordeal consists of the need to help others through their ordeals, such as caring for a family member with serious health problems.

For example, I supported my mother on a daily basis through eleven years of Alzheimer's; this was an ordeal for her, me, and our other family members. Not just an ordeal in the sense of the suffering it caused, but also in the sense that each of us, my mother included, did our personal best to deal with the situation wisely, courageously, compassionately, patiently, supportively, and lovingly: by honing our own best qualities and strengths to meet this ordeal and face it to the end. The orlog of family ties of love and loyalty, layers that my mother fostered as she interacted with family throughout her life, led directly to the strengths we all were able to bring to support her and each other as she faced her orlog-while, the difficult end of her life.

Working with the Knots

One metaphor I use to illustrate the concept of the ordeal is macrame, with complex patterns of strands that are knotted together at certain points. Those knots, those nexus-points, are where strands of orlog come together to create a significant event or situation for us, which may be something really challenging and difficult, a 'knotty problem' that we must deal with somehow.

Ordeal: Dealing with Orlog Today

Knots can cause problems and challenges, being difficult to untangle. But knots also hold the strands of our life together and create patterns—patterns that we can choose how to shape. Patterns, and their beauty and symmetry, are made by twists, loops, bindings, knots, interweavings: in fabric arts, and in the way we deal with our lives.

We're all called to deal with orlog and wyrd in our lives, and as Heathens it makes sense to *work with* these patterns rather than pulling against them or running away from them. How do we deal with ordeals, struggles, challenges, in this quintessentially Heathen way? My view is that we do not regard these ordeals as afflictions and persecutions; we avoid taking a victim stance here. Embracing victimhood is not 'dealing' with orlog and ordeals. It overcomes nothing; instead, it is overcome by events and left helpless.

I don't at all mean that we should fail in compassionate and supportive responses toward others who have become victims of terrible events. There are many times in life when helping others who are overwhelmed by circumstances, or standing together as a group against adversity, is the right thing to do. We should be compassionate toward ourselves when needed, too, but do that in practical, supportive, and problem-solving ways. When I suggest that we avoid taking a victimhood stance ourselves, I'm talking about our choice of attitude toward the events of our own life. We can regard ordeals, challenges and difficulties as an honorable warrior regards a worthy opponent or a skilled sparring partner: as a situation where we are called upon to bring everything we have, everything we are capable of, in order to face our challenge.

We may 'win' in the sense of overcoming the challenge, dealing with it, resolving the problem. Or we may not win; sometimes the challenge is too great for us to overcome, at least at that time. In that case, we can still face the situation with courage, learn from it, and grow our inner qualities and resources so we can continue to face these challenges with courage and wisdom. *And* we keep a sharp eye out for future possibilities to resolve the situation! Just because we can't prevail today, doesn't necessarily mean we can't do so in the future, after we've developed more wisdom, inner strength and resources from facing the situation today.

We don't fall back in despair, or run away from our ordeals. Instead we seek to understand the patterns, the lessons, the guidance, that our Gods and Goddesses, Norns and ancestors, are presenting to us through the ordeals and challenges of our lives. This follows the understanding that orlog contains the significance and meaning of events. What we do here, how wisely and well we deal with our ordeals, *matters:* it matters to us and to those around us, in mundane ways and in spiritual ways, which are both important. We may be handed knots to deal with in our lives, but we can use them to recreate the patterns that shape us, enhancing their strength, significance, and even their beauty.

The Formal Ordeal

My concept of the Heathen ordeal does not involve the deliberate infliction of pain, as 'ordeal' is sometimes understood in other contexts. An artificially-created episode of deliberately inflicted pain or struggle is not likely to be rooted in wyrd and orlog, nor dealt out to us by the

Ordeal: Dealing with Orlog Today

Norns as part of our path toward wisdom. Thus, I do not consider this kind of artificial ordeal as a true Heathen ordeal in the philosophical sense: an ordeal which is rooted in and arises out of orlog, and leads us toward the wisdom of the Norns.

Sometimes, however, we may choose to go through a deliberate, ceremonial ordeal, a spiritual challenge to grow our Heathen might and main. This often involves the imitation of some challenge that our Holy Ones have endured. Not using one hand for a period of time to temporarily imitate Tyr's challenge is one example, or standing / sitting under (or ideally up in) a tree and fasting for a significant period of time while meditating on the runes is a way to imitate Odin's challenge. A spiritual seeking for some dimly-seen spiritual goal would imitate Freya's challenge of her search for Óðr, while working to mitigate danger and harm to others would imitate Frigg's efforts to save her son Baldr.

Frigg with her companions, clearly preparing for action! The armed Goddess may be Hlin, who provides refuge and protection to those in danger. By Emil Doepler.

For any of our Deities we can come up with a ceremonial ordeal, dedicated to them, to bring us closer to them and their wisdom. Our choice to engage in such a ceremonial ordeal would likely be the result of our own orlog nudging us in that direction. It is certainly not a requirement for Heathen practice, however; it's just a choice that some people may make.

We may also, at some point in our life, choose to enter a situation or take up a task that is truly daunting, challenging, perhaps dangerous or life-changing, involving real personal sacrifice—a true ordeal—for some overwhelmingly good reason or to support a cause we believe in with all our heart. This is another type of ordeal that we may choose for ourselves—one that grows out of the values and meaningfulness of the layers of orlog that we and the Norns have laid during our life.

Another type of voluntary ordeal is the initiatory ceremony or ordeal, which should be done with respect for the worth of human life and dignity, and respect for dedicated effort, rather than being an exercise in abuse and degradation. An ordeal of initiation is, in fact, a way of weaving a person into the orlog of the group, organization, or practice (such as an esoteric path) that the person wants to join or follow. The initiation ceremony or ordeal should reflect the values of the group or practice, giving the neophyte a sense of what that group stands for, or what the practice involves. It involves more than just joining a group: what the neophyte is doing, during initiation, is joining their orlog with the orlog of the group.

For this reason, it's important to think carefully about the group or the practice beforehand: do you want to be part of their orlog? Is it a good match with your own orlog and your values—will it support you in laying good orlog in your life, and help you express and live your values? Or will your membership end up being a source of constant inner conflict between your values, your orlog, and those of the group or practice?

Considering an initiatory ordeal, before agreeing to undertake it, is the time to ask oneself these important questions. If the ordeal involves abuse and degrading behavior, it's reasonable to ask: are these actions and experiences layers that I want to lay in my own orlog, and do I want to join with people and a group that is shaped and represented by these actions? An initiatory ordeal is a significant, orlog-influencing event, likely to be laid in the Well, and should be approached with serious thought and intent.

All forms of ordeal, whether forced upon us or chosen by us, are things that we need to or choose to 'deal with,' and thereby develop our qualities of character such as courage, wisdom, determination, patience, compassion, insight, devotion, spiritual discernment, or whatever qualities are called for in that situation. Calling on the Norns, Tyr / Tiw, and our other Holy Ones can help us perceive the deeper meaning of the ordeal and its connection to our orlog, whether the ordeal is forced upon us or whether we choose it, and help us face it with courage, strength, and wisdom.

Heroes of Our Own Time

To summarize: the Heathen attitude toward orlog and wyrd in the form of necessity, ordeals, and challenging circumstances is neither to collapse under it, nor to try to flee it in ways that in the end make the situation worse (for example: through addictions, taking the problem out on others, or abdicating our responsibilities). Instead, we can

Ordeal: Dealing with Orlog Today

use the ordeal as a foil or a 'worthy opponent,' to hone our own essential qualities, our uniqueness and our power, our own moral choices, as we face the pressures of necessity.

Thus, orlog shapes our path, and our path in turn shapes orlog that is coming into being. In this way, we orient ourselves to a Heathen path of strength, wisdom and resilience, able to face the ordeals that orlog deals out to us and use them to grow our might and main. By regarding the difficulties of our lives as Heathen spiritual ordeals rooted in orlog, and dealing with them according to Heathen values, we each become heroes in our own unique ways, on our own unique path of life: heroes in—and of—our own time.

Ordeal: Dealing with Orlog Today

It's a tough climb...use everything you've got to get yourself through the ordeal!

29. *Sara:* Tools for Working with Orlog

By Sara Axtell

The Big, Sticky Velcro Ball of Orlog

We often think of orlog as a tapestry, with our actions as threads that help to create the whole. We can also think of ways that orlog can operate like a big ball of velcro rolling in wool fibers: a situation we are experiencing in the present sticks to other patterns that are deeper in the Well. This can help us to understand our own reactions, as well as others' reactions to what we say and do. For example, what is happening in the present might stick to my own family patterns: an interaction I am having might remind me of how my father and I interacted when I was a child. And my reactions and emotions I experience in the current situation might be rooted there. This doesn't mean my pain isn't real; it just helps me to understand all of the places the pain is coming from and allows me to be more present to the current situation.

A situation in the present might also snag a deeper cultural pattern. I might realize that the person I am interacting with is reacting to what I said because it is what people in my position often say and suggests an assumption or expectation. For example, I might say to a young father, "Wow, you are really good with your baby." If he reacts negatively, he may be reacting not just to my statement, but to the repeated statements that many people have made, suggesting an assumption that we do not expect him to be able to care for his baby, perhaps due to his age or gender. When I realize this, I can ask, "is that actually a pattern I want to contribute to and make stronger with my actions, or is that a pattern I would like to help transform or heal?"

Some Tools for Working with Orlog

Recognizing and beginning to untangle all of these threads of orlog is part of a healing process, a part of becoming more whole, more fully ourselves and present to those around us. It is hard work, and we need tools and resources to help us. What follows are some of the resources that we've been working with in circles that I am a part of. I offer them to spark conversation and sharing across different Heathen communities doing this work. Please use your own knowledge and intuition to guide your own use of any of these resources.

Runes

Runes are one resource that I have found helpful in my own journey. I have learned a lot about using runes in this way from my participation in the Rune and Virtues Study Group, started by Bee Bletsian and now facilitated by Kristina Kvarnlov-Leverty.

For example, **Ansuz** is for the breaking of fetters, for letting go of things that bind us. It can help loosen the hold that a pattern in the orlog has on us.

Uruz teaches that, just as metal becomes stronger as the slag comes off of it, we become stronger and more rooted when we let go of patterns that don't serve us.

Mannaz helps us to heal the disconnections within us. It helps us to be more whole. It reminds us that we are not trying to be perfect in this work, but more fully human and alive.

Runes can remind me of the changes I am trying to make. I write them on my skin. Create bind runes. Stitch them into a talisman to carry with me. They remind me of what new patterns I am trying to lay. Runes can help hold the emotions that come up while we are doing healing work. I sing and chant them, breathe them in and out.

I visualize them:
The flow of **Laguz** helps the anxiety, stress, or fear to run out to my body, out the soles of my feet into the Earth.

Othala, like the fence around the yard, can help to create or strengthen boundaries when I need them. (Thanks, Michelle Ray, for sharing this interpretation of Kveldulf Gundarsson's (1990) image.)

Spells or Charms

I have also found that there are some spells or charms that can be spiritual supports in the healing process. For example, this 9th century Old Saxon charm discussed in Ben Waggoner's *Norse Healing* (p.xv-xvi) can help when there is an emotion or pattern in the orlog that I am having trouble releasing. The charm reveals a lot about the theories of sickness and healing at that time when disease was conceptualized as a worm that the body needs to expel. I have found it can be a helpful support (sometimes in combination with Ansuz) for breaking the hold that a pattern has on me. I say it (or even yell it) to aid in letting go of the pattern.

Go out, worm, with your nine wormlings
Out from the marrow to the bone;
From the bone to the flesh;
Out from the flesh to the skin;
Out from the skin to the hoof!

Ritual and Ceremony

Many people are working with rituals and ceremonies that can help to heal and shift orlog. In Healing Roots, a learning community I am a part of, we are working with ways to use symbel as a healing ceremony specifically for healing and shifting orlog. Sometimes we do this in combination with Winifred's nine-fold process as discussed in Chapter 31. Symbel is a time to be witnessed and supported by community. We can speak over the horn about the changes we are trying to make, receive support from others, and talk about progress and setbacks. Perhaps there are other groups working with symbel in this way as well.

In my own kindred, Gullveig's Hearth, we have started working with a brief ceremony based on the moon cycle. Building on another idea presented in Waggoner's *Norse*

Healing, the ceremony is designed to be held on the sixth or seventh day of each moon cycle, said to be good days for healing. It is very simple and draws language from Larrington's translation of *Sigdrifumal* (verse 11) and *Hávamál* (verse 149), and Bellows' translation of *Hávamál* (verse 157) in the Poetic Edda.

We sing to Eir and to Menglad, we sing to the healers among our ancestors and to the spirits of this place with whom we share our luck.

[Light candle]

We sing branch-runes to mend our wounds, runes written on the bark of trees with their boughs bent eastward.

We sing runes to loosen patterns of harm. The fetters springing from our feet, bonds breaking from our hands.

We sing runes to remain whole.
Whole to the field of fight,
Whole from the field of fight,
And whole when we arrive back home.

[Each person speaks what is on their heart. What are you trying to heal tonight? What is one rune that symbolizes this healing for you?]

[Burn healing herb]

[Galdr: chant the runes that have been shared by each person. For example, in our Sunday morning Galdr group, we chant a 3x3 weaving of the runes: rune 1 three times, rune 2 three times, rune 3 three times. And through this same cycle 2 times more.]

For mending, for loosening, for wholeness.

[Go outside to make an offering.]

Shild

Shild can also help us to heal orlog. Shild is a process of restoring balances in the relationships between people. If my cows cross the creek into the fields of the neighboring farm and eat all their grass, the damage that my cows have created to my neighbor's livelihood causes an imbalance in our relationship. Payment of a shild can help to restore the balance in that relationship. In this example, perhaps half of the cheese that I make with the milk from those cows is given to that neighbor.

Winifred conceptualizes shild as threads that the Norn Skuld attaches to our wyrd or orlog. These threads can limit the directions along which our orlog can unfold. As she writes in Chapter 31 about wyrd and shild, "if we hope to create a change in our wyrd, we must first settle any shild––any moral debt or obligation––that our deeds or lack of deeds may have brought about. Or, it may be that we have made an oath, promise or commitment, that has not been fulfilled, and which we can now determine to fulfill. When this has been done, there is a greater degree of freedom, an opportunity, that opens up out of the pattern of That-Which-Is, just as it is shaping into That-Which-Is-Becoming."

Tools for Working with Orlog

In that way, the payment of shild can be about repairing our relationship with ourselves, repairing our own wholeness. My own experience with paying shild is varied and complex. Some shild I have paid on behalf of myself. Some I have helped to pay on behalf of a group. Some I have been asked to pay when I did not believe the debt was mine. Some I am still struggling to fulfill after years of work (which may actually reflect our lack of capacity and infrastructure needed to effectively utilize these tools).

In modern Heathenry, we often see shild as a form of restorative justice. But our current context is much less relational than the communities in which shild practices developed. It is difficult to step outside the mindset of our highly punitive system of 'law and justice.' Simply transplanting a practice of shild into our communities as they as are now risks replicating our punitive system on a community level. It will not have the reparative effects that it did in earlier times. We will have to build the relational context that is needed to support a system of shild.

How can we build the context that is needed to renew shild as a reparative practice? In restorative justice, the use of community-building circles is advocated to build a foundation for reparative practices *(Crisis and Trauma Resource Institute, n.d.).* Community-building circles invite participants to authentically share their thoughts, emotions, and experiences with others in the circle; each person has the opportunity to speak uninterrupted until they pass to the next person. The circles that are used in restorative justice draw on teachings from Indigenous cultures in North America. *Living Justice Press* recounts some of the history of cultural sharing that has led to circles being used in non-Indigenous contexts. There are traditional cultures around the world which have similar approaches to community-based restorative justice.

I think we can build on what many Heathen groups already do in symbel to practice this kind of community circle. We can also invest in Heathen communities by taking advantage of available learning opportunities about restorative justice. That will help us to gain the skills and perspectives we need if we are to renew and adapt the practice of shild for our communities today in a way that will bring healing and repair.

Sara's Bind Rune

A Bind Rune to Hold this Work

We may hold shild on the individual level (for a way we have harmed another individual) or collective level (when we are a member of a group that has harmed another group.) I have found this bind rune to be helpful in that work of collective shild, specifically, to help me be fully present when I am listening to someone recount historical and current wrongs that have been committed and the suffering that those actions have caused. We may often become defensive or immobilized in the face of difficult truths. This bind rune can help me to stay present and listen deeply.

The bindrune is rooted in **Perthro,** which represents the Well of Wyrd. **Eihwaz** allows me to bend but not break with the weight of what I am learning. **Ansuz** helps to loosen the fetters of the patterns of action that have created the harm. **Berkana** speaks to what I would like to grow out of the listening process: a laying of new patterns of healing and collective well-being.

References for this chapter

Bellows, Henry Adams. (1923) *The Poetic Edda*. Translated from the Icelandic with an introduction and notes. The American-Scandinavian Foundation.

Crisis and Trauma Resource Institute. (n.d.) *Restorative Justice: Facilitating dialogue.*

Gundarsson, K. (1990). *Teutonic Magic*. Llewellyn Publications.

Larrington, C. (2014). *The Poetic Edda*. Oxford University Press.

Living Justice Press. (n.d.) *The Origin of Circles.* https://livingjusticepress.org/

Waggoner, B. (Ed.). (2011). *Norse magical and herbal healing.* Troth Publications.

30. *Sara:* Healing Orlog Journaling Questions

By Sara Axtell, for the Rune and Virtues Group

I know an ash-tree, named Yggdrasil:
Sparkling showers are shed on its leaves
That drip dew into the dales below,
By Urd's Well it waves evergreen,
Stands over that still pool,
Near it a bower whence now there come
The Fate Maidens, first Urd,
Skuld second, scorer of runes
Then Verdandi, third of the Norns:
The laws that determine the lives of men
They fixed forever and their fate sealed.
    -Völuspá (Auden and Taylor translation)

The concept of orlog gives us a way of thinking about ancestral healing. Orlog describes the influence of the past on the present. The great tree Yggdrasil holds the cosmos. Dew drips from the leaves, and falls into the Well of Urð at the foot of the tree. Water from the Well is taken up by the roots of the Tree. This cycle of water between the Well and the Tree is a metaphor for our own actions (Bauschatz Ch. IV).

Generation after generation we lay our actions into the Well where they create patterns with the other actions that have already been laid. Like threads creating a pattern in a tapestry. These patterns create the foundations for the actions that continue to unfold. Some of these patterns may unfold in individuals and families, and others affect whole communities and cultural groups. Some patterns that we inherit bring health and abundance to our lives and the lives of those around us. These are the patterns that teach us to support each other and create strong families and communities. But other patterns may cause great damage to ourselves and to others, like patterns of addiction and violence, or patterns that support and reinforce the impacts of structural inequalities or political and state violence.

What could it mean to heal orlog? In Chapter 31, Winifred describes a process for healing orlog using ceremony, reflection, and action in the world. The process builds on weaving as a metaphor for shaping orlog. Kari Tauring's (2010) tradition of Völva Stav uses sound, rhythm, and music to influence multiple dimensions of the soul and heal wounds that have been passed to us from earlier generations.

What follows is a series of reflection, journaling, and discussion questions. The questions are designed to support a process for healing orlog that involves understanding and transforming unhealthy patterns, and repairing harm that they have caused to ourselves and to other people. As we do this work in our own lives, the healing ripples back in the tapestry to our ancestors, and helps to create a healthier foundation for the next generation.

The process is organized into three sections, one section for each of the Norns, or beings who tend the Well and the Tree. Each of the Norns represents a part of the fabric of orlog. Verðandi's name means 'becoming.' She represents what is unfolding in the present moment. Urð represents what has already been laid into the Well. Skuld's name means 'debt' or 'obligation.' She represents what is obligated to happen based on what has already been laid down. "It is also said that those norns who live beside Urd's Well draw water every day from the spring and that they splash this, mixed with the mud that lies beside the well, over the ash so that it branches will not wither or decay." *(Gylfaginning* in the Prose Edda, Byock translation, p. 27.)

Verðandi: Feelings and Conditions Unfolding in the Present Moment

1. What are the actions, situations, conditions that have led to your understanding about the need for healing? What is the Nauthiz, or compelling need, that you feel?

Urð: Understanding the Patterns in the Well

1. What are all of the personal, family, and cultural patterns that led to that action/situation/condition? If you can identify personal and family patterns, how do those patterns fit into larger cultural patterns? If you can identify cultural patterns, how do you participate in those patterns on a personal or family level?

2. What is the history of those patterns? How did they develop over generations? What were the conditions that gave rise to the patterns? A response to trauma? A response to particular conditions and structures that existed at certain times / cycles in our history?

3. What have been the impacts of these patterns over time? On you? On your ancestors? On others in your family and community? On communities that you are not a part of, but who have been affected by the patterns? On the land?

Skuld: Healing, Transformation, Coming into Balance

How can damaging patterns in the Well be healed or transformed? How can a balance be restored that will bring weal and well-being to those who have been harmed by the pattern, to you and your own family and to the community as a whole?

1. What are new patterns of thought and action that you are trying to lay in the well?

2. What are the cultural and spiritual resources (e.g., teachings, practices, symbols) that can help you to lay those actions?

> a. Are there runes that hold teachings about these new patterns?

> b. Are there runes that can help you hold feelings, reactions, emotions as you do this work?

c. Who can you call on to support you in this work? Friends, kindred members, family, ancestors, land spirits, Elder Kin?

d. Are there practices, rituals, or ceremonies that can support you as you lay the new patterns? For example, symbel is a ritual for truth telling, for making oaths or commitments, and for bringing together a community of support.

3. Is there shild (reparation or compensation) that needs to be paid? If so, what do you think can help to restore the balance? The previous chapter offers additional guidance regarding the following questions.

a. Are you able to talk directly to a specific person who has been harmed by the pattern? If so, what shild do they think would help to heal and restore balance to your relationship? Note that in some cases having a direct conversation would add to the harm. Use your best judgement and discernment, and guidance from the individual themselves or elders or other community members.

b. How could you contribute to repairing the harm and preventing additional harms?

c. How can you contribute to bringing weal to persons harmed, to the community, to the land?

d. How might the payment of shild help to lay healthy patterns in the Well?

This is long-term, iterative work. Work that we can do together in community. It can help us to repair and heal harms, and relearn positive, healthy practices within our ancestral cultures. It helps to re-weave threads in the tapestry that have been frayed or broken, so that we can live more fully, deeply connected lives.

Acknowledgements

The process of reflection, journaling, and discussion questions described in this chapter is based on the work of the Rune and Virtues Study Group, a small grassroots learning community. The group was started by Bee Bletsian and is currently facilitated by Kristina Kvarnlov-Leverty. The work that we do is strongly influenced by what we have learned in the Healing Roots Learning Community. I (Sara Axtell) have woven the threads of our study together in order to share these journaling exercises.

References for this chapter

Bauschatz, P. C. (1982). *The Well and the Tree: World and Time in Early Germanic Culture.* University of Massachusetts Press.

Mimisbrunnr.info. (2017). "Paul B. Taylor & W. H. Auden, 1967 & 1981". Eddic to English, Mimisbrunnr.info. URL: https://www.mimisbrunnr.info/eddic-to-english-taylor-auden-1967-1981

Sturluson, Snorri. (2006). *The Prose Edda: Norse Mythology.* Translated and introduced by Jesse L. Byock, Penguin Classics.

Tauring, K. (2010). Völva Stav Manual.
https://www.karitauring.com/about-5

Healing Orlog Journaling Questions

Two of the cords I (Winifred) use for Heathen work. The larger one is my soul-cord, with clusters of strands representing each of my souls. The smaller one is a runic tally-string, with runes painted on wooden beads.

The meditative creation and use of magical cords is a very useful practice, including blessing-cords, protective cords, and cords which carry specific symbolic meanings. In the following chapter I suggest making and using symbolic cords to help untangle harmful orlog and to lay new threads onto the loom of your wyrd.

31. Wyrd and Shild: A Ninefold Rite of Life Renewal

Note: There are several chapters in this book that can provide helpful background and preparation for the work described here. Chapter 21, "The Work of the Three Wells," gives a theoretical background for the ritual work in this chapter. Chapters 29 and 30, concerning tools and journaling questions for working with orlog, are useful on their own but can also provide structure for the steps outlined in the ritual here.

Here is a process and a set of rituals that serve two purposes. One is to discuss and illustrate aspects of the workings of orlog and of Wyrd and Scyld, in the context of how one might apply such knowledge in one's own life. 'Scyld' or Shild is the Anglo-Saxon equivalent of Skuld, one of the three Norns. Her name is related to 'should,' and her realm of action is 'what should be,' the consequences arising from past actions. Scyld or shild in Anglo-Saxon meant 'responsible for, liable for, in debt to,' among other meanings. The ethical meaning of 'shild' that I focus on here is 'moral debt or obligation.'

The second purpose of this chapter is to provide a specific ritual based on this knowledge, which can be used to help you address problematic aspects of your orlog if you choose to do so. When you find yourself in a position where bad luck, mistakes, wrongful deeds, problems of personal, familial, or cultural history, or other kinds of unhappy situations are constraining your ability to live a worthy life, this ritual can help you redesign your life and to offer a better life-thread to be woven on Wyrd's loom. Or, you may simply feel the need for a 'spiritual housecleaning' and a fresh start in your life: this ritual can also serve that purpose.

Please keep in mind that there is not enough strength in the words or ritual actions alone to effect such a change. The change must come about within yourself, affecting your understanding of and intentions toward yourself and the world around you, especially with respect to the Norns and your own orlog.

The Symbolism of the Ninefold Rite

The extended ritual provided here is intended to reach all the different parts of your body-soul complex. The prose explanations provided in the discussion are for the sake of your conscious, rational mind, and are also meant to help strengthen and direct your will and intentionality. The 'spells' or poetic portions of the ritual are directed toward the trans-rational aspects of your souls, that deal less with logic and words, and more with imagery and symbolism, mystical consciousness, and hidden memory. The actions that are called for in the spells bring in the participation of the physical body–the Lich.

Wyrd and Shild: A Ninefold Rite of Life Renewal

Thus, with rational prose, mytho-imagic poetry, and physical action, three major aspects of the body-soul complex are brought to bear in concert toward one's intention. If you can make up your own tune or chant for the spell parts of the ritual, and if you wish to add more poetry or songs of your own composition or selection that is meaningful to you, this will further help the self-tuning and focusing process. These actions of weaving together the different parts of yourself and focusing them on your purpose is a personal enactment or mirroring of the weaving of the manifold strands of Wyrd in the world.

This is called a 'Ninefold Rite' because it involves three Wells, three Norns, and three steps. The Wells are the *Well of Wyrd, Mimir's Well,* and *Hvergelmir.* You might find it useful to review Chapter 21 on "The Work of the Three Wells" as you continue with this ninefold rite.

The *Well of Wyrd* holds the pattern of That-Which-Is, created by the strands of all significant deeds and events that have occurred, including your own: the orlog you have laid in the Well. All that is now coming into being is influenced by the pattern of orlog that has already been laid. To change the influence of orlog for the better, it is necessary for you to add another deed—a life-changing deed and a deed of might—to this pattern, which will hopefully help to turn That-Which-Is-Becoming into a better direction for you. What has been woven in the past cannot be erased, but what is woven in the present can catch up the threads dangling from the past and weave them into a new pattern.

Mimir's Well is the collective memory of Heathenry and much else as well, perhaps all memories. It's the collective unconscious, to use another frame of reference. It contains all wisdom, knowledge and memory that have been. Odin's eye lies in this Well, the price for his draught of wisdom from it. People go to this Well to seek wisdom and understanding, and in turn, wisdom, memory and understanding that we gain during the course of our lives eventually finds its way into the treasure-hoard of Mimir's Well. Gaining even a small amount of wisdom and transpersonal memory from Mimir's Well often allows us to better understand and interpret the events and conditions of our life, and casts the whole pattern of it into a clearer perspective.

Hvergelmir, meaning 'the roaring cauldron,' is the churning cauldron, the whirling source of the great Wells: a mighty entity that is beyond any close-up human perception and knowledge. I believe that the whelming and stirring of this well is powered by the perpetual creative force that occurs when the primal Ice and Fire meet in Ginnungagap—the chasm of unbeing within which the worlds are born. I think that Hvergelmir can be a source of randomness, newness and change, that can sometimes appear and surge up through the other Wells, subtly affecting their contents and patterns.

Shild and the Actions of the Norns

Wyrd or *Urðr* is the Norn who rules the Well of Wyrd and That-Which-Is, creating a pattern out of all our deeds and events that shapes the process of becoming. *Verðandi* is the Norn who presides over That-Which-Is-Becoming, the very instant when a being or a deed comes into existence. *Skuld* spins the thread that is formed from the 'shild,' the moral debt or obligation, that we incur by our choices, commitments and deeds or lack thereof, in our lives, current and past, and sometimes indirectly from the lives of any whose wyrd has been woven together with ours through kinship or oath bonds.

The shild or moral debt we incur can be of a positive nature, something we have earned by our efforts, as would be contained in the main (soul-power) and the luck that are generated by an oath given and kept or a good deed done. Or, it can be of a negative nature, such as the moral debt (including loss of main—soul power—and luck) generated by an oath forsworn or an ill deed done. This chapter will primarily focus on the effects of negative shild, or moral debt.

Shild-threads are attached to any deed, action, or being that arises in the moment of Becoming, and again at any time during their span of existence that the being, deed, or action generates shild. Through these threads, Skuld tugs upon that deed or being, affecting their path and outcome, according to the shild that has accumulated from their past. More shild may be added, strengthening the thread, as the being or the deed continues its existence and effects.

Looking at this effect from the outside, it may seem to us that Skuld is 'the future,' inevitable and set, but this is not necessarily the case. It is often possible to pay at least some of our negative shild in some way, which then reduces the strength of the shild-thread that tugs at our wyrd, leaving us with more freedom of choice for our future directions.

Thus, if we hope to create a change in our wyrd, we must first settle any shild—any moral debt or obligation—that our deeds or lack of deeds may have brought about. Or, it may be that we have made an oath, promise or commitment that has not been fulfilled, and which we can now determine to fulfill. When this has been done, there is a greater degree of freedom, an opportunity, that opens up out of the pattern of That-Which-Is-Becoming.

If there are no threads of shild, or fewer, thinner ones, attached to this new Becoming, it is more free to move in a different direction, according to one's will. This degree of freedom that comes about, seized with true-hearted intent and strength of soul, offers a chance to turn one's wyrd toward the better.

It is not complete freedom or randomness, indeed: all that comes about is shaped by the patterns of orlog that have already been laid, and this pattern cannot be torn out or uprooted. But the beginnings of a new pattern can often be woven onto the tail-ends of the old pattern, if we have the insight and determination to go about it rightly. The steps of the ritual described here are intended to help guide you in this process.

'Turning'

You will notice that in the final part of the spell associated with each step is the process of 'turning.' There is deep meaning associated with this process. The word *wyrd* itself is derived from an ancient Germanic word meaning 'to turn, to wind.' In a rite of renewal, what one wishes to do is turn away from the old, negative patterns and ways, and turn toward a new and better path. Spinning—the process of turning, twisting, winding raw fiber into thread—is one of the mightiest deeds of power and magic recognized by the Heathen forebears. Spinning was thought to influence wyrd itself. Even today, many folktales and fairy tales survive in which a spindle and / or thread plays a fateful role in the story, or appear in the tale as an indicator that mighty magic or mystery is about to occur.

Wyrd and Shild: A Ninefold Rite of Life Renewal

The inclusion of the 'turning verse' in each spell of this ritual is therefore intended to align you with this mystery of turning, of winding wyrd. If you are able, physically perform the action of turning around as you speak or chant the verse, holding in your focused mind a perception of the 'power of turning' on all the planes of existence as you do so.

Imagine yourself as a spindle, and hold the image of the Tree itself: the Spindle of Wyrd, the Axis of the Worlds, around which they turn and have their being. You may continue to repeat the turning verse, until you feel that the stated intention of the verse has been brought about. (It is advisable to turn around slowly, however, to avoid dizziness! Alternatively, make these turns in your imagination.) If you have the skill, you could use a distaff and spindle to spin thread instead, as you chant the turning verses.

Step One: Forming Your Intent

It is best to act out each of these steps to the extent possible. Try to find a body of water, a hole in the ground, a cave, a cliffside, or some other location that could symbolize the Hvergelmir and Mimir's Well for this step. If you have to, dig a hole yourself, or find some other creative alternative.

Before you begin the rite, braid, spin or twist for yourself a cord or thread in colors that symbolize for you what it is you want to change or overcome in your life.

If you do not have access to any of these things, work with images of them in your imagination, or find simple objects or locations that can symbolize these things for you. For example, a cup or a bowl, even a circle drawn on a piece of paper, can symbolize the Wells. A sock can stand in place of a cord, if you have no access to string or thread. Anything that you decide is your chosen symbol will work for you in this ritual.

The thing you want to change through this ritual could be one or more deeds you did that were wrong or badly mistaken, a negative attitude, a run of bad luck, failure or neglect of some obligation or duty, some part of yourself that has developed in undesirable ways even if that was not all your own doing, or whatever else is wrong.

As you braid or twist your cord (or wring and twist your sock-cord), put into the cord all the feelings and consequences that arise from the aspect you are trying to change. Chant over your cord, shout at it (in private!), cry tears on it, grind it in your teeth, tie it in knots, stomp on it, do a rune-working with it, carry it around with you and live with it for awhile. Do whatever you need to, to make sure you've really inserted into the cord the negative energy you're trying to change. This is no longer just a plain old string, but something a good deal more.

If you are going to throw this cord into a body of water or other natural area, choose something natural or biodegradable to make your cord out of. For example: twisted grass or thin flexible twigs, seaweed, bread dough twisted and baked, taffy that you make, stretch and twist yourself. These materials may not stand up to all of the rough treatment I suggest above, but some creative thought will lead you to other options. For example, you could keep your bread dough in the refrigerator for several days and take it out from time to time to pound and knead your feelings into it, before you bake it.

As you begin the rite, go to the place you have chosen at a time that is meaningful to you. Enact the rite by holding the cord tightly in one hand, then pulling it out slowly with difficulty and force, using your other hand. If your 'cord' is made of delicate material, pull more gently but tense your muscles hard to make your body feel the work, like isotonic exercise. Take as long as you need, repeating the verse and / or adding more poetry or your own words to it, to visualize and feel this drawing-out from yourself of the aspects you want to change. If there is pain, anger, or other ill feelings associated with the drawing-out process, allow yourself to feel them as fully as is safe for you. Then throw the cord into the water, hole, bowl, circle, or wherever you have chosen, representing Hvergelmir.

Then as you chant the words aloud, envision the transformation of this thread as it passes through the Wells: its unraveling and unwinding in the violent churning of Hvergelmir, then the shredded strands floating up from Hvergelmir into Mimir's quiet cavern-well, there to combine with strands of wisdom and memory from the past, and begin to reassemble itself into a new configuration.

If you are scientifically inclined, you can envision this as sort of a metaphysical 'recombinant DNA' process, with the shredded strands representing bits of DNA from an outworn chromosome, the wisdom and memory from Mimir's Well as the genes that guide the re-assembly, and the new configuration becoming a new chromosome with different characteristics, that will guide the development of new soul-qualities in you.

Pause as long as you wish between the phrases of the spell, to meditate on the images that come to mind. When you come to the turning-chant, physically turn yourself around if you can. ('Hvergelmir' is pronounced *VAIR-gel-meer,* with a hard 'g', and with the addition of a strong, huffing H-sound at the beginning. Or if it is hard to say that way, you can leave the 'H' off.) Repeat the spell as many times as you wish, perhaps with the addition of other poetic lines of your choice, until you feel a sense of completion and closure for this step of the rite.

Words to speak or chant:

Pull out and cast off cursed woe-working threads,
Thrown to Hvergelmir's spinning deeps:

    Whelmed....

        Torn asunder.....

            Re-spun....

New-shaped to ripple and shimmer
Through Mimir's moss-cool cavern,
Through World-Mind's echoing dimness,
Spinning new wisdom out of ancient strands.

Turn and turn again,
Turn and turn again,
Bind off old threads
Wind and weave anew.

If the place you have thrown your cord is not a place that will 'take it away' as a river or the ocean would do, or a hole in the ground that you can bury, then first dry the cord if it is wet, and afterwards burn it in a fireproof container. If you cannot do that, then 'decommission' your cord / sock / whatever, by declaring that it has served its purpose and now is no longer a symbol of anything. Put it aside, unused, for as long as you can, so its symbolic force can dissipate.

Step Two: Paying Your Shild

This step must be taken with the utmost seriousness, taking all the time you need to do it right. It could take weeks, months, or more, if your shild is heavy. Even if the thing that is wrong, that you are trying to change, seems not to be your fault or not entirely your fault, it is still important to look for traces of shild, from this life, past lives, or from the orlog of your kin.

The paying of shild is in part the great deed you will do, to repattern the weavings of wyrd in your life. (The other part of the deed is your firm intention to change your life, and then doing it.) Try to stand outside yourself, looking at the situation objectively so that you place neither too much nor too little responsibility on yourself for the thing you are trying to change. If you have a wise and trusted friend who is not too closely involved in the situation, you might seek this person's rede to make sure you are taking a well-balanced view of the circumstances.

Examining your shild

Meditate on the situation, letting your mind roam back to the roots of what has happened in your life, and follow those threads through your life until you understand at least the basic nature of the causes-and-effects that brought you where you are. Mentally placing yourself in Mimir's cavern as you do this, seated next to his dark Well, may help to infuse ancient wisdom and the knowledge of your forebears into your process of life-examination. You may also wish to make an offering to the Norns, Mimir, and/or to any of our

Wyrd and Shild: A Ninefold Rite of Life Renewal

Goddesses or Gods whom you think could best help you do the needed work, and ask their aid: their clear sight and fair judgement to guide you.

Two runes can be of special help in your efforts here: Nauthiz or 'Need,' and Fehu or 'Fee.' Strive to recognize the shape and nature of what is needed, and what fee would balance or redress that need. *Fee often can balance need:* this is the principle that lies behind *wergild*—the fee paid for damages done to person, property, or reputation, or even to one's dignity in some cases. This principle in fact goes much deeper into the metaphysical realms, having to do with the balance of *hamingja,* or spiritual power and luck, between persons and other beings and processes, and how injury, damage or insult throws the balance off.

Wergild, in the past, was not intended as a punishment *per se,* but rather as a way to redress an imbalance in how hamingja and luck were distributed between one person and another, caused by their deeds and injuries. This is why ancient Heathens generally required wergild regardless of whether the injury was caused deliberately or accidentally, or even completely unknowingly. Fault, blame, and punishment were not the basic issue, nor the primary reason for requiring wergild, at least not during Heathen times. Rather, wergild was intended to right the imbalance of spiritual power—and also the dishonor—caused by the injury, however that injury came about.

In our own lives, if the fee owed is not honored, if shild is not acknowledged and addressed, then the heavy weight of need generated by shild can throw the whole pattern of one's wyrd out of kilter, causing many distressing effects in one's life.

Going deeper

Use the words of the Shild-Rite, given below, to focus your meditation and thought, until it becomes clear to you whether you have any unmet obligations, or whether any shild is owed, and if so what an appropriate wergild or payment of the shild would be. Usually, the best form in which to make the payment is one which is as much like the cause of the shild as possible (though you may wish to multiply your fee severalfold greater than the shild you perceive, in accordance with the Heathen thew or virtue of generosity).

For example, if you caused someone to lose something they valued (material or non-material), try to find something to give them that they will value as much as, or preferably more than, that which they lost. If you harmed someone—whether intentionally or not (you still have responsibility, even if you do not have 'fault 'or 'blame,'), then find some way to be of service to them or to someone else who could represent them.

You cannot always reach the one who was harmed, and may sometimes need to find a logical substitute. For example, if you harmed or neglected a child who is now grown or is unreachable, then do something good for another child or for children in general. If bad luck which has been plaguing you has made the world seem an ugly place, create beauty in some way that will bring joy to others—to humans and/or other beings such as landwights or housewights. (Not uncommonly, 'bad luck' can be caused by offending or neglecting some of the other beings who inhabit the worlds with us, but whose presence is often not obvious to us.)

Wyrd and Shild: A Ninefold Rite of Life Renewal

It is not always possible to make up for some harm you did to the same person or entity to whom you caused the harm. This is especially true if the shild attached to your life was originally generated by some ill-fated pattern in your family line, that might go back many generations. For example, some of my family's genealogical research indicates that I am descended from the 8th century emperor Charlemagne. As was pointed out to me by one Heathen, only half-jokingly, it may take the efforts of a good number of Heathen generations of Charlemagne's offspring to repay or rebalance the enormous shild he earned for his family line by his oppressive treatment of Heathen folk during his lifetime!

As a more modern example, it is unfortunately all too easy to find ill-fated, shild-generating patterns running through a family line, such as generation after generation of spouse or child abusers, as well as less lurid but still harmful patterns such as selfishness and neglect of one's proper obligations in life.

Thus, it may be that the shild that is unbalancing your life was not even earned by you, or not entirely by you, in addition to the fact that you may not be able to reach whoever was harmed in order to repay them. And, easily enough, if the shild is something that runs in your family line, you may well have been the recipient of harm yourself, in addition to owning your share of the family shild for harm done to others.

This seems a bit unfair on first glance, does it not? Sort of a double-whammy situation, a nasty tangle of wyrd- and shild-threads. Yet there is no denying that—fault or no fault—if this is indeed the case then this load of shild is a burden on your life and your wyrd. It should be addressed with courage and determination, in order to make room for a new and better strand to be cast onto the loom of Wyrd to improve your lot and that of the generations to come after you.

Restitution

If you yourself suffered harm for which you also own some of the kin-shild, try to find another family member for whom you could do something good—especially a child, for whom you might try to break or mitigate the family pattern of ill before it is ingrained in the child. (It is also easier not to blame a child for any kin-grudges that you might hold, in contrast to dealing with older members of the family.) Regard this relative whom you are benefiting as being a substitute for yourself, when you were harmed in the past. This way, your chosen substitute will be gaining payment for the injury done to you, at the same time that you are paying off your share of the kin-shild, thus evening out two harmful imbalances in one fell swoop! If direct contact with a child is not advisable, other benefits can be arranged, such as beginning a savings account or savings bonds for the child's education.

Rest assured that this would be an authentically traditional Heathen way of dealing with your dilemma, if you have such a dilemma. Elder Heathens regularly acted on the assumption that kinfolk were very acceptable substitutes for each other when it came to vengeance, paying or accepting wergild, erasing dishonor, and other ways of rebalancing their situation.

This makes it very clear that they did not regard wergild, or even vengeance, as being 'punishment.' What would be the point of punishing someone who did not even commit the ill deed—who perhaps was totally unaware of it, or even tried to prevent it? But since kinfolk could stand for each other, then when they were trying to rebalance the situation—the loss of *hamingja*, other forms of luck, and honor—one kinsman was as good as another. It did not really matter who paid, as long as somebody did. And—bottom line in terms of Heathen belief—one way or another, Skuld received her due if this was done: balance was restored and the shild did not hang on and on to plague everybody.

If it is not possible to work in this way with your literal kin, you can 'adopt' someone informally, someone in need of your help, and work with this person to pay your shild through help and service. Likewise, you could work on behalf of a group or a cause, such as a charity. Or simply do something for your 'neighbor'—anyone who is available to you: offer help, support, understanding, a listening ear, acts of simple kindness.

So, what you are seeking to do in this step of the ritual is rebalance something that is out of balance, out of kilter: rebalance 'you' with 'the world' so you are in right relationship with the world again. This needs to be done whether the lack of balance seems to be your fault or not, or even if it is not clear whose fault it is, or whether it is anyone's fault. Even if you cannot figure out the cause and effect, or who owns the obvious responsibility for the situation, usually an act of rebalancing will address the problem.

If after all your careful thought and meditation, you still seem to have no reason to pay anyone anything as wergild, then make a gift to the world out of sheer Heathen generosity. Imagine that you are sitting on one side of a balance-scale. What should go in the dish on the other side of the scale, to 'balance' you? Try out various gifts to see which one looks or feels right in your imagination. A gift could be a deed of service, a donation or contribution, a work of your own craft or art, some gesture of generosity of spirit. It could be given to someone close to you, or to a needy stranger, to the environment or the landwights, to your community, to one God or Goddess or to all of them....the possibilities are endless!

The Shild-Rite

Seek and use the inner core of your healthiest instincts, your inner sense of rightness, to decide what is the best gift or wergild to give. You may want to make use of some art of divination, such as rune casting or spaeworking, to help you seek this knowledge. You can use the first two verses of the following spell to help you focus your meditation and determination on this work, repeating them as long as needed, and adding more to the verses if you wish. Then, repeat them together with the last verse (the turning spell) a final time, to mark your deed when the work of this step is done. If you complete this step of shild-knowing and shild-paying, truly you will have done a great deed to mark and honor, worthy of a song!

Seek now to know what's owed;
Skuld's rede lies deep and cold.
Nor think to stint her meed:
Give fee to balance need.

All wergild find
In coin or kind:
Skuld cleanses heart and mind.

Wyrd and Shild: A Ninefold Rite of Life Renewal

Turn and turn again,
Turn and turn again,
So Skuld is paid her due:
Now wind and weave anew.

(Notes: The word 'stint' in this sense means to give ungenerously, to hold back in your giving. 'Meed' means something that is deserved or earned, a person's rightful share. 'Coin or kind' is an old phrase that means 'you can pay with money, or with barter or service.')

Step Three: Weaving Anew

Now you have cleared the decks of your life, to the extent you can do so: you have consciously sought an understanding of your orlog, and have addressed to the best of your ability any shild that might be owing. These actions certainly do not erase your wyrd as a whole—one would not wish this to happen in any case. To be wyrdless is simply not to exist as a conscious, responsible being. But your actions have helped to 'clean out the closet,' so to speak, and make room for some new, brighter threads to be cast onto the loom of Wyrd.

Be aware that these new threads will of course become a part of your orlog, so think carefully about your new directions and choices, seeking always the most honorable and virtuous path according to Heathen thew (virtues and values). It is helpful to open your mind to godly guidance through meditation and perhaps an offering, and you could again make use of some form of divination, to give you indications for good choices. Your struggle, your effort to change your life, is itself a deed—a mighty one—laid in the Well or cast onto the loom to reshape your orlog. This deed of change should itself be done rightly and truly, as the first of the new and better threads to be attached to your wyrd.

Verðandi, as the Norn of Becoming, helps shape your present actions and decisions, and her help and blessing should be sought—perhaps with an offering, certainly with your acknowledgement and thanks. Skuld has helped you, in her often painful way, by forcing you to clean out and rebalance that which needed such action.

Though dealing with these requirements is not pleasant, it is necessary to do so. Keeping the fibers of the Worlds taut and properly balanced is Skuld's task. Difficult though we might find the experience as individuals, the well-being of the Worlds depends on her actions of balancing, of getting the tensions just right. As you lay the new strands of your worthy deeds into the hands of the Norns, ask Wyrd herself to take them up and weave them into the fabric of That-Which-Is, continuing the process of orlog and of life.

As your final act, now braid, spin or twist a new cord, symbolizing the new strand of wyrd that you want to attach to your life-patterns. Speak or chant the first verse of the final spell as you wind this new cord, pausing to meditate as needed:

New patterns out of ancient Wyrd-might flow;
On darker web, now weave a brighter hue.
From pain and struggle bring forth a new birth—
And bid Verðandi's blessing on the new strand's worth.

Then, place the cord into a bowl of water. If possible, the bowl should be beautiful and / or of special meaning to you—perhaps an heirloom of your family or a gift from someone you care about. You might wish to draw the water from a stream, lake or well, if one is available. Place the cord in the bowl as you begin the second part of the spell, meditating on the actions of the Wells. If you are not able to do these things, use whatever you can, and envision the Well in your imagination.

Pause for as long as you wish between the phrases of the following spell, or repeat them, to let the meanings and images sink in. Feel deep in yourself the strength of your intention to turn your life around, fed by the power of the Wells, as you reach in and draw forth your cord: washed, blessed, and charged with the might of the Wells. Then, perform your final turnings, turning toward a new and better wyrd and pattern for your life.

Three Wells draw in
Three Wells flow out
Shaping mighty deeds of worth.
Now: bring true honor forth!

Turn and turn again,
Turn and turn again,
Ever old and ever new:
In Wyrd, all deeds come due.

Know that your new deeds, deeds of Heathen worth, are likely to be taken up by Wyrd and woven into the pattern of all that is, creating a new and better wyrd for you and for those whose lives you touch. Save the cord you have wound in some honored place—perhaps on your harrow / altar—to remind you of your new path of life. As you close your rite of renewal, give honor from your heart and soul to the great Wells, to Mimir and the Norns: embodiments of the processes of existence itself. It is no small thing to try to deal directly with these powers. As Heathens, we are fortunate to have ways to grasp and communicate some understanding of these patterns and powers, and have the might of soul to be able to work with them to better our own lot.

Sara: Testimonials on Using the Ninefold Rite
By Sara Axtell

Emily's Experience, as told to Sara

At the time I first tried out the Ninefold Rite of Renewal (in 2022), I had been attending Healing Roots circles with Sara Axtell for about a year and was involved in the work of the Cultural Wellness Center in Minneapolis for longer. I was drawn to these groups because I wanted a space to tend to grief circling in my family's and my people's (European American) orlog. I reached out to Elder Sara to ask if there was a ritual I could undergo to heal and ease some of the abuse inflicted by members of my maternal family upon others within the family. I also saw this abuse ripple out in the way our family was able to and did steal Indigenous land and participate in a forgetting of our own healthy ways once we came to Turtle Island. She introduced me to Winifred's Ninefold Rite. I decided to commit to it over a period of four months.

Using Winifred's template, I designed a ritual that could help me sit with some of the pain in my family's orlog and mixed it with some of my own practices around fire and water. I also used the four months to do some family research, travel to ancestors' graves and reflect on my experiences. I scheduled the moments of intentional ritual around three new moon dates.

On the first new moon, when I let go of the cord that I had worn for three weeks into a lake, it started to rain. I found this to be a synchronous moment of cleansing. I noticed other symbols throughout the span of time I did the ritual - some in dreams, some in the natural world. I also participated in a clearing ritual with another elder a couple of weeks after I wrapped up the ninefold rite of passage.

Overall, the experience helped me stick with a thread for a period of time, bring intention to my healing process, and move at a speed that was conducive to integrating the experience. I definitely have felt more at peace since I went through the ritual.

– from Emily, as shared with Sara

Sara's Experience

I would like to share an experience of how the Ninefold Rite can support deep listening and reparations. The year 2008 marked the 150th anniversary of Minnesota becoming a state. There was a celebratory tone to events commemorating the anniversary. But Dakota and Ojibwe Nations were telling a different history of the state, one that described the depth of the brutality and loss that paved the way for the state's founding, and the strength of their Nations in resisting the forces of settler colonialism.

A community organization that I was a part of, the Cultural Wellness Center, was hosting a Dakota elder and professor of Dakota Studies, to share the history of the formation of the state of Minnesota and the devastating impacts on Dakota people. We hosted a 'preparation for listening' process during the four months preceding the gathering.

On the day of the teaching (which we called a truth-telling) a friend and I spent the day together to help prepare food for the evening's meal. During the day, we enacted Step 1 of the Rite. We created our cords. We told our own stories

Wyrd and Shild: A Ninefold Rite of Life Renewal

of our families' settling in Minnesota, and how our family stories are woven into the broader history of the harms and losses suffered by the Dakota people. We spoke the first spell of the Rite. We turned the cords into bracelets that served as a reminder of the spiritual work that we would engage in as we participated in the truth-telling.

These things reminded us that we engaged in listening not only for ourselves but for our ancestors and for our communities living now in Midgard. Even after all these years we have not closed the ritual. We continue to live our lives within the shild and the weaving anew.

--*Sara*

https://www.culturalwellnesscenter.org/

32. Unfolding Destiny, Weaving a Werold

Destiny Unfolding from Orlog

Is 'destiny' a fixed goal to be reached, like a mountain top? Or is it a repeated unfolding, like a flower in full bloom setting a seed that falls and grows again? The plant is rooted in layers of soil and compost laid by orlog; as our orlog reaches a stage of fulfillment the plant sets a bud. This budding destiny unfolds, revealing a flower with exquisite scent, vibrant color, delicate petals, complex shape. This is a state of fulfillment, a place or a state that we have achieved after a time of struggle and striving through the ordeals that our orlog lays out for us. As we strive, the plant grows, unfolds into a blossom, a full-blown fulfillment of our 'destiny.' But we don't stop there...destiny is not, it seems to me, a static endpoint like the peak of a mountain, but a series of stages that we strive to reach—perhaps reaching completion in this life, perhaps continuing through multiple lives and deaths and afterlives.

There are so many anecdotes, in many paths of life, about people who strive toward some kind of spiritual state or form of enlightenment and find 'something,' but then fall back from there and daily life takes over again. I assume the same might be said for the heroes who 'meet their destiny,' but once that's been achieved they still have to run their kingdom or act appropriately in whatever situation their destiny places them. This is the natural course, not a failure of intent. One doesn't live on the mountain-top forever—not in this Midgard life, at least.

This imagery of destiny unfolding, again and again, to me offers a different and more realistic pattern of spiritual movement. The flower blooms, the seed falls into the soil of orlog, watered by the Norns and the Well, and grows again. If we tend this process rightly, the bloom of destiny becomes more beautiful and more intensely real every time it grows, through a process of refinement resulting from tending the soil of our orlog, laying fresh, rich layers full of nourishment.

I realize that growing a flower might not have the same motivational and imaginative impact that climbing a mountain peak might have, but it depends on the shape we perceive our 'destiny' taking: a recurring unfoldment, or a mighty but static state. For many of us, I think, 'destiny' is more a path of unfolding beauty and meaning, rather than a mighty struggle, especially if we look at it in the context of many lifetimes and afterlife experiences. It depends on our own souls, our life, our orlog, our Werold, as to the shape our 'destiny' might take and the metaphors that are most meaningful to us. I offer this imagery as just one example among many that could be used.

Another image I use is very abstract and hard to describe: sort of a whelming, billowing, burgeoning fractal state where new patterns repeatedly burst out of old ones. It reminds me of Hvergelmir, with its forces of creation perpetually billowing out of Ginnungagap. This image is very powerful, very dynamic, difficult to grasp. It has a high level of energy and a sense of spiritual power which I also find motivating.

All the images of 'destiny' that my souls present to me, whether I can describe them or not, are patterns of ever-repeating unfoldment, an endless mystery of Being, that burst upwards and outwards out of layers of orlog, rather than being something separate and distant from orlog.

Werold

Our Werold is our lifetime and everything it contains: the interwoven shape of all our thoughts and deeds, choices and experiences. We may think of everything that has happened with us up until now as 'the past', but in fact, it is the Werold we have woven, the garment or soul-skin of our Aldr soul. It is not 'gone', but still here with us, transformed for better or for worse by how we deal with all the matters of our life.

We can see our Werold as a tapestry of threads. Some of these threads were spun by ourselves, others were spun by the Norns, and by people who have influenced us or touched our lives significantly, for good or ill. Others are spun by the society and culture we live in, by the history of our kin and culture, and by many other factors, such as genetics. We do not have full control over every one of the threads of orlog we are handed in this life, but what we can choose is how to pattern those threads into the work of art that is our life.

Werold as a Work of Art

Consider this exercise. Can you draw or paint a symbolic image of what your life-tapestry looks like, the colors and patterns that are woven there? Can you embroider or weave something that looks like it? Or use any other form of art? A tapestry is a visual, tactile thing, but you might perceive your Werold more like a poem or song, or a piece of music, a sculpture, a garden with flowers and weeds, an architectural or geometric pattern, or a dance. Try rendering your Werold, your life woven into Time and Wyrd, into a form of art, a symbolic representation in some form. If you don't have the artistic skills for this, or if you feel the scope is too large for something you can work with materially, then you can work in your imagination as I do in the following example.

Mosaic: An Example

I've gone through many iterations of this exercise at different times of my life; they've all been different. The first time happened in a dream, during a time when I was going through difficult changes in my life. In my dream I held a very beautiful vase made of blown glass, iridescent with rainbow colors, admiring it as I walked. But then I stumbled and dropped the vase, which broke into thousands of colored pieces, many more pieces and colors than it had seemed to contain originally. I was upset at the loss; I started sadly picking up the pieces of glass, and then had the idea of making a mosaic out of them.

In my dream I was in a cave, dimly lit by fire or torches, and I started pressing pieces of broken glass into the moist clay wall of the cave. I eventually filled the whole wall with this mosaic, a rich tapestry of dark and bright colors and swirling patterns, lit by flickering firelight. I couldn't see the whole pattern, some of it was tantalizingly obscure, but I loved this beautiful, expressive mosaic as a whole. The glass vase had been a lovely, small container, shaping my perceived desire for a simple, beautiful life-pattern. But this pattern broke—in my life and in my dream—and what I made out of the pieces turned out to be much larger, grander, more complex and far-reaching, reflecting my real inner life more accurately than the lovely little vase ever did.

I return in spiritual work, from time to time, to this cave with my firelit mosaic. Each time it seems richer and deeper, extending into darkness on either end, endlessly fascinating even though I could not express in words what it means to me. It is my Aldr-soul, my Time-Body, who loves this mosaic, and who continues creating it, out of sight, while the rest of me and my other souls are busy with other things.

I think that the otherworldly cave where the mosaic lies is close to the Well of Wyrd; it is the water from this Well which seeps through and moistens the clay of the cave wall, allowing it to accept and hold the pieces of my mosaic. I feel that this is a subtle gift of help and blessing from the Norns,

Unfolding Destiny, Weaving a Werold

supporting my efforts to understand my Aldr, my Werold, and how they relate to larger patterns of orlog and Wyrd.

The wall of the cave is Time itself—my time of life; its beginnings and its ending are obscured by shadows. But Aldr knows those shadows; the Norns know; the Holy Ones know. The mosaic is a spiritual map that unfolds year by year, bringing into my awareness the mysteries that shape my life.

Meditations

⊰ ◯ ⊱

33. Meditations

Here are four separate meditations provided by Svartheiðrinn, Sara, and myself. Don't try to use them all at once! Each one is unique, and requires deep attention to your inner experiences. Svartheiðrinn's and Sara's beautiful meditations are immersive ones, calling on body-sensations and awareness-experiences to deepen your perception of the workings of orlog and wyrd.

"Being Shaped by Orlog," the third meditation, is more focused on deep thought, a way of exploring specific experiential questions about your orlog and directing them toward a life-review that will require multiple sessions.

The last meditation here takes you on a journey through time, beginning in the farthest past and leading through the present into the perpetual Now.

Read through each of them before actually proceeding with the meditation, and make sure it is an exercise that would not take you outside the boundaries of what you can handle at the present time of your life. If you are doubtful about any meditation here, put it aside and consider revisiting it after you have done more work with orlog and have integrated the resulting changes in your life.

Meditations

Svartheiðrinn: Meditating on the Web of Wyrd

By Daniela Svartheiðrinn Simina

Preparations:

For this meditation you'll need to find a space where you can settle comfortably for about 30 minutes, free of any distractions. You may want to record yourself reading the following steps of the meditation so you can close your eyes and focus as you listen.

Have something to drink and a bite to eat for when you are done meditating. Food and drink will help you ground back into consensus reality.

You may want to have a journal and something to write with in case you wish to record your experiences from this meditation.

You may choose to "go under the cloak" in which case you will need an item that fulfills the same purpose as a cloak would have served in this specific context. Depending on personal preference and the ambient temperature of the space where you will meditate, you can substitute an actual cloak with a blanket or any lighter or heavier piece of fabric that feels comfortable on you. Make sure that you can breathe while under the "cloak" and that your eyes are shielded from light. If a full body cover – soles of your feet to the top of your head - is not an option, then, as a minimum, drape a light covering over your eyes.

Meditations

Meditation:

Now, make yourself comfortable sitting or lying down under your cloak... The purpose of this meditation is to make you keenly aware about yourself as an intrinsic part of the Web of Wyrd. You will experience yourself as being part of a greater reality in which everyone and everything is connected throughout time and space...[2-3 breaths]

Take a slow, deep breath... hold it for one or two seconds, and then passively let the air flow out. Let the breath settle and allow yourself to settle while mentally following the flow of your breath...[2-3 breaths]

Feel yourself getting lighter with each inhale and more relaxed, more settled with each exhale.... [2-3 breaths]

Bring your awareness to the soles of your feet... As you breathe in, feel the breath traveling upward from the soles of your feet ...all the way to the top of your head.

Breath out from the top of your head, farther out, skyward... Do this again... In through the feet, upward... out through the top of the head, outward... Repeat...[2-3 breaths]

The movement of air through the body feels velvety and warming. It may even happen that in your mind's eyes this "ascending" flow acquires a warming color. If this occurs spontaneously, just go with it. If it doesn't happen, don't force it. Simply stay with your warming breath...[2-3 breaths]

Meditations

Set this upward-going flow on a default mode, firmly convinced that, for the rest of the meditation, it will continue to go this way whether you specifically think of it or not...

Bring now your awareness to the top of your head. As you breathe in, slowly, feel the breath moving in through the top of your head and pouring itself downward, from the top of your head toward your feet... Breath out through the soles of your feet, downward, farther away... Repeat...[2-3 breaths]

The flow of your breath feels silky and cooling. It may happen that, in your mind's eyes, the "descending" flow acquires a cooling color. If this occurs spontaneously and you enjoy it, just go with it. If it doesn't happen, don't force any visualization. Simply stay with your downward-flowing, cooling breath...[2-3 breaths]

Set this downward-going flow on a default mode, firmly convinced that for the rest of the meditation, it will continue to go this way whether you specifically think of it or not...

Bring now your awareness to both the top of your head and the soles of your feet. As you breathe in, you feel the in-breath entering through your feet and head simultaneously. The two streams, coming from opposite directions, cross paths within you, their warming and cooling qualities balancing each other. Then, the incoming streams follow their pre-established paths and flow out and away... The primordial powers of Heat and Cold, of Fire and Ice move

Meditations

through you now, and with each breath-cycle you feel that you are dissolving into this flow…[2-3 breaths]

You are experiencing oneness with the primordial Powers from which everything emerged. You are of the same substance as the Nine Worlds before the Nine Worlds came into being.

With each inhale you feel lighter, buoyant even. With each exhale you feel dropping deeper within. [2-3 breaths]

Stay connected to your breath but let go of any attempt to control it. Listen to it…The farther and deeper you drop within, the more the sound of your own breath becomes amplified in the vastness of space that surrounds you.… The sound grown louder… and louder… until it becomes the roar of the wild primordial waters frothing inside the Ginnungagap… You feel there is no separation between your own breath and roaring breath of Hvergelmir.…[2-3 breaths]

You feel your breath extending into a thread that stretches out … and then divides into two strands… before entering the bodies of Askr and Embla. Through your breath, you are woven into the same fabric with the tree-people and the first humans, and the humans coming afterwards…[2-3 breaths]

You see many threads rise vertically around you. You cannot see where they begin nor where they end, but you sense clearly that many such threads run through you as well… You may not see it, but you feel it, thus you know it: these vertically running threads were set by the Norns themselves and by other, even older Powers whose names faded from memory eons ago.... See these threads as the warp in the Web of Wyrd and acknowledge that their presence, roles, and everything they determine is immutable .... They give the Web its structure and everything existing in the Nine Worlds is built essentially around the threads making up the Web's warp - everything and everyone, including you and your existence in Midgard... Sit for a moment with the thought of your own existence as it relates to cosmic-scale forces that shape our World and the Others.... [2-3 breaths]

From right and left, fibers of all colors and textures come in and weave themselves into the warp: they are the weft in the fabric of the Web.... . All kinds of textures and colors, threads of gold, silk, wool.... some smooth, some rough .... Get a sense of how they feel, look, smell, how your thoughts and emotions fluctuate when you contemplate or touch them...These are all the lives there have ever been lived and all the actions ever taken. Those lives and actions have directly and indirectly influenced the lives and actions of your own ancestors. All these threads also run through you, now.... [2-3 breaths]

You are a part in the Web as much as everyone and everything else is, but you are not a mere knot randomly occurring in the fabric of the Web of Wyrd. Your place is largely determined by what was there before, but also by what you are doing now and what you will do from now on. You are both weaver and intrinsic part of the pattern that is being woven. Sit with this reality for a moment. [2-3 breaths]

Meditations

Breathe, and draw in the power and knowledge that runs through the Web, feel these flowing into you, coursing through your body, through your existence and then reaching out, farther out and away. You are not a dead-end, a terminus point, but an artisan who skillfully contributes to the ever-growing Web, an artisan who makes the most out of the fibers handed to you by the Web of Wyrd itself…Breathe, feel, witness… let thoughts, feelings, emotions percolate through you…Acknowledge everything yet hold onto nothing. Be with the Web. Grow with the ever-growing Web of Wyrd [5-7 breaths or as long as desired]

Allow your breath to gradually deepen, making the inhaling and exhaling a little bit more intentional. Be aware of your chest rising and falling with the incoming and outgoing flow of air. Let your awareness pervade your entire body and notice how the whole body feels as you breathe. [2-3 breaths]

Feel how the breath anchors you into your physical form. [2-3 breaths]

Take one deep breath in, hold it for a second or two, then let it fall out and bring you back here. Do this again: take one deep breath in, hold it for a second or two, then let it fall out and come back fully. You are fully present, here and now. Wiggle, stretch, and whenever ready, open your eyes.

Meditations

Once you are back:
If your intent is to journal about your experience, I suggest you do so immediately because all the impressions will quickly fade away.

Grab a bite of food, a drink of water or juice, and if you still feel ungrounded, take a pinch of salt and dissolve in your mouth.

Sara: Healing from the Roots of the World: An Embodied Visualization

By Sara Axtell

Start by just moving your body gently. Find those places where you might be holding tension and see if you can move them gently. Allowing that energy to flow like Laguz. Now imagine roots growing out of the bottom of your feet down through the layers of earth until they reach the very roots of the cosmos. And the energy there underneath the great tree feels so welcoming, it draws you down to the roots.

See yourself now underneath the great tree, the sun shining down through the branches onto your face. You walk over to the bench where you usually sit. You take a seat to watch the Norns at their work. They are spinning on their spindles. They are weaving on their great loom.

You watch as they take up the fibers of your life, the moments, the emotions, the laughter, the fears, spinning them all together into one strong and beautiful thread. Your threads join others on the great loom and you watch the images unfold there. The stories that we are all living in our own lives, the stories that our elders told us when we were young, the stories that our ancestors whisper to us in our dreams. They are all there on the loom. Continuing to unfold as we continue to lay our actions in the well.

Meditations

You watch as one of the Norns bends over the Well and scoops up a handful of clear sweet water. She spreads the water over the bark of the tree wherever it is worn or wounded, and those places begin to heal and that healing ripples out across the face of the tree, high, high into her branches and deep down into her roots.

She spreads chains of runes that spell galdrs, galdrs that create healing songs that you can hear with your ears and feel in your bones. Those songs spread out across the root system of the tree and you take them up in your own root system. They travel up through the layers of Earth into your palms and legs and feet until they flow within your whole mind-body-heart-spirit, and you can breathe them in and out. You can sit quietly with them in the moments that you need them. You can sing them to others in your life.

As you reach up, you are so full of those healing songs that they radiate out the tips of your fingers, reaching out to our tree-kin here in Midgard, reaching up to Sunna. They share back their own songs of healing. All of these songs make a medicine circulating through your own mind-body-heart-spirit, healing all the hidden cracks with beauty and with wholeness. They flow back down to the roots of the cosmos to mingle with the other healing songs there, all flowing throughout the root system of the great tree, all flowing throughout your own root system so that you can take them up when you need them.

Now take the shape of Uruz with your body. Head hanging down, fingers touching toes, allowing your muscles to stretch and release, allowing you to release those patterns and emotions that no longer serve you. You learn from them and you let them go. Now roll your spine back up until you are upright again looking at that beautiful sun in the sky and hopefully taking some of this healing with you into your day.

Acknowledgements
This guided visualization developed out of a meditation group some friends and I started during the covid19 pandemic. We wanted a way to connect and to support each other to stay centered and rooted. We started by meeting twice daily via Zoom at the height of the pandemic, and now continue to meet once a week.

The images of roots coming out of the bottoms of our feet and sinking down to the roots of the world are openings to journeying work that I have experienced with groups like Healing Roots, the Volva Stav Guild, as well as Cat Heath's work.

Meditations

Being Shaped by Orlog

A deep, meditative examination of strands of orlog in your life.

Sit in silence, breathe, and gather your awareness.

You're an unborn, insubstantial consciousness floating deep within the dim, indistinct waters of the Well of Wyrd.

Somewhere in the distance, you hear an eerie chanting: the Norns are singing, gathering together the strands of your Aldr-soul, wrapping them around the spindle of yourself. Your lack of substance begins to fill with these strands, as your orlog is spun by the Norns.

How do these orlog strands feel?

Do they give you shape and substance?

A sense of direction, or a sense of challenges?

What are the colors of these strands, or what do you sense about them with your other senses? Are they, perhaps, strings that give out musical notes? Are they rough or smooth, tight or elastic, vibrating or still?

Do these strands constrict you?

Can you see how a band of constriction could be turned into a thread to weave into your tapestry of your life, your Werold?

Meditations

Can constrictions or limitations be transformed into resources, life-experience, wisdom, under the stern benevolence of the rune Need / Nauthiz and the gaze of the Norns?

Now move forward in time, to some significant event in your childhood (as long as this is safe for you). Keep that time in your awareness, and non-judgmentally examine the orlog-strands that played into this event: strands that came from recent or distant past, strands that might be pulling you forward in time, in a certain direction. Repeat the questions above on the basis of this life-event that you are remembering.

You can repeat this exercise as a life-and-orlog-review, working step by step through the events and meaning of your life up until now. This will take a long time and shouldn't be rushed—it is an ongoing exercise pursuing awareness of your orlog for as long as you are alive. Keep a record of your findings in your Daybook; you will find, I believe, that your whole life history and meaning of your life takes on shape and substance through these exercises.

This process reveals the 'Tale of Your Aldr' and the 'Weaving of your Werold.' You are examining your orlog honestly and with compassion here: learning from it, growing in wisdom, gaining insights into yourself, your choices and their consequences.

This activity, extended toward understanding the orlog of others as well as your own, helps you increase in compassion,

Meditations

acceptance, and understanding toward yourself and toward others.

Perhaps most importantly, when you begin to have a true sense of how orlog has shaped your life in the past, you can begin to make choices about future actions and directions with a fuller awareness of how orlog works in your own life. You gain insights into ways you can subtly influence it by the work of your awareness, your will, and your deeds.

Meditations

Layers of Time

A Meditation on the Aldr-Soul / Time-Body Embedded in Layers of Orlog

Here is a meditation for individual or group work that focuses on the Aldr-Soul or Time-Body, its experience of layers of Time, and its similarity to features of orlog. Change the pronouns as appropriate for group meditation.

Now relax, let your body feel heavy and loose, and take some deep, gentle breaths. In your imagination, sense that you are present with the Well and the Tree. From this holy place, your Aldr-soul is setting forth on a journey through Time, a journey of memory and mystery, beginning from the most ancient of ages, and moving to the present moment of time. (Read it out loud if possible.)

Eons. Great ages of Time. Strata building up layer by layer on the Earth, under the sea. Soils forming, and sediments, layer upon layer, containing within them histories of Earth's life.

Earth forms her **Ealdor-yard,** her mantle of power, that contains and protects her and the life upon her. Atmosphere, ionosphere, magnetosphere: layers of power held in place by gravity and the inner workings of our World.

Ages. Layer upon layer of lives: ocean lives, land lives, plant lives, animal lives, always evolving and taking shape. They build upon one another, are shaped by their surroundings, shape themselves.

Generations. The Gods and Goddesses, the Norns and the Great Spirits of many beings give a touch here, a tweak there, a gift, a push, at just the right time, in just the right place, to shape what is coming into being. And so the generations arise, lay down their influences, pass away.

We, the living, **Alda-beornum,** children of Aldr, Time-Children: we are shaped by all these layers.

My **Aldr** is sung and woven into being by the Norns as they, and I, take up the layers of What-Is and shape them into What-Is-Becoming. Day by day I shape the layers of my life.

The **World-Tree** grows, laying down its rings of life, ever-expanding. My own Werold grows, the tale of my life, shaped by all that I am, all I experience, all my deeds. Layer by layer, day by day, my Werold grows as the Great Tree grows.

Aldr. Being-In-Time. Intricate weaving of the Norns, of my ancestors going all the way back to the beginning. Rooted in the past, growing in the present, influencing what shall be, uniquely shaped into my own Aldr-Being, my Time-Body.

This day, this moment in time, to be shaped by me, blessed by the Holy Ones, laid as my Aldr's daily offering, here at the foot of the World Tree, at the Well of Wyrd.

Meditations

We are the **Time-Children,** together weaving Life into layers of Time, age upon age upon age.

And here is **Aldr's mystery:** it does its Time-work while standing in the sacred Now, the very instant of Becoming, the No-Time outside of Time, as it fills the drop of dew that hangs in the air…
…ever falling…
…ever falling…
…ever falling…

…from the boughs of the Tree into the deeps of the Well.

Meditations

34. The Song of the Norns

Expanding the Scope of *Sköp Norna*

During the years I worked on this book the subject matter and the chapters kept expanding, as I realized more and more how broad the effects of orlog and wyrd are in our lives. The contributions of Sara and Svartheiðrinn expanded that understanding even further. I came to realize in a very profound way why orlog, wyrd, the fabric of our lives, and Heathen troth itself can all be called *sköp Norna:* the shapings of the Norns.

It's quite clear that the concept of 'shaping' was seen as something wyrd-ful, fateful, in the old Germanic languages, a power that lies in the hands of supernatural beings as well as humans. We tend to focus on how the Norns influence the course of our individual lives, but they shape the larger tides of events and changes that occur in our collective lives as well, from the level of the family and kindred on up to national and world-wide events.

Our Heathen troth is not only a personal religious belief. The idea of the Heathen faith as *sköp Norna,* the shapings of the Norns, encompasses this wider influence on the world. If we extend a Heathen mindset into the domain of philosophy it becomes a way of comprehending the great sweep of human history: the history of the past, and the history-in-the-making that we experience as members of our societies and of humanity today.

The Anglo-Saxon word for historian, *gewyrd-writere* or 'wyrd-writer,' emphasizes this point. What a historian does is look for significance and meaning in the interrelationships of events and circumstances in the past, and link them with circumstances in the present, to deepen our collective understanding and wisdom. We, the authors, can say from personal experience that looking at any event, past or present, by asking "what are / were the Norns shaping here?" produces profound insights and a deeper sense of the connections among humans, human nature, Nature itself, and all the Holy Ones.

The Meaningfulness of Orlog

Orlog / wyrd does not 'reside' in time, but in the meaning and significance of events, which happen to occur in 'time as a container.' French writer Antoine de Saint-Exupery was a fighter pilot in both WWI and WWII, and knew something about staring Wyrd in the face, I would guess! He wrote: "We don't ask to be eternal: what we ask is not to see acts and objects abruptly lose their meaning" (quoted in Winterbourne p. 60).

I find this a very Heathen-like and orlog-oriented sentiment. Acts and objects, and our life as a whole, have meaning, not because of time and the length of time that we live, but because of how they relate to, arise from, lead into other acts, objects, events, and beings. It is this reality that the Heathen custom of speaking boasts, oaths, and other powerful words in symbel ties into. By ritually acknowledging the power of the past and tying our intended new deeds to the momentum created by meaningful deeds of the past, we place ourselves into that network of interrelationships and the power that flows forth from them: the power of the Well.

Earlier in this book I quoted the following passage from Winterbourne's book *When the Norns have Spoken,* but it's worth repeating it in a different context here. He contrasts the Germanic attitude toward wyrd with the ancient Greek idea of *hubris*. Hubris is the act of either stepping beyond the bounds that Gods have set for humans and helplessly suffering the punishment that results, or else attempting to escape fate, which is futile. In contrast, Winterbourne writes:

"What we see so often in Norse literature is something that is perhaps unique in European paganism: an attempt to escape fate by *living up to it*—the near-opposite of hubris. In other words, the acknowledgement of fate provides the necessary presupposition for facing the challenges of life, which…are precisely made meaningful by it. It is a hugely impressive humanistic vision." (p. 17).

Orlog / wyrd as death, as fate, as powers that reach beyond our ability to control: these understandings do not rob our lives and deeds of meaning. They *create* meaning by providing the arena of mortal life where we are called to live and act and be, in context with all else that lives, and acts, and is—within Midgard and outside of it. From these interactions arise the significance and meaning of our lives.

What the Norns Ask of Us

In my experience, the perspectives I've outlined here do not necessarily lead into some warm and fuzzy sense that 'all is right with the world,' just because 'the Norns are in charge and everything will turn out okay.' It would be difficult to gain a deeper understanding of any period in history, including the present, while sustaining that belief in any sort of literal sense. I would also suggest that taking that attitude amounts to abdicating our own human responsibilities in laying orlog: if we mess up and lay crummy orlog, the Norns are not going to sort it out for us! We'll have to work on that ourselves, though we may get a boost from them as we work if they see fit to do so.

Though the Norns take action to nurture and sustain the Worlds of the Tree, they are not what one might call warm and fuzzy beings. They are stern guides who attempt to teach us lessons that need to be learned again and again, over and over in our own lives and across the generations of human history. Lessons about consequences. About cause and effect. About obligations and responsibilities. About our self-inflicted difficulties and our unmanifested potentials, both personal and collective. About the big picture across time and space. About raising our heads above the swamp of details and short-sighted motivations within us and around us, to gain a larger view of *what was, what is, and what could be.*

The Norns / Wyrd guide us toward asking profound questions as we root ourselves in Heathen troth and philosophy: how shall we expand our awareness of *sköp Norna,* the shapings of the Norns? What might this mean to us as holistic beings, material and spiritual together, living in this world of Midgard that inextricably blends the spiritual with the material into subtle layers of orlog that shape all that is? What paths of wisdom might we walk—here, today—that will align our steps with the shapings of the Norns?

The Song of the Norns

In the previous section I presented a rather stern view of the Norns and their expectations of us; I do firmly believe in that understanding of them and take it seriously. Here I'll show a different side, a perspective that's recently arisen from a personal experience I had with them. It came out of some deep meditation I've been doing, trying to understand more about 'what the Norns really are'...or rather, how to imagine / experience them in ways other than human-shaped beings sitting around in a Midgard-like landscape, with all the implied limitations of those forms.

The result was seeing / feeling / perceiving the Norns as deep, gently rippling layers of water lying over the world, not drowning but sustaining us with this life-giving water. In a way, the whole world became the Well of Wyrd! The individual Norns and Wyrd seemed like separate layers of water, but not separate: a metaphysical riddle to explore. I heard faint echoing sounds in the water, which gradually crescendoed into the sounds of song or galdor. Though I heard the Norns singing, I did not see them.

Urðr and Verðandi each galdored their mighty tones of Being and Becoming which, vibrating together, created a harmonic overtone note. I realized that this overtone note 'necessarily' arises from the tones that these two sing; it would be impossible for them to sing those notes together and not have the overtone arise from the harmonic vibrations interacting. That overtone note is Skuld's song which she picks up in harmony with them: the Necessity, the What-Should-Be, that arises from all beings and life itself in ongoing action among the wide Worlds of the Tree.

This experience of the Norns' harmonic galdoring is creating a new feeling in me toward Skuld / shild / necessity: seeing her as an expression of what we all need, *the necessary needs of life itself,* and what is due to us so life on all levels, physical and spiritual, can be sustained. It leads to a deeper understanding of how the work of the Norns supports and nourishes all of us on the World-Tree in response to that existential need.

'What should be' takes on another tone—not only a stern, fatalistic one, but also a tone which acknowledges that we all—humans and all beings—'should' be living in circumstances that provide for our needs. Not for our 'greeds' necessarily, but for our true needs, material and spiritual.

Not that everything 'should be' provided to us without any effort on our part. It's more that what is needed and necessary, and what should-be, is something we all owe to one another. All of us: humans, Gods and Goddesses, Norns and ancestors, the beings of Nature, the other tribes of beings such as Landwights, Alfar, Dwarves, Jotnar and all, generate the life-forces, the sacred spaces of the Wells and Worlds and the Tree, that form the matrix of being within which we all exist. This matrix of life and being nourishes us all with life-force in different forms; we each contribute to it, we each draw from it. This balance is important, and Skuld is the one who manages it: balancing needs, obligations, debts, taking and giving, each in proper measure. She and her sisters do what they can to shape it all into what-should-be.

The Song of the Norns

For us, here and now, 'what should be' implies that working with the Norns / Wyrd, with orlog, with the Holy Ones, can help us reshape both our needs and our circumstances to be congruent with what is available to us, individually and collectively, from the orlog we've laid and that has been laid for us. We can focus on our true needs, especially the spiritual ones which tend to be neglected, rather than on our greeds.

And more: this insight implies slowly shaping the world, layer by layer, so that more and more true needs of all beings and their collectives can be met, in balance with one another—more of 'what should be,' in this sense, coming into being.

This, too, is what 'working with the Norns' can mean for us as Heathens, expanding out from our individual perspectives to encompass greater realms of Being. Thus, in troth and in truth, we may take our full part in the shapings of the Norns within this sacred world of Alda Vé.

~~~

Winifred
Sara
Svartheiðrinn
~~~

Harvest-Tide 2025

The Song of the Norns

Word Hoard / Glossary

Here I offer definitions for some of the important concepts discussed in this book. I include a list of the chapters where each concept is discussed at the end of each entry, except where the term is used very widely throughout the book.

Alda Vé
Alda Vé translates as the 'sanctuary or sacred place of Aldr,' of humans who possess the Aldr soul. As I understand it, the 'sanctuary of Aldr / humans' refers to Midgard itself: the place that Vé, son of Borr and Bestla, and his brothers Odin and Vili shaped out of Ymir's corpse as a sanctuary for human and earthly life in the midst of the cosmic chaos surrounding it.
(Chapter 16, 30.)

Aldr, Ealdor, Alda börnum, Eldi-barn
Aldr, Ealdor, and their variants in the old Germanic languages pertain to one's age, span of life, and to the life-force or life-soul that supports us during that lifespan. It also is used in descriptions of death, the end of the lifespan. In the lines about the creation of humans from trees or logs, the Norns "choose life for the children of *aldr*" *(Völuspá vs. 20).*

The word *aldr* comes from the Proto-Indo-European root **al*, 'to nourish,' related to *alan*, with the same meaning, a word found in Gothic, Anglo-Saxon and other Germanic languages. It also means 'to grow.' **Al* is the root for words relating to 'age' in the various Germanic languages, including English 'old' and 'elder.'

Old Norse *alda börnum* means 'children of Aldr;' Old Saxon *eldi-barn* means 'Eldi-child.' I translate these terms as 'mortal beings' because the context in which they are used in the old texts is that of mortality, of humans whose time in Midgard is limited by the shaping of the Norns / Wyrd. Another, more poetic way I translate these terms is 'Time-Children.'

(Chapters 5, 16, 19, 32, 33.)

Beowulf

The manuscript form of this epic Old English poem was written sometime between 975 and 1025 CE, based on older poetry whose original dates are unknown. Both the poem itself, and scholarly analyses of it, are of great importance for modern Heathenry, especially the analysis by Bauschatz in his book *The Well and the Tree: World and Time in Early Germanic Culture*. Wikipedia offers some background about this poem, as follows.

"Scholars have debated whether *Beowulf* was transmitted orally, affecting its interpretation: if it was composed early, in pagan times, then the paganism is central and the Christian elements were added later, whereas if it was composed later, in writing, by a Christian, then the pagan elements could be decorative archaising; some scholars also hold an intermediate position. *Beowulf* is written mostly in the Late West Saxon dialect of Old

Word-Hoard

English, but many other dialectal forms are present, suggesting that the poem may have had a long and complex transmission throughout the dialect areas of England.

"The story is set in pagan Scandinavia in the 5th and 6th centuries. Beowulf, a hero of the Geats, comes to the aid of Hrothgar, the king of the Danes, whose mead hall Heorot has been under attack by the monster Grendel for twelve years. After Beowulf slays him, Grendel's mother takes revenge and is in turn defeated. Victorious, Beowulf goes home to Geatland and becomes king of the Geats. Fifty years later, Beowulf defeats a dragon, but is mortally wounded in the battle. After his death, his attendants cremate his body and erect a barrow on a headland in his memory."
https://en.wikipedia.org/wiki/Beowulf

There is much to be pondered in this poem as regards wyrd, Heathen ethical values and behavior, and more, as we have discussed throughout this book.
(Chapters 1, 2, 3, 4, 5, 6, 8, 10, 16, 26, 27)

Determinism and Free Will
The philosophical concept of determinism and its converse, free will, comes in several forms. I'll quote a few simple definitions here.

Hard Determinism holds that "free will does not exist—our actions are shaped by external forces. ...things such as society, the environment, and our biology determine what we do, and we have no choice about it. ...Hard determinists think that people can't be responsible for their actions unless those actions are the result of free choice." (Fletcher, p. 136)

Soft Determinism, or *Compatibilism,* argues that everything is determined by a cause, but we can still exercise our will as long as external circumstances are not forcing us in a certain direction. This position allows for the existence of moral responsibility—we do have responsibility for our choices except in cases where no choice was possible.

"*Existentialist* philosophers think that people have freedom of conscience (i.e. the liberty to follow their beliefs) at all times. ... Sartre took an extreme view when he claimed that individuals are always free, even when they are persecuted or imprisoned, as they have the power to decide how to react to their environment. He thought free will could be a burden: we are always responsible for what we do, and this can cause great anxiety." (Fletcher p. 136) (Chapters 9, 10, 11.)

Disir, Idisi, Idesi

Disir (plural; the singular is Dis) are most often female ancestral spirits, though sometimes beings called 'Disir' are more like demi-goddesses, or fylgja: luck-bearing spirits who are attached to individuals. Likewise, Disir are sometimes considered equivalent to the Lesser Norns who attend people in person to shape their fates more individually.

Idisi (plural; the singular is Idis) or Idesi are similar beings seen in continental Germanic lands rather than in Scandinavia as the Disir are. Though the word *idis* technically just meant 'woman,' often a noblewoman, the word as used by modern Heathens holds the implication of arcane skills. There is an old German charm that was written in the 10th century, perhaps much older in oral form, that shows one kind of magic Idisi performed.

First Merseberg Charm
Once sat *Idisi,*
They sat here, then there.

Word-Hoard

Some fastened bonds,
Some impeded an army,
Some unraveled fetters:
Escape the bonds,
flee the enemy!
https://en.wikipedia.org/wiki/Merseburg_charms

Many of us assume this magic was done by the Idisi sitting near the battlefield using runes—some runes are known to be useful for fettering and unfettering. Caesar's writings and other old writings mention that women often stood on the sidelines of battle where their men were fighting, shouting to encourage them, but more than simple encouragement may have been going on. These Idisi did more: they fettered their foes and unfettered their own warriors. The 'bonds' mentioned in the charm are likely to have been magical attacks on the souls or psyches of the warriors, causing immobilizing panic attacks or deep confusion. Idisi on both sides of the battle would attack their enemies and release their own warriors from such attacks. A lot was happening on the so-called 'sidelines' of battle, apparently!

Disir and Idisi are considered to be knowledgeable about spells, orlog, and oracular knowledge. The Disa-Blót was celebrated annually in Scandinavia, indicating the widespread importance of these beings.
(Chapters 7, 12, 14, 16, 22.)

Drýgja / Dree
Based on the interpretation of *drýgja* and how it is used in conjunction with orlog in Eddic poetry, the word can mean 'to carry out, fulfill, accomplish orlog' (active sense); 'to endure orlog' (passive sense); and 'to align one's actions with

orlog.' Based on usage of the word in Anglo-Saxon, Gothic, Old Saxon, *dreógan* and its cognates can mean to 'endure, struggle with, work at, fight for, fight against, find fulfillment in, suffer through' and more. These words are useful when considering how we deal with our orlog. (Chapter 13, 28.)

Einherjar
Einherjar (plural) are the 'single-warriors,' the champions, who populate Odin's Hall Valhalla or Valhöll. They are selected from the battlefield by the Valkyrja—this selection brings about their death. Their spirits or Ghosts are then taken to Valhalla, where they train daily, and feast in the evenings, to prepare for the great battle of Ragnarök.
(Chapters 10, 16.)

Frith
Its simplest meaning is 'peace' in the sense of not fighting, arguing, or causing serious offense. Its deeper sense refers to the behaviors, attitudes, and commitments that support a closely-knit and well-functioning community.

Frithyard, frithstead
A place where people are required not to fight or shed blood. This usually referred to either a place of assembly, a Thing or a Moot, or most often to a sacred space for worship, such as an outdoor altar, sacred well, tree, or stone, or a temple.

Fylgja, Kin-fylgja
The fylgja is a spirit that accompanies an individual or family (kin-fylgja). Sometimes the fylgja is described as taking the shape of an animal who represents an important dimension

of a person's character (Ellis, 1943). In other stories, the fylgja is described as a female spirit being. She plays a protective role in a person's life, often accompanying them until they are near death, when she may leave to accompany another member of the same family, perhaps an embodiment of the luck or destiny of the family (Bek-Pedersen, 2011). The word fylgja is related to the Old Norse fylgja 'to follow' and also fulga, 'skin, covering, caul' and fylgja, 'afterbirth' (Simek, 1993). (Definition contributed by Sara.)
(Chapters 4, 9, 14, 15)

Galdor
Galdor is a form of chanting, singing, or intoning that is used for magical purposes. It is often used in combination with the runes for runic magic or meditation.
(Chapters 4, 6, 21, 34.)

Gefrain
The Anglo-Saxon word for 'reputation, fame.' I like to use it in place of the modern word 'reputation' to emphasize the spiritual importance of this concept for Heathens. It is pronounced yeh-FRAIN.
(Chapters 4, 15, 26.)

Ginnungagap
In Old Norse lore, Ginnungagap is a place of primal chaos or nothingness. At either end are the primal powers of Fire and Ice, and in the temperate center is where the World Tree takes root. The ancient Giant Ymir was formed from the frozen rime at the icier end of Ginnungagap. The ancient divine Cow, Auðhumla (whom I regard as the Ur-Mother)

also arose from Ginnungagap, as did the progenitor of the Gods, Buri.

Hamingja

Norse *hamingja* is a complex concept. It can refer to an out-of-body spirit-shape that some people can take on—often an animal form—to engage in magical or shamanistic activities such as fighting with an enemy in similar form, or scouting ahead during a journey. As Winterbourne describes, "*hamingja* carries three main characteristics—shape-shifting abilities, 'fortune' as such, and the guardian spirit" (pp. 38-9). It is sometimes considered part of one's own soul, other times as a more independent spirit attached to one. The term is used in similar ways to other terms for spirit-beings or shape-functions such as *fylgja, kinfylgja, hamr, hugr, hugham, vörðr*. Jan DeVries describes the *hamingja* as the indwelling luck, in the form of a protective spirit that accompanies a person life-long. It also takes the form of a power or energy that can radiate out from a person or other kind of being, as well as from objects such as heirlooms and features of the land. When someone had a lot of this kind of power, for example a chieftain or war-leader, they could lend it, send it, or spread it around among their followers. (deVries 1956, pp. 222ff.)
(Chapters 9, 14, 15, 16, 25, 26, 31.)

Holle, Frau Holle

A German Goddess much involved in all matters of daily Midgard life, especially those traditionally relating to women and children, and to food, agriculture and home. Her care for all humans extends before and after Midgard life, as well as during it. Her name is cognate with 'Hel', and

Holle's domains of action include not only Midgard and Midgard's sky, but Underworld as well. Other roots of her name include words for 'benevolent, kind, gracious'. Holle is especially revered by the modern Heathen sect called Urglaawe. (Chapters 8, 16, 21.)

Hugr
A powerful soul focused on Midgard activities, using faculties of thought and emotion to navigate the complexities of human social life. In my thought, Hugr is the soul which periodically reincarnates, and which continues its involvement with Midgard life even after death by becoming an ancestral spirit, an Alf or a Dis, or a guiding spirit, or if ill-natured, becoming an afflicting wight.
(Chapters 5, 8, 14, 16.)

Hvergelmir
In Norse mythology, a well or wellspring located in the cold, Niflheim side of Ginnungagap, under a root of the World-Tree, from which the Elivagar river(s) flows. In my thought, Hvergelmir is centered in Ginnungagap and is the source of the energy flows that form the cosmos. (21, 31, 33.)

Landwights, Landvættir
Land-spirits, beings who inhabit spiritual planes of Earth / Midgard, and involve themselves with the features and processes of landscapes and ecosystems. They range in size / power from smaller beings inhabiting trees, rocks, small spaces, up to mighty warders of large areas and phenomena such as mountains, lakes and storms. At the latter end, they merge into the domains of the Jotnar and Deities.
(Chapters 5, 14, 24, 16, 31, 34.)

Matronae, Matrons

A multitude of Goddesses, demi-Goddesses, patronesses of cities and regions, ancestral warding spirits of tribes and clans, and land- and river-warding spirits, whose worship flourished during the time of the Roman empire. Both Germanic and Celtic Matronae are recognized, as well as some whose provenance is not clear. Many stone altars and thanks-offerings to them have been found, especially in the region of what is now Germany, but extending all over Europe and Britain in the wake of the Roman Empire and their troops. These matronly beings are honored by modern Heathens, as well. (Chapters 7, 16.)

Might and main, mægen, megin

Power, force, energy that is inherent in living beings, magical objects, and otherworldly beings. Used in a modern Heathen context, these terms often refer to the spiritual power gained from living an ethical Heathen life. (Chapters 9, 10, 14, 15, 25, 26, 28, 31.)

Metod, Mjǫtuðr

Metod-sceaft, metod-gesceaft, means 'metod-shaping': "Decree of fate, doom, fate after death." *Metod* is a poetic term that refers sometimes to Wyrd or 'fate,' sometimes to Heathen Gods or the Christian God. When used in a Christian context, *metodsceaft* often referred to a person's fate after death: their God's spoken judgement and assignment to hell or heaven. Cognate words with the same meaning are Old Saxon *metod* and Old Norse *mjötuðr*. Another poetic term is *metod-wang*, 'metod-field,' meaning a battlefield, a field where fate / orlog happens according to the decrees of the Powers. Beowulf says that "Wyrd swept all my kin to *metodsceafte,"* to their doom that was shaped by otherworldly powers. (l. 2815)

"Metod, metud, meotud, meotod. A word found only in poetry. The earlier meaning of the word in heathen times may have been *fate, destiny, death* ... in this sense it seems to be used in its compounds, and in the Icelandic *mjötuðr* weird, bane, death (Cl. and Vig. mjötuðr, II). ... But the word, which occurs frequently, is generally an epithet of the Deity as the O. Sax. *metod;* so too Icel. *Mjötuðr*...is applied to heathen gods." (Bosworth-Toller Anglo-Saxon dictionary online.)
(Chapters 3, 8, 16)

Norns, Nornir

Three womanly beings, possibly Giants though their origins are unclear. In Norse lore they are named Urðr, Verðandi, and Skuld, representing 'What-Is', 'What Is Becoming', and 'Debt, or What Should Be.' They live beside the Well of Wyrd / destiny, called Urðarbrunnr, and nourish the World-Tree with mud and water from the Well. They speak ørlög or fate for humans, and the council or doom-stead of the Gods takes place near their Well; presumably they participate in these councils. There are also lesser norns, who appear as fairy Godmothers and similar beings involved with people's fates. In Anglo-Saxon, these beings are called the Wyrdæ.

The term 'Norns' is used only in the Norse languages. *Etymology of Norn:* "Old Norse *norn* (plural nornir), which is related to Swedish dialectal *norna* "to warn, to communicate secretly," perhaps ultimately imitative of low murmuring." (Etymology Online.)

As Svartheiðrinn writes in Chapter 12:
While Urð, Verðandi, and Skuld are the best-known ones, they are not the only Norns in Norse myth. In the Prose Edda, Snorri Sturluson mentions two categories: the greater Norns whose actions reverberate at a cosmic level, and the lesser Norns who apparently visit every child when it is born and speak its destiny. There is great diversity among Nornir:

"Which are those norns who go to help those in need
And bring forth children from their mothers?"

"From very different tribes I think the norns come,
They are not of the same kin;
Some come from the Æsir, some from the elves,
Some are daughters of Dvalin"
(*Fafnismál* v.12-13, Poetic Edda, Larrington translation)

Odal land and Odalsrett
Odal land is ancestral land, land that has been occupied, used, and cherished by one's personal or tribal ancestors. *Odalsrett,* meaning 'the rights associated with ancestral land' in traditional Norwegian law, describes an ancestral relationship with land in which generations of a family, including both living and dead members, had a relationship with a farm. One might think of this as generations of people laying the orlog of their work and activities into their land. (Chapter 24.) This also relates to the accumulation of Hamingja in the land as mentioned in Chapter 14.

Oðrœrir
Meaning: 'wode-stirrer.' This name refers to the Mead of Poetry, and to a vessel where it was contained. The Mead of

Poetry was made from the blood of Kvasir, considered the wisest of beings.
(Chapters 16, 21, 27.)

Ordeal
Here is the definition of 'ordeal' as I understand and use it in the context of Heathen life. An 'ordeal' has the connotation of a struggle, a challenge, a personal testing, and it is that, but it is more. It is fateful, it is a weaving of wyrd, a drawing-together of the strands of our life into a nexus-point of deep significance. This understanding of *an ordeal as an event that brings orlog into manifestation for us to deal with* can be applied to many of the difficulties and challenges in our own lives. (Chapters 13, 14, 27)

Orlog
Orlog is a concept of fate that developed among the old Germanic and Nordic peoples; there are cognate orlog-words in all the main old Germanic languages, though the meaning in Gothic is less developed. Orlog refers to the primal or originating layers of events and actions, out of which present causes and effects arise. It consists of layers of significant deeds and events laid in the past which form a substrate out of which fateful patterns, events, and circumstances arise, including but not limited to laws and other patterns of human behavior and social life. Though laid in the past, orlog still continues to have an active, 'conditioning' influence on the present. I envision orlog acting rather like yeast (orlog from the past) fermenting in bread dough (the present), conditioning the dough and causing to react in ways it would not do without the yeast.

Word-Hoard

In Bek-Pedersen's book, *The Norns in Old Norse Mythology,* she discusses a number of Old Norse terms that have meanings similar to ørlög: *skǫp, miǫtuðr, auðna, forlǫg, urðr.* I've discussed *skǫp* extensively in this book, and *metod / miǫtuðr* is mentioned here in this Word-Hoard. *Urðr* is cognate to wyrd.

Primstav
The Primstav or Runic calendar is a 'perpetual calendar' that can be used year after year, since it marks days and seasons but not numbered dates. It consists of a flat wooden stave shaped and sized like a large ruler, one side representing the days of summer, the other side winter. Nicks are made on the bottom edge to count the days of each half-year. Carved symbols along the length represent the tasks and events of the seasons, including farming and household tasks, holidays, and other observances. In earlier times the Primstav reminded people when seasonal tasks must begin, dating to a time when calendars as we know them were not commonly available to country folk. Its use today, individually designed and made by Heathens for their own purposes, helps connect one to the life of the land and the holy tides of the year.
(Chapter 24)

Proto-Germanic
A language which has been reconstructed by modern scholars; the prehistoric ancestor of Germanic languages such as Anglo-Saxon, Old Saxon, Old Norse, Frisian, Old High German, Frankish, etc. Proto-Germanic developed from Proto-Indo-European about 500 BCE, and from there branched off into its descendant Germanic languages over

the course of several centuries. Gothic is the closest historical language to Proto-Germanic. (Chapters 1, 2, 3, 8, 13, 14, 28.)

Proto-Indo-European, PIE
The prehistoric root of all Indo-European languages, ancient and modern. No writings exist in this language; it is reconstructed by linguists based on known patterns of language transformation. PIE was spoken beginning approximately 4500 BCE, and branched off into different languages at widely different time periods after that.

Quantum Physics / Mechanics
Quantum physics studies the nature and behavior of matter and energy at the subatomic level. (Chapters 20, 21)

"Quantum mechanics is the fundamental physical theory that describes the behavior of matter and of light; its unusual characteristics typically occur at and below the scale of atoms. ... Quantum mechanics can describe many systems that classical physics cannot. Classical physics can describe many aspects of nature at an ordinary (macroscopic and (optical) microscopic) scale, but is not sufficient for describing them at very small submicroscopic (atomic and subatomic) scales."
https://en.wikipedia.org/wiki/Quantum_mechanics

Quantum Theory Interpretations overview:
https://en.wikipedia.org/wiki/Interpretations_of_quantum_mechanics

Ragnarök:
'The destiny or fate of the Gods,' a great battle between the Gods and the Jotnar or Giants, with the dead from different realms participating on different sides. Some modern Heathens regard Ragnarök as having already happened, in the form of the forcible conversions from Heathenism to Christianity during the early Middle Ages. Others regard it as an event yet to come, and some see Ragnarök as a cyclical, recurrent event, having already happened in the past, and still to come again in the future. (Chapters 10, 11, 16, 21.)

Shild / scyld
Scyld in Anglo-Saxon meant 'responsible for, liable for, in debt to,' among other meanings. The spelling is modernized as 'shild,' which is how it is pronounced. The ethical meaning of 'shild' that we focus on in this book is 'moral debt or obligation,' which might be accrued by one's own deeds and choices, or by those of one's kin, ancestors, or culture. Scyld is the form that the Norn Skuld's name would take in Anglo-Saxon, and shild is part of what Skuld and the Norns deal with.
(Chapters 4, 14, 20, 21, 23, 25, 26, 27, 29, 30, 31.)

Spákona, Spámaðr, Spaewife, Seer/ess, Völva, Seiðkona, Seiðmaðr
Terms such as Spákona, Spaewife, Seeress, Völva, and Seiðkona for women and Spámaðr, Seiðmaðr, and Seer for men refer to practitioners of divination or sorcery. A prominent example is Þorbjǫrg in Erik the Red's Saga: a woman held in high esteem who travelled from farm to farm answering people's questions about the future, a service often provided in return for gifts or payment. In some

stories, it is unclear whether the practitioner was believed to simply predict or to actually cause future events, and sometimes the figures appeared to be feared or mistrusted. In addition to prophecy, practitioners were also associated with forms of sorcery like manipulating the weather. They are thought to have used songs, chants, and perhaps trance in their magic and are described as both sending souls out from their bodies and calling spirits to them in their workings (Price, 2019). (Contributed by Sara.)
(Chapters 7, 11, 12, 13, 14, 15.)

Symbel, Sumble
A Heathen ritual of community, attested in ancient times and practiced today. Participants sit together and make toasts, boasts and oaths, offer prayers, remembrances, poetry or songs, give gifts, and witness events such as agreements, betrothals or weddings, new members being sworn in or accepted to the group, anniversaries, and the like. Sacred drinks, often imbibed from drinking horns, are raised and drunk from to hail and acknowledge the words spoken in sumble. Among modern Heathens, usually the first round of drinks and speeches hails the Deities, the second hails ancestors and heroes, those we admire and are grateful toward. The third and any subsequent rounds are 'speaker's choice' as to subject matter. Some Heathens consider that the words spoken in sumble are 'laid in the Well of Wyrd.' Therefore, great care should be taken in considering one's words, especially with regard to oaths and commitments, since they are likely to become part of wyrd and have powerful impacts on our lives. (See Chapter 13 in Waggoner for more detail.)

Bauschatz suggests the following etymology for symbel: "...the term *symbel* itself may very well find its own roots in ale. The word is quite probably a compound of *sum-* or *sam-* (which represents a collecting or gathering): MHG *sament, samt* 'along with'; ON *samka, samna* 'to gather; etc. and the form **alu* 'ale' (ON *ǫl*, OE *ealu*, etc.)" (Bauschatz p. 76.) The overall sense is thus 'a gathering over ale, gathering together to drink ale,' a meaning that mirrors Old Norse *ölmól*, 'ale-speech.' The Old Norse phrase *munu verða ölmól:* "ale-speech must become"— must come into being—emphasizes the idea that words spoken in symbel are linked to orlog. *(Helgi Hjorvardsson)* vs. 32 ON, vs. 33 in translation, Poetic Edda.)
(Chapters 3, 4, 10, 15, 23, 26-27, 29, 30, 34.)

Thyle, Thul or Thulr
In modern Heathenry this person is, in effect, both master of ceremonies and master of arms at a symbel. He or she must be a person of wise judgement and good reputation, and an experienced and knowledgeable Heathen. Their function at symbel is to monitor oaths and promises by challenging and testing anyone who proposes to swear an oath, as to their ability to follow through with the oath. They must also moderate any arguments or challenges that might occur, and handle any conflicts appropriately, according to the values and customs of the group who is hosting the symbel. People proposing to make an oath in sumble are advised to consult with the Thyle beforehand; this helps the process to go smoothly. It should be noted that not all Heathen groups make use of a Thyle at symbel; some consider it unnecessary, or feel it is not in accordance with their values and customs.

(See Chapter 13 in Waggoner Vol. 3 for more detail about the Thyle's role in symbel.)
(Chapters 4, 26.)

Time-Body

I envision that we have something I call a Time-Body that is analogous to our physical body, but exists in time rather than in three-dimensional space. I suggest, further, that this Time-Body is the same thing as our Aldr life-force or life-soul. Our Time-Body occupies its place in time through the process of continuity: the continuity of who we are, our life-span, our Werold, our experiences, our sense of self, our life-story, our body itself, all maintained throughout our life. The continuity of who we are holds and shapes our place in time, as our physical body shapes our place in space. The characteristics of our Time-Body change over time and so does our physical body. They both—physical and time bodies—are affected by all our experiences in life as well as by our processes of growth, maturation and aging.
(Chapters 5, 16, 19, 32, 33)

Werold

Werold is an Anglo-Saxon and Old Saxon word that means 'man-age.' Our modern word 'world' comes from it, but has a different meaning. The old 'werold' referred to each person's own personal world, not 'the world out there' as the word means today. Our Werold is composed of the years, events, and experiences of our full life-span. It is the 'world' within which our Time-Body / Aldr lives, and it is what we mean when we talk about our 'life' and 'lifetime.' For example, "never in my life have I seen such a thing" would

be expressed, in the old languages, by saying "never in my werold have I seen such a thing."
(Chapters 5, 10, 13, 14, 16, 19, 32, 33)

Wode, Oðr: One of the gifts given by Hœnir / Odin's brother when two trees or logs were transformed into the humans Ask and Embla. Wode refers to an ecstatic state of heightened spiritual—and sometimes physical—energy, which can take forms ranging from inspired eloquence and prophecy, artistic and intellectual genius, warrior focus and strength, to berserker rage, or outright madness. I see the gift of wode as a divine spark or a bridge, that enables humans to reach divine consciousness and communication with the Deities. If the person is not fit nor prepared for this, if their motives are skewed, or if they approach the Deities in inappropriate, offensive ways, the resulting flow of wode may backfire into negative forms.
(Chapters 21, 27.)

World-Tree, Yggdrasil: The cosmic Tree, the structure of Space and all that exists within space. It is rooted in the three great Wells of power in Norse myth: Hvergelmir, Mimir's Well, and Urðr's Well, and the Nine Worlds are supported by its branches and roots.

Worlds, Nine Worlds: Norse mythology envisions nine worlds as the home-bases for different kinds of beings: Asgard for the Æsir, Vanaheim for the Vanir, Alfheim for the Alfar or elves, Midgard for humans, Svartalfheim for the Dwarves, Hel for the dead, Jotunheim for the Giants, and the Worlds of the primal energies: the World of ice and cold, Niflheim, and the World of Fire, Muspelheim.

Word-Hoard

Wyrd

I think of Wyrd as a being, a singularity who expresses what the Norns express in their triplicity. In some ways, I see Wyrd as being the same thing as the Norns collectively are; in other ways she seems to stand on her own, possessing her own mysterious nature. It's as though these views, Three or One, are different facets of the full Being that is Wyrd. To add to the ambiguity, Wyrd herself, in my perception, seems to have no issue with sometimes appearing as a person, other times as a phenomenon. I seems as though she is presenting us with an existential riddle, challenging us to plunge more deeply in our efforts to understand who and what she / it is. As one contributor to this book, Svartheiðrinn, notes, Wyrd is rather like the quantum phenomenon of light being both a wave and a particle, depending on the method one uses to observe it: sometimes she appears as a personal being, other times as an impersonal phenomenon.

Yggdrasil: The 'steed of Ygg'. 'Ygg' means the 'terrible one', and is a byname of Odin. His 'steed' here is the World-Tree upon which he hung for nine days and nights to win the Runes. (Chapters 3, 6, 12, 16, 17, 21, 27, 30.)

Word-Hoard

Book-Hoard: References and Further Reading

Barber, Charles Clyde. *An Old High German Reader.* Basil Blackwell, 1964.

Bauschatz, Paul C. *The Well and the Tree: World and Time in Early Germanic Culture.* The University of Massachusetts Press, 1982.

Bek-Pedersen, Karen. *The Norns in Old Norse Mythology.* Dunedin Academic Press Ltd., 2011.

Berr, Samuel. *An Etymological Glossary to the Old Saxon* Heliand. Herbert Lang & Co. Ltd., 1971.

Bosworth-Toller *An Anglo-Saxon Dictionary* online at the University of Texas: https://lrc.la.utexas.edu/books/asd/dict

Boucher, Alan. *The Saga of Hallfred.* Iceland Review, 1981.

Byock, Jesse L. *The Saga of the Volsungs: The Norse Epic of Sigurd the Dragon Slayer.* The University of California Press, 1990.

Chickering, Howell D. Jr., transl. *Beowulf.* Doubleday, 1977. (Dual language edition)

Cleasby, Richard, and Gudbrand Vigfusson. *An Icelandic-English Dictionary.* Clarendon Press, Oxford, 1874. https://old-norse.net/search.php

Damico, Helen. *Beowulf's Wealhtheow and the Valkyrie Tradition.* The University of Wisconsin Press, 1984.

Day, David. *The Illustrated World of Tolkien: The Second Age.* Thunder Bay Press, 2023.

de Santillana, Giorgio, and Hertha von Dechend. *Hamlet's Mill: An Essay on Myth and the Frame of Time.* Gambit, 1969.

deVries, Jan. *Altgermanische Religionsgeschichte, Band I.* Walter de Gruyter & Co., Berlin, 1956

deVries, Jan. *Altgermanische Religionsgeschichte, Band II.* Walter de Gruyter & Co., Berlin, 1957.

deVries, Jan. *Altgermanische Religionsgeschichte, Einleitung: Die Vorgeschichtliche Zeit.* Walter de Gruyter & Co., 1935.

deVries, Jan. *Altnordisches Etymologisches Wörterbuch.* E.J. Brill, 1961.

Dowden, Ken. *European Paganism: The Realities of Cult from Antiquity to the Middle Ages.* Routledge, 1999.

Edda (prose Edda) see Sturluson.

Egil's Saga. Transl. Hermann Pálsson and Paul Edwards. Penguin Books USA, 1976.

Egil's Saga in Old Norse: https://www.Voluspa.org/egil78.htm

Ellis, Hilda Roderick. *The Road to Hel: A Study of the Conception of the Dead in Old Norse Literature.* Cambridge University Press, 1943. (Note: some editions of this book are published under the author's married name, Hilda Ellis Davidson.)

Book-Hoard

Erik the Red:
The Saga of Erik the Red. J. Sephton, *Icelandic Saga Database*, Sveinbjorn Thordarson (ed.)
http://www.sagadb.org/eiriks_saga_rauda.en

Flateyjarbók, ed. by Guðbrandur Vigfússon and C.R. Unger: volume 1 (1860), volume 2 (1862), volume 3 (1868)

Fletcher, Robert, Paola Romero, Marianne Talbot, Nigel Warburton, and Anna Whiston. *Philosophy: A Visual Encyclopedia.* DK Penguin Random House, 2020.

Grimm, Jacob. *Teutonic Mythology, Vol. 1.* Transl. James Stephen Stalleybrass. London: George Bell and Sons, 1882.

Grønbech, Vilhelm. *The Culture of the Teutons.* Humphrey Milford, Oxford University Press, 1931.

Hall, J.R. Clark. *A Concise Anglo-Saxon Dictionary, Fourth Edition.* University of Toronto Press, Toronto, 1960.

Hallfred Saga:

> *Hallfreðarsaga Vandræðaskálds,* Möðruvallabok version.
> https://www.snerpa.is/net/isl/hallf.htm
>
> *The Saga of Hallfred the Troublesome Scald,* transl. Alan Boucher, Iceland Review Saga Series, 1981.

Heath, Cat. *Elves, Witches, & Gods: Spinning Old Heathen Magic in the Modern Day.* Llewellyn Publications, 2021.

Heliand:
https://www.hieronymus.us.com/latinweb/Mediaevum/Heliand.htm#top

Hêliand: Text and Commentary, James E. Cathey, editor. West Virginia University Press, 2002.

Himma Daga *English to Gothic Dictionary.* https://airushimmadaga.wordpress.com/wp-content/uploads/2020/09/english-to-gothic-dictionary.pdf

Hostetter, Aaron, accessed June 12, 2025. https://oldenglishpoetry.camden.rutgers.edu/2017/06/08/wyrd-bid-ful-araed-the-wanderer-line-5b/

Jonsson, Finnur, ed. *Edda Snorra Sturlusonar.* Udgivnet efter Handskrifterne af Kommissionen for det Arnamagnaeanske Legat. København: Gyldendalske Boghandel – Nordisk Forlag, 1931.

Jonsson, Finnur, ed. *De Gamle Eddadigte.* København: G.E.C. Gads Forlag, 1932.

Jordanes, transl. Charles Christopher Mierow. *The Origin and Deeds of the Goths*, 1908. (The original history by Jordanes was written in the 6th century CE in Latin; the original title is *Getica*.) Text is available in English at: https://www.gutenberg.org/cache/epub/14809/pg14809-images.html

Kellogg, Robert. *A Concordance to Eddic Poetry.* Colleagues Press 1988.

Kroonen, Guus. *Etymological Dictionary of Proto-Germanic.* Brill, 2013.

Larrington, Carolyne, transl. *The Poetic Edda*, revised edition. Oxford University Press, 2014.

Lecouteux, Claude. *The Return of the Dead: Ghosts, Ancestors, and the Transparent Veil of the Pagan Mind.* Inner Traditions, 2009.

Mallory, J.P. and D.Q. Adams. *Encyclopedia of Indo-European Culture.* Fitzroy Dearborn Publishers, 1997.

Maxims II (in Anglo-Saxon):
https://sacred-texts.com/neu/ascp/a15.htm

McKernan, Matthew Ash. *Wyrdcraft: Healing Self & Nature through the Mysteries of the Fates.* Llewellyn Publications, 2023.

Njal's Saga, transl. Magnus Magnusson and Herman Palsson. Penguin Classics, 1960.

Poetic Edda: See Larrington (English), Jonsson (Old Norse).

Price, Neil. *The Viking Way: Magic and Mind in Late Iron Age Scandinavia.* Oxbow Books, 2019

Quantum Theory Interpretations overview:
https://en.wikipedia.org/wiki/Interpretations_of_quantum_mechanics

Rose, Winifred Hodge. *Heathen Soul Lore Foundations: Ancient and Modern Germanic Pagan Concepts of the Souls.* Wordfruma Press, 2020.

Rose, Winifred Hodge. *Oaths, Shild, Frith, Luck & Wyrd: Five Essays Exploring Heathen Ethical Concepts and their Use Today.* Wordfruma Press, 2022.

Book-Hoard

Russell, James C. *The Germanization of Early Medieval Christianity: A Sociohistorical Approach to Religious Transformation.* Oxford University Press, 1994.

Rydberg, Viktor, transl. Rasmus B. Anderson. *Teutonic Mythology vol. II.* New York: Norrœna Society, 1906.
Saxo Grammaticus. *The Danish History.* Translated by Oliver Elton, Project Gutenberg, 2004.
www.gutenberg.org/files/1150/1150-h/1150-h.htm.

Schreiwer, Robert, and Ammerili Eckhart. *A Dictionary of Urglaawe Terminology.* Urglaawe, 2012.

Sehrt, Edward H. *Vollständiges Wörterbuch zum Heliand und zur Altsächsischen Genesis.* Vandenhœk & Ruprecht in Göttingen, 1966.

Simek, Rudolf. *Dictionary of Northern Mythology.* D.S. Brewer, 1993.

Skeat, W.W. *A Mœso-Gothic Glossary.* London UK: Asher & Co., 1868.

Stokker, K. *Marking Time: The Primstav Murals of Sigmund Aarseth.* Vesterheim Norwegian American Museum, 2003.

Strömback, Dag. "The Concept of the Soul in Nordic Tradition" in *ARV: Journal of Scandinavian Folklore, Vol. 31, 1975.* The Almqvist & Wiksell Periodical Company.

Sturlason, Snorri. "History of Olaf Tryggvason" in *Heimskringla or the Lives of the Norse Kings*, edited with notes by Erling Monsen and translated with the assistance of A.H. Smith, Dover Publications, 1990.

Sturluson, Snorri, *transl.* Anthony Faulkes. *Edda.* Charles E. Tuttle Co., 1995.

Tacitus' *Agricola, Germany, and Dialogue on Orators.* Transl. Herbert Benario. University of Oklahoma Press, 1991.

The Seafarer Old English poem:
https://clasp.ell.ox.ac.uk/db-latest/poem/A.3.9#115

Tolkien, J.R.R., ed. Christopher Tolkien. *The Legend of Sigurd and Gudrun.* Houghton Mifflin Harcourt, 2009.

Völsungasaga: see Byock.

Waggoner, Ben, transl. *Hávamál: A New Translation.* Troth Publications, 2017.

Waggoner, Ben (Ed.). (2011). Norse magical and herbal healing. Troth Publications.

Waggoner, Ben, et al. *Our Troth 3rd Edition*
    Vol. 1: Heathen History, 2020.
    Vol. 2: Heathen Gods, 2021.
    Vol. 3: Heathen Life, 2022.
The Troth Publications

Watkins, Calvert. *The American Heritage Dictionary of Indo-European Roots.* Houghton Mifflin Harcourt, 2011.

Winterbourne, Anthony. *When the Norns have Spoken: Time and Fate in Germanic Paganism.* Associated University Presses, 2004.

Wright, Thomas. *Anglo-Saxon and Old English Vocabularies.* London: Trübner & Co., 1883.

Book-Hoard

Wulfila Gothic Bible: http://www.wulfila.be/gothic/browse/

Young, G.V.C. and Cynthia R. Clewer. *Føroysk-Ensk Orðabok Faroese-English Dictionary with folk-lore and proverbs.* Mansk-Svenska Publishing Co. Ltd., 1985.

Photo Credits

Where photo credits are required, they are listed here.

Cover image
Murray Foubister, CC BY-SA 2.0
<https://creativecommons.org/licenses/by-sa/2.0>, via Wikimedia Commons
https://upload.wikimedia.org/wikipedia/commons/8/8f/At_the_Hamelin_Pool_Stromatolites_preserv

Frontispiece
Ribe Vikinge Center, The 3 Norns
Västgöten, CC BY-SA 3.0 <https://creativecommons.org/licenses/by-sa/3.0>, via Wikimedia Commons
https://upload.wikimedia.org/wikipedia/commons/7/7c/Ribe_VikingeCenter_-_the_3_norns.jpg

page 8
Beowulf manuscript
British Library, CC BY-SA 4.0
<https://creativecommons.org/licenses/by-sa/4.0>, via Wikimedia Commons
https://upload.wikimedia.org/wikipedia/commons/0/0f/Beowulf_Manuscript.jpg

page 45
"Kongshornet," king's drinking horn
Lennart Larsen, CC BY-SA 4.0
<https://creativecommons.org/licenses/by-sa/4.0>, via Wikimedia Commons
https://upload.wikimedia.org/wikipedia/commons/1/14/Kongshornet%2C_DMR-167969.jpg

Photo Credits

page 54
Askr och Embla
Bengt Oberger, CC BY-SA 3.0
<https://creativecommons.org/licenses/by-sa/3.0>, via Wikimedia Commons
https://upload.wikimedia.org/wikipedia/commons/1/17/Ask_och_Embla_Nyk%C3%B6ping.JPG

page 140
"Völva," by Vangland.
Vangland, CC BY-SA 4.0 <https://creativecommons.org/licenses/by-sa/4.0>, via Wikimedia Commons
https://upload.wikimedia.org/wikipedia/commons/7/78/V%C3%B6lva.jpg

page 148
Franks casket, front.
John W. Schulze, CC BY 2.0
<https://creativecommons.org/licenses/by/2.0>, via Wikimedia Commons
https://upload.wikimedia.org/wikipedia/commons/7/7e/Franks_Casket_front.jpg

page 190
Relief sculpture of Egil Skallagrimsson carrying his son
https://upload.wikimedia.org/wikipedia/commons/c/cd/Egill_Skallagr%C3%ADmsson_1995-IS-0

page 209
Cypress tree rings
[[File:Tree rings in Taxodium distichum wood (bald cypress) 4 (24518375307).jpg|Tree_rings_in_Taxodium_distichum_wood_(bald_cypress)_4_(24518375307)]]

Page 210
Tree-rings in an ancient wooden beam
Weathered growth rings at Aztec Ruins National Monument, New Mexico USA

Photo Credits

https://upload.wikimedia.org/wikipedia/commons/4/45/Weathered_growth_rings_at_Aztec_Ruins_National_Monument.jpg
I, Michael Gäbler, CC BY 3.0
<https://creativecommons.org/licenses/by/3.0>, via Wikimedia Commons

Page 211
Folded layers of rock
File:Visible folded layers in Amman.JPG
High Contrast, CC BY 3.0 DE
<https://creativecommons.org/licenses/by/3.0/de/deed.en>, via Wikimedia Commons
https://upload.wikimedia.org/wikipedia/commons/a/ab/Visible_folded_layers_in_Amman.JPG

page 213
Brown and tan soil profile
Petr Kinšt, CC BY-SA 3.0 <https://creativecommons.org/licenses/by-sa/3.0>, via Wikimedia Commons
https://upload.wikimedia.org/wikipedia/commons/4/46/Lib%C4%9Bdice_2015-04-19_P%C5%AFdn%C3%AD_profil.jpg

p. 222
Clock-face draped over feet
Horst J. Meuter, CC BY-SA 4.0
<https://creativecommons.org/licenses/by-sa/4.0>, via Wikimedia Commons
https://upload.wikimedia.org/wikipedia/commons/d/db/ Ruhezeit.jpg

page 234
The Quantum Leap
The Quantum Leap, Shrewsbury by Stephen Craven, CC BY-SA 2.0
<https://creativecommons.org/licenses/by-sa/2.0>, via Wikimedia Commons
https://upload.wikimedia.org/wikipedia/commons/9/91/The_Quantum_Leap%2C_Shrewsbury_-_geograph.org.uk_-_7325659.jpg

Photo Credits

page 236
Fractal
Optoskept, CC BY 4.0 <https://creativecommons.org/licenses/by/4".0>, via Wikimedia Commons
https://upload.wikimedia.org/wikipedia/commons/5/5c/Fractal_Detail_No_1_by_Optoskept.jpg

page 252
Wooden carving of "The Well (Quantum Corral)"
Julian Voss-Andreae, CC BY-SA 3.0
<https://creativecommons.org/licenses/by-sa/3.0>, via Wikimedia Commons
https://upload.wikimedia.org/wikipedia/commons/e/e3/The_Well_%28Quantum_Corral%29.jpg

page 266
Ancient enclosed well
Grant Sherman / St Nectan's Well, Welcombe
https://upload.wikimedia.org/wikipedia/commons/b/b5/St_Nectan%27s_Well%2C_Welcombe_-_geograph.org.uk_-_75518.jpg

page 268
Tilted rock layers
https://upload.wikimedia.org/wikipedia/commons/4/42/Tilted_Rock_Layers_near_Tasselmante_i
Ronny (https://www.geodiversite.net/auteur137), CC BY-SA 3.0
<https://creativecommons.org/licenses/by-sa/3.0>, via Wikimedia Commons

page 285
Primstav summer side
https://www.wikidata.org/wiki/Q20084081
Primstav NF.1987-0460 c.jpg
[[File:Primstav NF.1987-0460 c.jpg|Primstav_NF.1987-0460_c]]
https://en.wikipedia.org/wiki/en:Norwegian_Museum_of_Cultural_History

Photo Credits

Primstav winter side
https://www.wikidata.org/wiki/Q20084081
Primstav NF.1987-0460 d.jpg
https://en.wikipedia.org/wiki/en:Norwegian_Museum_of_Cultural_History

page 388
Spring rose blooming
Audrey from Central Pennsylvania, USA, CC BY 2.0
<https://creativecommons.org/licenses/by/2.0>, via Wikimedia Commons
https://upload.wikimedia.org/wikipedia/commons/3/33/Spring_Rose_Blooming_%28520190731%29.jpg

page 407
Water droplet hanging from a twig.
Vijayanrajapuram, CC BY-SA 4.0
<https://creativecommons.org/licenses/by-sa/4.0>, via Wikimedia Commons
https://upload.wikimedia.org/wikipedia/commons/5/5a/Water_drop_art_vijayanrajapuram_04.jpg

Authors

Winifred Hodge Rose

Winifred Hodge Rose is a Heathen Elder and has followed a Heathen path for more than thirty years, serving as a scholar, writer, leader, teacher, priestess, and oracular spaewife in many Heathen venues.

Winifred grew up as the daughter of a US diplomat stationed in various countries during the 1950s and 1960s, and later lived for years in Greece and Germany. She learned foreign languages through immersion, and learned to observe and adapt to different cultures and world-views.

These experiences have supported her efforts to understand, as well as possible, ancient Heathen world-views and adapt them for modern Heathen use, and led to her self-study of ancient Germanic languages, literature, and etymology.

She has Bachelor's and Master's degrees in the natural sciences, and a Master's degree in political science, focusing on the study of conflict resolution and cooperation.

Winifred is now retired from her career as a senior research scientist working on methods for watershed and natural resources management on military installations in the US and Germany. She's blessed with two grown children, three growing grandsons, and a good life in the Illinois countryside with her blacksmith husband Dean Rose (and various critters, wild and tame).

Winifred is deeply grateful for the years of support and encouragement for her Heathen work from her Heathen husband, and her non-Heathen children, grandchildren, siblings, and large extended family—those living in Midgard today, and those who have passed on. Her extended family members represent a very large range of religions and philosophies, but find this a matter of mutual interest rather than a reason for arguments and hard feelings among them. Winifred profoundly wishes the rest of the world could do the same! She offers her profound thanks to her colleagues, Sara and Svartheiðrinn, for their inspiring contributions to the book as well as their background support throughout the preparation of the book.

Nowadays Winifred considers herself an independent scholar of Heathen theology and philosophy, and spends most of her time involved with thinking, studying, spiritual practice, writing and publishing on these topics. Her website is HeathenSoulLore.net.

Sara Axtell

I am the descendant of Norwegian settlers living in Imnížaska / St Paul, Minnesota on Dakota land in a place where there once was an oak savanna. My partner and I navigate life with my two fabulous adult children, their wonderful partners, and our beautiful, complicated network of family and friends.

I love to learn and teach with others, and I am fortunate to live in a place where there are lots of opportunities to create and share knowledge together. I am part of a learning community called Healing Roots, which brings people together to learn about the role of culture in our lives, how it can support our well-being, and be a resource in our racial justice work.

I am deeply grateful to be guided and nurtured by elders and teachers in my community—at Healing Roots, the Cultural Wellness Center, the Decolonization Roundtable, the North American Water Office, and the National Native American Boarding School Healing Coalition.

In my day job, I teach about culture and community in the Department of Family Social Science at the University of Minnesota.

When I was first coming up in Heathenry 25 years ago, I was fascinated, challenged, and nourished by Winifred's writing and it has been an honor and a joy to be able to work with her on this project.

Thanks to everyone who read and commented on versions of my essays, especially friends from Healing Roots, the Runes and Virtues Study Group, the Primstav study circle, Gullveig's Hearth Kindred, and the Sunday Morning Galdr Group.

Daniela Svartheiðrinn Simina

Daniela 'Svartheiðrinn' Simina is a Norse-Germanic Pagan, native of Romania. As the granddaughter of a Fairy Seer and medicine woman, Svartheiðrinn grew up immersed in folk traditions of healing and magic, and since very young, she developed a vested interest in both Romanian and Norse-Germanic myths and folklore. Growing up, Svartheiðrinn explored various European nature-based traditions of spiritual healing.

She teaches courses and workshops on various modalities of energetic rebalancing, esoteric subjects, and topics pertaining to Norse-Germanic Paganism. Svartheiðrinn was recently ordained as Heathen clergy by the Troth, an international organization promoting inclusive Heathenry.

Svartheiðrinn is the author of:

Where Fairies Meet: Parallels Between Irish and Romanian Fairy Traditions

A Fairy Path: The Memoir of a Young Fairy Seer in Training

Fairy Herbs for Fairy Magic: A Practical Guide to Fairy Herbal Magic

A Word about Wordfruma Press

Fruma means 'origin, beginning' in Anglo-Saxon, and *ordfruma* means the fount or the source. The Anglo-Saxon word *Os* refers to a God of the Esa or Æsir tribe, and the Rune Poem for the rune Os / Ansuz goes as follows:

> *Os is 'ordfruma' of every speech,*
> *The support of wisdom and the benefit of the wise,*
> *And for every earl, prosperity and hope.*
> (my translation)

The Esa-God referred to here is Woden or Odin, the fount and origin of speech, eloquence and wisdom. Since my work relies in large part on understanding the roots and sources of words, I have made a play on words here, changing *ordfruma* to *wordfruma:* "the origin of words". The origin or wellspring of meaningful words flows from godly inspiration: a divine gift that underlies the formation and emergence of our entire species, *homo sapiens*. Wordfruma Press thus honors the gift of speech, and the origins of the gift: all of the Holy Ones.

The trademark logo pictured here, conceptualized by myself and created by Forest Hawkins, shows the rune Ansuz, an analog of Os, rising up from a wellspring. Ansuz takes shape as a fountain that represents the power of speech and wisdom. The shape of the logo also represents the Well of Wyrd and the World-Tree, with dew from the Tree dropping into the Well. Wordfruma Press publishes scholarly and inspirational Heathen works.

Other Publications from Wordfruma Press

Heathen Soul Lore Foundations: Ancient and Modern Germanic Pagan Concepts of the Souls, 2021 (575 pages)

Heathen Soul Lore: A Personal Approach, 2022 (423 pages)

Heathen Soul Lore Workbook I: To Support the Study and Practice of Heathen Soul Lore Foundations and *Heathen Soul Lore: A Personal Approach,* 2024 (234 pages)

Wandering on Heathen Ways: Writings on Heathen Holy Ones, Wights, and Spiritual Practice, 2023 (510 pages)

Oaths, Shild, Frith, Luck & Wyrd: Five Essays Exploring Heathen Ethical Concepts and their Use Today, 2022. (164 pages)

Idunn's Trees: A New Tale of the Norse Goddess Idunn, 2022 (children's illustrated story and activity book, 52 pages)

Celebrating Heathen Yule, 2023 (booklet, 45 pages)

Mothers-Night Blot and Yule Celebration, with Heathen Words for Yule Songs, 2022 (booklet, 28 pages)

www.ingramcontent.com/pod-product-compliance
Lightning Source LLC
Chambersburg PA
CBHW071221230426

43668CB00011B/1262